THE
FINAL
FOUR

THE FINAL FOUR

NATIONAL COLLEGIATE ATHLETIC ASSOCIATION

A RICH CLARKSON BOOK

Compiled by Billy Reed ✍ Photographs by Rich Clarkson

CONTENTS

PHOTO AT RIGHT:
San Francisco's Bill Russell is
carried from the floor in celebration
of the Dons' 1955 championship.

PRECEDING SPREAD:
In basketball's most glorious moment,
Connecticut players begin their
post-game celebration after
winning the 1999 championship.

STAFF FOR THIS BOOK
Editor RICH CLARKSON
Art Director KATE GLASSNER BRAINERD
Production Coordinator JENNIFER FINCH
For the NCAA DAVID PICKLE

PUBLISHED BY
THE NATIONAL COLLEGIATE ATHLETIC ASSOCIATION

PRINTED IN THE USA BY
HOST COMMUNICATIONS, INC.
All rights reserved.

Copyright © 2001, First Edition
ISBN: 1-57640-060-3
Library of Congress
Cataloging-in-Publication Data on file.

NATIONAL COLLEGIATE ATHLETIC ASSOCIATION
P.O. Box 6222
INDIANAPOLIS, INDIANA 46206

"The Final Four is now, in my opinion,
the major sporting event of the year."

— C.M. Newton
Tournament Committee Chairman 1997-99

FOREWORD

THE FINAL FOUR   **by John Wooden**

The Final Four never got old for me.

One reason, I suppose, is that I understood how hard it was to get there. Early in my career at UCLA, I told my old friend, Indiana coach Branch McCracken, that I was afraid I would never win a championship. The other reason was that every team, every season, was unique. So while I finally grew tired of coaching when I reached the age of 64, I never grew tired of the Final Four.

I'm often asked to name my favorite national championship team. While each of the 10 was special, I would have to say the first and the last. The first, in 1964, because, well, it was the first. Besides that, without any starter taller than 6-5, we were the shortest team to win the championship. Early in the year, that team was not expected to be a contender. But we played as well together as a team could play. Without much size, we had to use our quickness. We introduced the 2-2-1 fullcourt press to the nation, and, in Keith Erickson, we had the perfect player to play the No. 5, or safety position, in the press.

My last championship team, like the first one, was not expected to do well. We had lost four starters, including two superstars in Bill Walton and Keith Wilkes, from the 1974 team that had lost to North Carolina State in the national semifinals. David Meyers was the only returning starter. But we improved as the season went along. To do the unexpected is sometimes more exciting than doing the expected.

There were special moments between those first and last championships. At the end of our 68-62 win over Villanova in the 1971 championship game, a photographer, Rich Clarkson of Sports Illustrated, took a picture of Sidney Wicks and me that I particularly liked. It was taken at the end of the game. We had it won and we were shooting free throws. During a timeout, I told the players, "When the game's over, let's keep our cool and not be foolish." I wanted them to get the nets, but I didn't believe in any excessive exuberance.

When we broke the huddle, Wicks came over to shake my hand. In the Astrodome, the benches were below the floor, so I had to look up at him. He leaned over and said, "Coach, congratulations for another championship." Then he left, but he turned around and came back. Leaning down again, he said, "Coach, you're really sumpin'!" That brought tears to my eyes. Only a week earlier, I had disciplined him for something minor. But the way he said, "sumpin' " ... I really liked that.

As I said, my final season was special because nobody expected us to do much. In the semifinals, we had a great game against Louisville, which was coached by Denny Crum, one of my former players and assistants. We won, 75-74, in overtime. Neither team deserved to lose, but the proper one did, at least from my standpoint. If a Louisville player hadn't missed a one-and-one at the end of regulation play, our chances would have been just about gone. I was unhappy for Denny because he was, and is, very dear to me.

My decision to retire was very much a spur-of-the-moment thing. Before the game, I would have said that I was going to coach two more years. With what we had coming back and what we had coming in, I knew we had the chance to have outstanding teams. I didn't want to leave the cupboard bare, because that would have put extra pressure on whoever succeeded me.

After I visited with Denny following the semifinal, I felt good, but also sorry for him. I hadn't been feeling good at all—I was tired—and my wife, Nell, hadn't been well. "Now," I thought, "I've got to go meet the press." Then I thought, "If this is a bother to me, it's time to get out." So I just went in there and announced it.

That overshadowed our championship game against Kentucky. It turned out to be a hard-fought game, but we won, 92-85. Of all my teams, that one gave me as much pleasure as any. They were absolutely no trouble on or off the court, and that's a nice thing to be able to say about your last team.

In the years since that last game, I've often been asked if I think anybody will ever break our records of 10 titles in 12 years and seven in a row. Well, if somebody had told you 10 years ago that Lou Gehrig's record of consecutive games played would be broken and that it would be done by a shortstop (Cal Ripken Jr.), you would have said it could never happen. But it did. That's sort of the way I feel about those records. It'll be very difficult, but most records are broken.

I pretty much stopped going to the Final Four after Nell died in 1985. It wasn't that I no longer enjoyed it, because I did. It's just that it wasn't the same without her. Although I returned in 1995, I've been content to watch from afar. It's still the best event there is. I'm just pleased that I was fortunate enough to be a part of it for so many years.

John R. Wooden

Senior Sidney Wicks thanks coach John Wooden as he leaves the court at the end of Wicks' final game in 1971.

PORTFOLIO

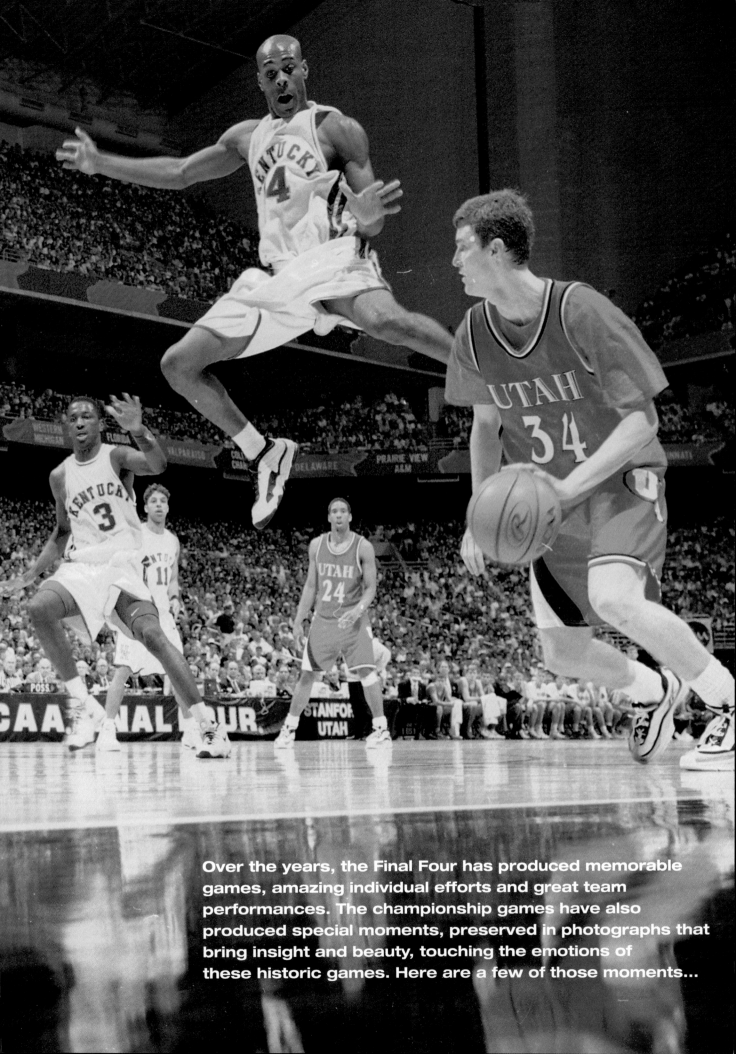

Over the years, the Final Four has produced memorable games, amazing individual efforts and great team performances. The championship games have also produced special moments, preserved in photographs that bring insight and beauty, touching the emotions of these historic games. Here are a few of those moments...

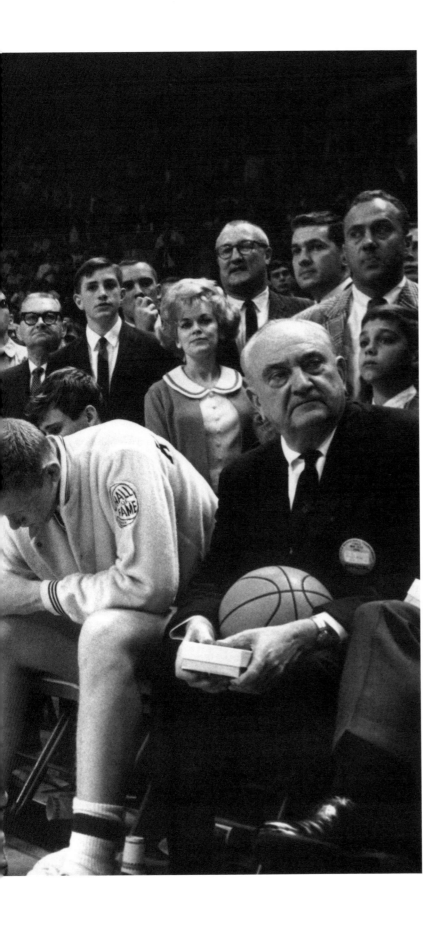

1966
KENTUCKY VS. TEXAS WESTERN

It was a stunned and disappointed Kentucky team that sat with a second place plaque, watching Texas Western receive the championship trophy in a historic turn of the college game. Texas Western, behind the shooting of David Lattin and the playmaking of Bobby Joe Hill, brought a largely black team to College Park, Md., defeating the all-white Wildcats. It has since been called basketball's "Brown v. Board of Education" turning point.

1998
KENTUCKY VS. UTAH

PREVIOUS SPREAD
Kentucky's Wildcats were sky high as they surprised their tournament opponents as well as the nation. New coach Tubby Smith built a team that marched to the school's seventh national championship. In the championship game, Heshimu Evans leaped high, cutting off a pass by Utah's Drew Hansen in San Antonio's Alamodome. Kentucky, behind the shooting of Scott Padgett and Jeff Sheppard, pulled away in the second half for the 78-69 victory and a renewed serving of championship glory.

1957

NORTH CAROLINA VS. KANSAS

The Jayhawks had the game's dominant player in Wilt Chamberlain and a perceived home court advantage playing 40 miles from their campus in Kansas City's Municipal Auditorium. Many experts conceded the championship to Kansas. But what ensued was a historic game with three overtimes in which the Tar Heels held Chamberlain to 23 points and went on to win the championship 54-53. Chamberlain, feeling responsible for the loss, left school and stayed away from the Kansas program for 40 years.

1983
HOUSTON VS. LOUISVILLE

Many experts figured Houston, with Akeem Olajuwon, was the favorite when the basketball world centered on Albuquerque's Pit. They faced the Louisville Cardinals in the semifinal game. Louisville had upset Kentucky to advance to the Final Four but Olajuwon led Phi Slamma Jamma past the Cardinals to face North Carolina State in one of the epic Final Four games.

1984
GEORGETOWN VS. KENTUCKY

PREVIOUS SPREAD
The dominating player of the mid-'80s was Georgetown's Patrick Ewing, and his Hoyas disposed of Kentucky in short order in the semifinal game in Seattle's Kingdome. Two nights later, a talented Georgetown team marched to their only championship, defeating Houston, 84-75. Houston made three straight Final Four appearances without winning the title. Georgetown returned to defend its title the next year but was defeated by upstart Villanova.

INTRODUCTION

THE GREAT AMERICAN DREAM   by Billy Reed

The walk from the locker room to the floor isn't a long one. Maybe 100 yards. But during that time, if you're a college basketball coach who has a team good enough to make it to the Final Four of the NCAA tournament, it's the walk of a lifetime.

Your players go ahead of you, and when they leave the darkness of the tunnel and burst into the bright lights of the cavernous domed stadium, your fans go berserk with pride and excitement. You hear the school band strike up the fight song. And then here you are, moving as if on a cloud. Your fans roar and call your name. Maybe you smile and wave, maybe you don't. Later you won't remember. All you know is that you have arrived at the pinnacle of the sport that has been your life since you were a kid, shooting hoops in the driveway or on the playground. "The walk onto the floor," former Marquette coach Al McGuire once said. "Savor it. It's the best. You're there!"

Former Marquette coach Al McGuire.

It never gets old, this walk on the last Saturday of the college season. It doesn't make any difference how many times a coach makes it. That's because it's so dog-goned hard to get there. As college basketball has expanded into a truly national game, parity has become as much a part of every season as the slam dunk and the three-point jumper.

Every year new programs jump up to challenge the perennial contenders—and every year the early tournament rounds are riddled with stunning upsets that have fans from coast-to-coast ripping up their office-pool bracket sheets. Since the end of the surreal UCLA dynasty (10 titles in 12 years) in 1975, only Duke, in 1991-92, has achieved back-to-back championships.

Heading into the new millennium, no sport owns a month the way the NCAA basketball tournament owns March. It begins with the conference tournaments, which theoretically give almost every member of Division I a chance to play its way into the 65-team field. On what has become known as "Selection Sunday," the field, seedings, and pairings are announced on CBS, touching off a wild scramble for airline, hotel and rental-car reservations. In the tournament's formative years, teams were assigned to regions on a geographical basis. But as the tournament expanded, geographical considerations became virtually non-existent. The committee's goal is to properly seed the teams based on performance, even if it means, say, sending UCLA to Orlando or Syracuse to San Jose.

After the first and second rounds, the 16 survivors advance to four regionals. One of the regionals usually is held at the site of the next year's Final Four, giving the NCAA staff and the local organizing committee an opportunity to hold a sort of "trial run." At this stage of the tournament, there's almost no such thing as an upset because everybody is a legitimate contender. With the Final Four so close, emotions elevate the quality of play. The best example came in the final of the 1992 East Regional, when Duke needed a last-second, miraculous turn-around jumper by Christian Laettner in overtime to subdue Kentucky, 104-103, in Philadelphia. Some veteran observers consider it to be the finest college game ever.

Then, finally, comes the Final Four.

When the quartet of regional champions arrive under the same roof with their pom-pon girls, cheerleaders, pep bands, fans and mascots, the college game reaches its pinnacle. Everywhere you look, hopes and dreams and backgrounds and traditions are colliding in a riot of noise and color. For a few hours, America seems to grind to a halt, just as it used to do in the long-gone days when baseball's World Series was unchallenged as the nation's premier sporting event. Now, arguably, the Final Four has replaced the World Series. It has fans from every state, not to mention every social and economic class. To enable more fans to participate in the event, the tournament committee mandated that it would be held every year in a domed stadium. Nevertheless, the NCAA receives far more requests for tickets year after year than it can possibly fill.

"The Final Four is now, in my opinion, the major sporting event of the year," said former Kentucky Athletics Director C.M. Newton, who chaired the tournament committee from 1997 through '99. "A lot of sports have one-day events such as the Kentucky Derby or the Super Bowl, but this is a national championship that runs over three weeks. For those of us who remember the days when the tournament was mainly a regional thing and didn't even have a national TV deal for the Final Four, the growth has been staggering."

Although college basketball had been around since Dr. James Naismith nailed up his peach basket at Springfield College before the turn of the 20th century, there was no recognized national championship until 1939, when the National Coaches Association staged the inaugural edition of what was to become the NCAA tournament. As early as March 1945, a whopping crowd of 18,035 pushed through the turnstiles at Madison Square Garden in New York City to see Oklahoma A&M and its seven-foot center Bob "Foothills" Kurland defeat New York University for the NCAA title. By 1949, the tournament celebrated its 10th anniversary with 66,077 total attendance and a $60,848 net profit.

In 1951, the NCAA made what was to be a fateful decision, hiring Walter Byers, then only 29 years old, as its first executive director. Byers had attended Rice and Iowa before enlisting in World War II. After being discharged, he worked a few years for United Press International before being hired in 1947 to assist Kenneth L. "Tug" Wilson, then commissioner of the Big Ten and secretary-treasurer of the NCAA. When the NCAA broke away from the Big Ten and named Byers as its executive director, he moved headquarters to Kansas City. In his first year, the basketball tournament field was doubled to 16 teams.

Nevertheless, the NIT, held at Madison Square Garden, was regarded as a more prestigious postseason championship. But then came the shocking news that in the late 1940s, a number of college games had been "fixed" by gamblers who paid certain players

NCAA Executive Director Walter Byers presided over almost all the details of the early championships, including passing out the trophy to Dr. Forrest C. Allen, who led his Kansas team to the 1952 championship title.

From the early years of the tournament, two of the game's most influential coaches returned to Kansas City for the 1988 tournament and the celebration of the Final Four's 50th anniversary. Oklahoma A&M coach Henry Iba (left), who took the Cowboys to championships in 1945 and '46, and Oregon's Howard Hobson, winner of the first tournament in 1939, were among those saluted. Both have since died.

to see to it that their team failed to get above the gambling point spread in certain games. Since most of the tainted games had taken place in the Garden, the point-shaving scandal effectively killed the NIT and opened the way for the NCAA to become the postseason tournament of choice.

The tournament's growth was slow but steady. In 1954, the first telecast of a championship game found only a handful of East Coast stations showing Tom Gola's virtuoso performance in leading La Salle to victory over Bradley. Two years later, 6-9 Bill Russell made "intimidation" a part of the game's vocabulary and established the black player's growing influence by leading San Francisco to its second consecutive title.

In the 1957 title game in Kansas City, unbeaten North Carolina's triple-overtime victory over Kansas and its seven-foot sophomore, Wilt Chamberlain, focused unprecedented national attention on the college game. Considering the cast of characters and the stakes, this has to be regarded as the best game ever.

The game's greatest dynasty began in 1964 when guards Walt Hazzard and Gail Goodrich led UCLA to its first title. Under coach John Wooden, a former All-American at Purdue, the Bruins captured 10 titles in 12 years, including seven in a row from 1967-73. The run was broken only by Texas Western, which in 1966 became the first team with an all-black starting lineup to win the title, and N.C. State, which upset the Bruins in the

1974 semifinals.

The Final Four made its debut in a domed stadium, the Houston Astrodome, in 1971. It didn't return to a dome until 1982, which was especially unfortunate in 1979, the year that Earvin "Magic" Johnson led Michigan State against Larry Bird's unbeaten Indiana State team in the title game at the Salt Palace in Salt Lake City. Although neither the game (Michigan State won, 75-64) nor the matchup lived up to expectations, the excitement generated by Johnson and Bird set the tone for the tournament's popularity explosion in the 1980s.

As the tournament committee expanded the field from 25 teams to 32, then 48, and finally to its current 65, fans everywhere began discovering what the folks in hoops hotbeds such as North Carolina, Kansas, Kentucky and Indiana had known for years—namely, that college basketball was as colorful, exciting, beautiful, emotional, and rewarding as a game can get. The tournament turned out to be a ratings bonanza for CBS, the tournament's television partner since 1982. Analyst Billy Packer, who was the point guard for Wake Forest when the Demon Deacons played in the 1962 Final Four, developed into Mr. March for millions of television viewers. Also profiting enormously from the college hoops explosion was ESPN, a cable network that was founded in 1979. Where Packer became known for his cogent analysis of the game's Xs and Os, his counterpart on ESPN was a bald, one-eyed former coach (he took Detroit to the 1977 Mideast Regional) who shouted his love for the game incessantly, much to the delight—or consternation—of the viewing public. Or, as Dick Vitale himself might put it in that modest way of his, "When it comes to college hoops, I'm a P-T-P'er, ba-bee!"

Today the Final Four is a four-day carnival that features everything from banquets to conventions to a street fair for the fans. There are all sorts of ways to measure its popularity, one of the most oft-quoted being the $6 billion that CBS paid to retain television rights to the tournament through the 2012-13 season. But beyond the glitz, crowds and money, the event still is about basketball—and the people who play and coach it. The stage is bigger and brighter, but the court still is 94 feet and the baskets still 10 feet off the floor. And victory usually goes to the team most able to do the little things that don't show up in the boxscore—come up with the loose balls, take the charge, deny easy shots and find the open man.

For veteran sports writers, the Final Four always is a sentimental journey—a time to honor the past while celebrating the present. It's impossible to attend a Final Four without remembering Bill Bradley's 58-point performance for Princeton against Wichita State in the 1965 consolation game ... the 44-point effort by UCLA's Bill Walton against Memphis State in the 1973 title game ... N.C. State coach Jim Valvano, running around the floor in Albuquerque, looking for somebody to hug after his team's upset of Houston in the 1983 title game … and Arizona's gripping overtime win over defending champ Kentucky in the 1997 final game.

Unlike other major sporting events, the Final Four never fails to deliver excitement and drama. Never. It probably has something to do with the unpredictable, improbable nature of college athletes and basketball itself. Some nights the best team doesn't get the bounces. Other nights a team will rise up far above its head, the way Villanova did in 1985 when it upset Georgetown during the title game in Lexington, Ky.

How tough is it to make the Final Four?

Well, consider Jim Calhoun of Connecticut. For more than a decade he produced one Top 10 team after another. But every year the Huskies came up short of the Final Four. However, just when it seemed as if Calhoun was destined to remain forever on the list of great coaches who never made it to the big show (Ralph Miller, Lefty Driesell, Uncle Ed Diddle, C.M. Newton, Clair Bee, Ray Mears, Peck Hickman, Bob Boyd, Press Maravich, and Pete Carril, to name a few), the Huskies broke through in 1999 and put Calhoun into the sport's most exclusive club by shocking heavily-favored Duke to win the national title.

The walk isn't that long. But getting to it requires years of highs and lows, successes and failures, surprises and disappointments. How many potential championship teams have been ruined by an injury? Thwarted by a bad officiating call? Caught off guard by an opponent playing the game of its life? All a coach can do is suck it up and start over again.

It's a heart-breaking cycle, this thing we call college basketball. At the start of every season, there are a lot of coaches who talk the talk. But on the last Saturday, only the most fortunate get to walk that emotional walk.

1939-1949
WAR AND PEACE AND THE BARON REIGNS

Adolph Rupp

The year 1939 was hardly the best time to begin a new sporting endeavor. Even as America finally was pulling itself out of the throes of the Great Depression because of President Franklin D. Roosevelt's New Deal, war clouds were overtaking Europe. On December 7, 1941, the Japanese attacked Pearl Harbor to plunge the U.S. into World War II.

During the war years, the anxious nation was hungry for entertainment that would divert its attention from the battles in Europe and the Pacific. It was the Big Band era of Glenn Miller, Benny Goodman and Tommy Dorsey, among others. The teens' heartthrob was a skinny young crooner named Sinatra, and Hollywood was in its heyday with sexy leading men such as Clark Gable and Humphrey Bogart starring with bombshells such as Betty Grable, Lana Turner and Rita Hayworth.

The only big-time sport as we know it today was major league baseball, and even the national pastime was diluted when many of its stars, including Joe DiMaggio, Ted Williams and Stan Musial, were called into service. The heavyweight boxing champion, Joe Louis, the renowned "Brown Bomber," also was a soldier who spent his tour of duty fighting exhibition bouts.

From the beginning, the college basketball tournament was truly national in scope. The first champion in 1939 was Oregon, coached by Howard Hobson. Nevertheless, most of the best coaches and teams were to be found either in the East or the Midwest, perhaps because the severe winters created a greater need for an exciting indoor game to help pass the long, cold nights.

When Oklahoma A&M won its back-to-back titles in 1945 and '46, it was coached by Henry Iba, who tailored his ball-control offense and man-to-man defense to take advantage of seven-foot Bob "Foothills" Kurland's size and dominance. But when Kurland graduated the game came to be dominated by teams that employed a more up-tempo style that emphasized passing, shooting and ballhandling.

The epitome of this style was found at Kentucky. Its coach, Adolph Rupp, had played for the great Forrest "Phog" Allen at Kansas in the 1920s. Allen, in turn, had learned the game directly from its inventor, Dr. James Naismith. When Kentucky's so-called "Fabulous Five" won back-to-back titles in 1948 and '49, it did so not with size—the tallest starter was 6-7—but with speed and skill.

Rupp was a clever, sarcastic individual who ruled through intimidation and fear. To this day, his former players love to tell stories about the man known as "The Baron." When guard Ralph Beard came to Rupp as a freshman and told him he was thinking of transferring to Louisville, Rupp snorted and said, "Well, Ralph, I don't know why you would want to go to that normal school, but I can promise you we don't plan on canceling our schedule." Beard stayed and became a two-time All-America.

At the end of the decade, after his 1949-50 Kentucky team had suffered a 39-point trashing at the hands of the City College of New York in the final of the National Invitation Tournament, Rupp told his players, "Thanks, boys, you bring me up here and then you embarrass the hell out of me." A member of the Kentucky state legislature proposed that state flags fly at half-mast.

During the war years, the anxious nation was hungry for entertainment that would divert its attention from the battles in Europe and the Pacific. It was the Big Band era of Glenn Miller...

Oregon's Tall Firs returned to Eugene four days after the championship where they were met by a crowd of several thousand fans. University President Donald Erb declared the day a school holiday.

1939
THE TALL FIRS

By Earl Luebker

The trophy was somewhat battered and bruised, in two pieces, when it arrived in Eugene, Ore., in the spring of 1939. As had happened to so many things that had come into contact with Bobby Anet, it had come out second-best.

The beat-up condition of the trophy, however, did nothing to detract from its significance. It became symbolic of the first NCAA basketball championship. (The first tournament was actually under the auspices of the National Association of Basketball Coaches with the NCAA taking over control of the tournament the following year.)

Other teams such as the UCLA Bruins, Kentucky Wildcats and North Carolina Tar Heels would come along later to earn their places in the basketball history book. But nobody else could ever lay claim to being the first.

That honor cannot be taken away from coach Howard Hobson and his Oregon Ducks, the "Tall Firs" who beat the Ohio State Buckeyes, 46-33, in Evanston, Ill., on the night of March 27, 1939.

Just what kind of team was this to come out of the Pacific Northwest and cruise to three relatively easy victories—the smallest margin was the 13 points in the championship game—against college basketball's elite?

For one thing, it was big, at least according to 1939's standards. They might be dubbed the Elfin Elms today, but they were the Tall Firs in 1939.

Urgel "Slim" Wintermute was the giant at 6-8 when that was king-sized for centers, not point guards.

"Forwards Laddie Gale and John Dick measured in at around the 6-4 mark, maybe a little taller, so it was Wintermute, Gale and Dick who put the Tall into the nickname. Most teams rarely had any one player with those Herculean dimensions, let alone three," wrote Ken Rappoport in his book, "The Classic: The History of the NCAA Basketball Championships."

The two guards, Anet at 5-8 and Wallace Johansen, came closer to fitting the usual basketball mold of the era and did the job of making the Firs' fast break something special.

The fast break was a vital part of the Tall Firs' game plan. With Wintermute, Dick and Gale dominating the backboards and Anet and Johansen keeping things under control, the Firs were in business.

"Our fast break was a little unusual in that we looked for it on every possession," Hobson said. "We used it all the time until the opportunity closed. It was a break that we always attempted after we gained pos-

session, with the two guards handling the ball most of the time, the two forwards down ahead and the center trailing and coming in on the rebound."

Gale explained it further to Rappoport. "I'd call it a controlled fast break," he said. "There was nothing reckless about it. We knew where we were going, and we knew where to expect our teammates to be. When the situation would present itself, we were there. Prior to that, many who used fast breaks would just have five men run down the floor, get a long pass or something and just throw the ball up."

The Firs however were not just a free-wheeling offensive unit. Dick, in fact, thinks that defense was their strongest point.

Hobson was a bit of a con man when it came to defense. Deceit was part of his game.

Playing against Oklahoma in the Western playoff final in San Francisco, the Firs opened with a zone defense. After a few minutes, a shift to a man-to-man was signaled, but all the Firs continued to play with their hands held high so that Oklahoma continued to take it for a zone defense and worked for outside shots.

The same ploy worked in the title game against Ohio State.

Hobson took particular pride in the fact that the Firs were home grown. He was a native Oregonian as were the five starters. Wintermute had attended high school in Longview, Wash., but the other four were Oregon through and through.

Hobson attributed much of his team's success to a grueling 10-game, 22-day trip to New York and back by train. They learned the facts of basketball life on the road.

The Firs won seven of those 10 games, and Hobson told Rappoport, "Because of playing all through the rest of the country, we were ready for any kind of officiating on any kind of court." Hobson felt that the first NCAA tournament was a relative piece of cake for his Tall Firs. They had to work harder against the Washington Huskies and California Bears en route to the Pacific Coast Conference championship than they did in any three of their tournament games—a 56-41 win over Texas, a 55-37 victory over Oklahoma and the 46-33 triumph over Ohio State.

In his book, "Shooting Ducks: A History of University of Oregon Basketball," Hobson wrote, "Had the Huskies gotten into the playoffs, they would have won the NCAA title because they were superior to the other teams in the playoffs."

One of Hobson's favorite stories concerning the championship game involves Anet, the sparkplug playmaking guard and captain.

"I talked to Bobby before the game," Hobson recalled. "He was a great team leader and led our fast break. I told Bobby to make Ohio State call the first timeout and not to call any until we were really tired. Ohio State called five timeouts, and we didn't call any.

"After the game I said to Bobby, 'Why didn't you call a timeout and take a little rest when the game was pretty well in hand?' He said to me, 'You told me not to call a timeout unless we were tired, and hell, we're not tired.' "

Anet was that type of guy and it figures that he would be the Fir to go flying through the air and hit the trophy sitting on a court-side table. Anet went over the table and clipped off the figure of a basketball player that was on top of the trophy.

Dick said, "When they presented the trophy to us at the end, they had to hold the little figure on top. We had to bring the trophy back home in two pieces and get a jeweler to mend it."

While the Tall Firs played a special kind of basketball, they also had that special name. It was given to them by L.H. Gregory, longtime Portland Oregonian sports columnist.

"Greg had taken to calling the team the 'Alley Cats' when they lost and the 'Bear Cats' when they won," Hobson said.

"Fortunately it was his later name that stuck. He used Tall Firs first in a column on March 5, 1938, and it remained with the team from then onward."

The 1939 tournament was the start of something big, although there was little indication of such at the time. That first tournament, sponsored by the NABC, lost $2,531. The NCAA agreed to pick up the tab in return for sponsorship of future tournaments.

"One of the great bargains in sports history," Hobson said.

Earl Luebker retired as associate editor of the Tacoma News-Tribune after 37 years, covering Final Fours as sports editor for much of that time. He was a graduate of the University of Oklahoma.

1940

HAIL THOSE HURRYIN' HOOSIERS

By Joe McGuff

The only thing scoring a point a minute would get you today in college basketball is a lot of one-

sided losses. Not so in 1940. Like the dollar, a point went a lot further in those pre-inflationary times.

The Indiana team that defeated Kansas for the NCAA championship that year was considered something of a wonder team because of its offensive ability. Indiana was known as the Hurryin' Hoosiers because of its fiery fast break and as the point-a-minute team because of its prolific scoring.

As the decade of the 1940s began, college basketball was just starting to take on the look of the game we know today, with rapid changes taking place on and off the court.

Indiana was one of the forerunners of a new wide-open style of play. The NCAA tournament and other postseason events were steering the structure of the game in new directions.

The concept of college basketball as a tournament sport was starting to take hold. Ned Irish had established the National Invitation Tournament (NIT) in New York's Madison Square Garden and Emil Liston had started a small-college tournament in Kansas City.

Surprisingly, the National Association of Basketball Coaches (NABC) was for the most part indifferent to starting a tournament, but a few progressive-minded members prevailed and the first tournament was held on the Northwestern campus. When the 1939 event attracted only limited attention, the coaches asked the NCAA to assume responsibility for future tournaments.

The tournament was looking for both acceptance and financial stability in 1940. It found both in Kansas City. The championship game drew a standing-room-only crowd of 10,000 to the Municipal

Marvin Huffman was named the Most Outstanding Player for the Indiana 1940 championship team that came to be known as the "Hurryin' Hoosiers." The first of Indiana's five national championships, it was the most decisive as the Hoosiers defeated Kansas, 60-42.

Auditorium. The tournament, which even turned a profit of $9,523, had taken its first steps toward becoming one of the nation's greatest sporting events.

The changes taking place on the court were equally dramatic. The championship game between Indiana and Kansas generated unusual interest because it matched a leading exponent of the newly developed run-and-shoot game with a team that believed in the fundamentals of the traditional ball-control game.

"All we care about is getting the ball in the enemy basket in the shortest possible time," Branch McCracken said in summing up his philosophy.

The running game suited McCracken's combative personality. He earned three varsity football letters at Indiana even though he supposedly had never seen a football game before arriving on campus. He was recruited as a basketball player from the farming community of Monrovia, Ind.

Throughout his career, McCracken was an innovator. He was the first coach to break the color line in the Big Ten, he was a pioneer in using air travel and was one of the first coaches to recognize the value of television.

Another Hoosier coach, Bob Knight, would recognize a kindred spirit in McCracken, who drove himself relentlessly, put his players through non-stop two-hour scrimmages and battled with officials. On one occasion, he became so enraged at an officiating decision that he ran on the court to pursue the official. An assistant coach grabbed him by the coat to restrain him and he dragged the assistant onto the court with him.

McCracken was especially fond of his 1940 team.

"They could really run and shoot," he said, recalling that championship season. "They were good on defense. All of 'em were real hustlers. They worked all the time and there was no selfishness. That was a team."

Indiana did not win the Big Ten title in 1940 but defeated Purdue, the league champion, twice and was named the conference representative for the NCAA tournament.

The Hoosiers were not extended on their way to the final. They defeated Springfield (Mass.) College, 48-24, in the quarterfinals and scored a 39-30 victory over Duquesne in the semifinals.

Kansas possessed good speed but played a more conservative possession game. The Jayhawks were known as the "Pony Express" team, a name that Allen gave them because they were small but fast. The Jayhawks also had exceptional outside shooters in Bill Hogben, Don Ebling, Howard Engleman and Bob Allen, the coach's son. Dick Harp, who later coached the Jayhawks, played on the team as did Ralph Miller, who later enjoyed a long and distinguished coaching career.

Kansas lost its final conference game at Oklahoma and finished in a three-way tie for the Big Six championship with Oklahoma and Missouri. The three teams met in a play-off. Kansas drew a bye and Oklahoma defeated Missouri, 52-41. Kansas then defeated Oklahoma, 45-39. The Jayhawks gained the fifth district spot by defeating Oklahoma A&M (now Oklahoma State), 45-43, in overtime.

The Jayhawks eliminated Rice, 50-44, in the first round of the NCAA tournament, but seemingly that was as far as the Jayhawks were going to go. Southern California was the Jayhawks' semifinal opponent and the Trojans were widely regarded as the best team in the country.

"I told 'em USC was great but had a reputation of just playing hard enough to win," Allen noted. "Then I said if they had any ideas about things they wanted to try, go ahead and try 'em, don't look at the bench to see if the old man would approve."

Southern Cal led, 42-41, late in the game, but Engleman hit from the corner with 16 seconds left to put Kansas ahead. The Trojans called a timeout and planned their strategy.

They developed a wedge at the center circle and gave the ball to Jack Morrison, their best outside shooter. He got his shot off, but it hit the back of the rim and bounced away. Astonishingly, the Jayhawks were in the NCAA championship final.

The story is told that a late-night conversation among McCracken and two old coaching friends, Sam Barry of Southern California and Everett Dean of Stanford, had an important bearing on the outcome of the title game.

Dean asked McCracken what kind of defense he was going to play and McCracken told him shifting man-to-man. Barry asked McCracken if he had scouted Kansas and McCracken said no. Barry recommended a switch to a pressing fullcourt defense and Dean concurred.

"We pressed them from the moment the ball changed hands," McCracken said later. "It took stamina and condition. It meant high speed for 40 minutes. But it wrecked Kansas' set shots and let us play our fireball game." Indiana also had one other advantage, a canine mascot named Tootsie. The dog, a cross between a fox terrier and a spitz, was brought to Kansas City by 71-year-old

---

Ohio State center John Schick scored his only field goal in the first half of the 1939 championship game in an era when scores were low and the games slow and deliberate. Oregon led 21-16 at halftime. The game's leading scorer was Oregon's John Dick with 13 points.

Charles P. McNabb, who said the dog had been to seven games and Indiana had won all of them.

Tootsie's record would soon be 8-0. The game started with promise for Kansas, which took a 10-4 lead in the first seven minutes. The Hoosiers, who came into the game lighthearted and confident, called a timeout to reflect on what was going wrong. Guard Marv Huffman said the Hoosiers just looked at each other and didn't say a word.

"We just knew that we weren't playing ball," he said. "We weren't doing the job. We weren't blocking out good and we weren't running fast enough." Huffman said the Hoosiers were determined to go out and do the job right. They did just that and for all practical purposes the outcome was decided by halftime.

The Kansas City Star recorded the Hoosiers' performance this way: "Scorching the floor with smooth speed and slicing the air with zipping passes, they moved through the Kansas defense for easy setups, dropped spectacular one-handed shots from all angles and buried longshots from the outside while Allen's lads looked on powerless to do anything about it."

Kansas was never able to get close in the second half and Indiana won, 60-42. "We didn't know what to expect because we had never seen Indiana," Engleman recalled later. "The only scouting report we had was a letter from a KU alumnus back there. They hit us with a fast break a little different than anything we had seen."

Joe McGuff was sports editor of The Kansas City Star for much of his career, which ended as the editor and vice-president of the company. He was president of the Baseball Writers of America.

1941

'HELL, WE'VE FORGOTTEN HOW TO LOSE'

By Tom Butler

Joe DiMaggio and Ted Williams were revving up for monumental baseball exploits and Pearl Harbor was a little more than eight months off when Wisconsin won its only NCAA basketball championship.

The Badgers capped a 20-3 season with a 39-34 victory over Washington State in the NCAA final at Kansas City on March 29, 1941. Basketball hadn't evolved into the free-wheeling game we know today, but Badger fans consistently jammed the Wisconsin Field House to its 13,000 capacity during that memorable season.

Wisconsin coach Bud Foster taught a methodical, disciplined brand of basketball that relied on deft passing, tight screens and sharp cuts. The team was paced by All-America center Gene Englund and deadeye sophomore John Kotz, the first one-hand shooter of prominence in Wisconsin history.

"We played more ball control," Englund said. "We passed the ball and kept the ball because the other team couldn't score while we had the ball."

Kotz was taught to shoot with one hand by his Rhinelander (Wis.) High School coach, Russ Leksell, who theorized that everyone has one "dominant" hand and shooting with two hands on the ball resulted in less accuracy. It worked for Kotz. He led Rhinelander to a 20-0 record and the Wisconsin Class A state championship in 1939, scoring 467 of his team's 952 points. His

total was just nine points fewer than all Rhinelander opponents combined.

Sophomores played a prominent role as the Badgers charged toward the national championship. Kotz and guard Fred Rehm teamed with seniors Englund and guard Ted Strain and junior forward Charley Epperson in the starting lineup. Reserves included giant center Don Timmerman, sparkplug guard Bob Alwin and swingman Ed Scheiwe, along with Harlo Scott, Bob Sullivan, Warren Schrage and Bob Roth.

The Badgers showed little of their championship caliber early that season when they lost three of their first eight games, including the Big Ten opener at Minnesota, 44-27.

"We got waxed, absolutely stomped," said Englund, recalling that opening loss at Minneapolis.

So inept were the Badgers that night they failed to get a field goal in the second half. Foster expressed disgust afterward. When asked if his team had a chance to finish in the Big Ten's first division, the coach replied, "Never! Not after that dismal exhibition."

There was little to cheer about. Wisconsin, which had finished with a 5-15 record the year before, ninth (3-9) in the conference, lost to Pittsburgh, 36-34, at Madison and to Marquette, 40-30, in Milwaukee during December.

The Badgers rekindled hope after returning home from Minnesota by defeating Iowa and Purdue, the latter by 48-42 in overtime. That launched a 15-game winning streak that culminated with the victory at Kansas City.

"I really think the turning point was the overtime game with

Purdue," said Englund, the Big Ten's most valuable player that year. "That's what turned the whole thing around as far as giving us the confidence we needed."

Kotz's three-point play in the waning moments of regulation sent the Purdue game into overtime with the teams deadlocked at 38-38. Baskets by Englund, Kotz and Alwin in the first two minutes of the extra period sparked the Badgers to victory.

Wisconsin won another overtime game at Northwestern, 48-46, and avenged the loss at Minnesota by trouncing the Gophers, 42-32, at Madison in the final conference game of the season. It gave Foster his second of three Big Ten titles as Badger coach.

Wisconsin then was chosen to host the NCAA Eastern Regional that included Dartmouth, Pittsburgh and North Carolina. The tournament featured such standouts as North Carolina's George Glamack, Pitt's Ed Straloski, and Dartmouth's Gus Broberg.

Wisconsin shaded Dartmouth, 51-50, and Pitt knocked off the Tar Heels, 60-59, despite Glamack's 31 points in the opening round. The Badgers earned a trip to the final by avenging their earlier loss to the Panthers, 36-30, before a record crowd of 14,000 in the Field House.

The Badgers were cocky and confident heading for their showdown with Washington State. When the Wisconsin party arrived in Chicago on the way to Kansas City, some hometown friends met Scheiwe at the train station and one hollered, "Good luck! I hope you win in Kansas City!"

The often brash reserve guard shrugged and replied, "Hell, we've forgotten how to lose."

It wasn't that easy, however,

against the Cougars. The Badgers rallied from a 23-18 deficit early in the second half by running off 10 unanswered points, six by Kotz, to gain the upper hand.

Washington State featured 6-7, 230-pound center Paul Lindman, a big man in that era, who scored 40 points while leading them to victories over Creighton and Arkansas in the Western Regional. The Badgers stymied him without a field goal. He sank three free throws.

Englund contributed 13 points and Kotz 12 to Wisconsin's victory and the Rhinelander sophomore, who was to earn All-America recognition the next year, was named the tournament's Most Outstanding Player.

Wisconsin relied on teamwork, tenacity and a knack for working the ball inside consistently for good percentage shots. Cougar guard Kirk Gebert sank 10 field goals, but Wisconsin's persistent defense denied Lindeman the ball in good position—which proved instrumental in the victory.

"We had plays that set up all the guys and we mixed them up," Englund said. "In fact, I'd say that teams we played scouted us enough so they knew exactly what our plays were, but we ran them so well we were able to score anyway. There was no doubt everybody knew what we were going to do."

When the Badgers returned from Kansas City the next night, a crowd estimated by Madison police at between 10,000 and 20,000 greeted them uproariously at the North Western depot and on the route back to the university campus.

Reflecting on what has transpired since that tournament, Englund said, "To tell you the truth, I don't think I could even play with those kids today. I don't

think I have enough ability. I couldn't run fast enough and playing under the basket, those guys would make mincemeat out of me."

But Englund and his teammates reigned supreme during that magical last season before World War II sent most of them into military service.

Tom Butler covered the University of Wisconsin football and basketball teams for 34 years at the Wisconsin State Journal before retiring in 1987.

1942
THOSE LONG-LEGGED, GANGLY INDIANS

By Art Rosenbaum

In 1942, basketball was a growth industry. When Stanford players alighted from the train in Kansas City for the fourth NCAA championship, they were greeted by gasps from a welcoming committee. How could one team have so many tall men—all agile, all coordinated and all able to pass, rebound and shoot?

Typically, newspaper accounts at the tournament site always included words like tall, lanky, long-legged, angular and gangly, just as West Coast sportswriters had described Stanford all season. They were giants for their time. Center Ed Voss was all of 6-5, forward Jim Pollard 6-5, guard Howie Dallmar 6-4, forward Don Burness 6-3 and guard Bill Cowden 6-3. More than a half century later, they'd all be small guards.

To make the Final Four hardly meant megabucks in 1942.

Coach Everett Dean, noted as an innovator of defenses, was also the holder of the exchequer. Stanford's winning net share was $93.75 and a trophy that honors the school's best all-time basketball team.

There were other differences in 1942. The NCAA tournament was mushrooming but still less publicized than New York's prestigious National Invitation Tournament (NIT). While media applications in the 1990s could fill an entire arena, even northern California newspapers used only wire service stories in those early years.

Additionally, there was a war going on. "We had a lot on our minds," recalled Dallmar. "We were only a few months beyond what President Roosevelt had called the 'Day of Infamy'—December 7, 1941. Should we enlist or wait to be drafted? What were we doing there playing games when guys our age were defending their country? Remember, too, our regional was held in Kansas City and in those days we didn't fly, so we stayed on that full week and had regular study periods to prepare for final exams as soon as we got home."

In 1942, before the term "Final Four" was coined, it was the Final Two. In one regional, Stanford muscled and sped past Colorado, 46-35, behind Pollard's 17 points. Meanwhile, in the regional at New Orleans, Dartmouth was trouncing Adolph Rupp's heavily favored Kentucky Wildcats, 47-28, and automatically became the favorite of the Final Two.

Some unknowing commentators guessed Stanford would benefit by remaining for a second weekend in Kansas City, with what amounted to a home court.

"Not so," said Dallmar. "We hated their new parquet floor. It had no give and was hard on the feet. We practiced at another gym."

Coach Dean was a master at devising defenses but this Stanford team was special—it could run. One must remember the times. The fast break was something of a novelty. Nobody dunked. The one-handed jump shot, popularized by Stanford's Hank Luisetti only a few years earlier, was still experimental for many schools. Long shots were rarely taken. And scores, of course, were low.

"We were," said Dallmar, "the first big team that could move faster than our opponents. With our success, the basketball world began to realize a big team could not only rebound but also run a good fast break."

Pollard had starred in the semifinal but he was sidelined by the flu and did not suit up for Dartmouth. Burness' sprained ankle did not respond despite a week's rest and though he started, he was out within two minutes. In their places came 6-4 Jack Dana and 5-9 Fred Linari with a different but just as effective style. Against Rice, Stanford had used a zone for a 53-47 win; against Colorado, a shifting man-for-man for a 46-35 victory; and against Dartmouth, a combination of both for the runaway 53-38 win.

With two first stringers gone, Dean decided on a different tempo: no setting up plays, fast break and shoot as often as possible, free-lance all the way. It worked—eventually. Dartmouth led five minutes into the second half, 27-26, but suddenly the Indians of Dartmouth collapsed to the Indians of Stanford. Dallmar, Dana, Voss and Linari all scored quickly and in the end, Dartmouth had been held to a 19.3 percent shooting average

while Stanford shot 38.7, outstanding for the type of basketball in that era.

In that tournament, much was made of Stanford's height, smoothness and skills during an era of low scoring. The following paragraph form the Associated Press report of the finale capsuled the tremendous change in the game of basketball:

"In the closing 10-minute surge, Voss, Dana and Linari collaborated for 15 points in one of the greatest sprees of point tabulating seen in this college basketball capital."

The talent of that Stanford team was re-emphasized later when both Pollard and Burness were named All-America; Dallmar was the NCAA tournament's Most Outstanding Player and later Stanford coach. Pollard moved on to the pros for an illustrious career capped by his selection to the NBA Hall of Fame.

Art Rosenbaum was the sports columnist of the San Francisco Chronicle for many years and was sports editor from 1954-77. Eleven of his stories were selected for the anthology "Best Sports Stories."

1943
WAR-TIME WYOMING TAKES THE PRIZE

By Dick Connor

They weren't strangers, exactly. They had, after all, barnstormed the East a couple of times, the most recent trip only a few months earlier as the war deepened and America began to tighten itself for what it recog-

nized would be a long and bloody siege.

It was the winter of 1942-43, and the American public was looking for something, anything, to give it a few moments away from the gloomy news on Page One.

Maybe that's why Wyoming and its basketball Cowboys struck such a responsive chord. From the time in 1939, as freshmen, when they had challenged and beaten the varsity, they knew they were special. So did their coach, Everett Shelton. After that exhibition, he began scheduling his team into the big population centers of the East.

Or maybe it was Kenny Sailors, unleashing what would become the standard weapon for all basketball players of the future—the jump shot.

Perhaps it was the fluid, almost flamboyant style of these home-grown Westerners from the windy plains of the high country. In a time when the stationary, two-handed set shot was almost an act of faith, they all shot one-handed. Even free throws.

They ran the pick-and-roll, set screens as if they were blocks of granite on the ridges along the mountains next to Laramie, and they throttled that war-torn basketball season as few teams have ever managed, before or since. Consider this:

In the 1942-43 season, they played 33 games and lost just two. They beat Georgetown for the NCAA championship. Then they defeated St. John's, the NIT champions, in the Red Cross fundraiser that packed Madison Square Garden a couple of nights later. A little more than a week before, they had finished third in the AAU tournament against the best of the past.

"We should have won that," recalled Sailors. "We got beat in

Wyoming's Kenny Sailors went after a loose ball against St. John's in the Red Cross fundraiser a few nights after the Cowboys claimed their only national championship, defeating Georgetown in New York's Madison Square Garden. A wartime nation listened in fascination as the Cowboys, led by Sailors' jump shots, came from behind in four straight games to become the NCAA champion.

the semifinals by a team that wasn't as good as us, and we beat the eventual champions (Phillips 66) twice during the season."

A half century later, Sailors taught in Angoon and coached girls' basketball. During summers and falls he was a fishing and hunting guide and outfitter. And he still played basketball in the city league. "I still shoot the jump shot. Not as often, and I don't jump as high, but I still shoot it."

Six decades ago, that shot and his dribbling wizardry took the blond kid from southeastern Wyoming to the Most Outstand-

ing Player award of the 1943 NCAA championship.

No less an authority than Ray Meyer of DePaul credits Sailors with the creation of the modern shot. Many lean toward Hank Luisetti, but Sailors notes a critical difference:

"Hank never shot a jump shot. All the old-timers I have talked to credit him with starting the one-handed set shot, and I would agree. But he never shot a jump shot in his life."

Sailors did. "I had to start it as a kid. My older brother was 6-5, and it was the only way I could get the ball over him."

The rest of his Cowboy teammates—all but two of them homegrown Wyomingites—each featured the one-handed set shot, and few college teams came close to them until they reached the NCAA Western division tournament in Kansas City in March. They had rolled over everybody in the Mountain States Conference, beaten Brigham Young in a special three-game title series, then came within a whisker of winning the AAU before heading for Kansas City.

There they faced Texas and Oklahoma.

This, remember, was not a

normal season. Illinois, the scourge of the Midwest, and Notre Dame each passed up both the NIT and the NCAA. Washington arrived in Kansas City as the fourth member of the Western championships, but it arrived sans its captain. Walk Leask had been called into service. Texas had a 17-year-old guard, 5-9 Roy Cox, as one of its key elements. Oklahoma had finished second in the Big Six that abbreviated season, but it had a legitimate star in 6-4 Gerald Tucker.

It was the Cowboys, beaten just once, with 6-7 Milo Komenich and the clever Sailors, who were favored. After a 43-33 loss to Duquesne to open a six-game barnstorming tour of the East just after Christmas, Wyoming had not lost again until the semifinals of the AAU the week before.

The Cowboys would not lose another game, but none would be easy. As a wartime nation watched with fascination, Wyoming came from behind in four straight games to claim not only the NCAA but a special post-tournament game against St. John's, the NIT champion.

Against Oklahoma, they sent the mobile Komenich into a highly physical game that saw the Sooners' Tucker foul out before half-time. Komenich then rolled in 16 points in the second half and the Cowboys won, 53-50.

Texas, meanwhile, saw Washington sprint out to a 21-8 lead before following John Hargis' 30 points to a 59-55 win to set up the title game.

For a while on that long ago Saturday night, it appeared Wyoming's one-handed magic had ended.

"I remember coming into the dressing room at halftime," said Sailors. "We were down 10 or 15 points, which were a lot of points in those days." Actually, they had trailed by 13 at one point, 26-13, and were still behind by six, 33-27.

"Ev Shelton was our coach, and he was a master psychologist. He walked in and never said a word, until he finally turned to us. 'Well, boys, it looks like this is it. We didn't go all the way like I thought we might. I'll just tell you what: I'll go back up to the hotel and start packing things up, and I'll see you toward the end of the game.'

"And he didn't come back until the end of the third quarter. By then, we had finally gone ahead."

Their 58-54 victory sent them back aboard the train for the East and a date in the old Garden against Georgetown in what the papers of the time called "The Big Game."

The Hoyas had defeated George Mikan and DePaul and blistered New York University (NYU) to qualify as the Eastern representative. Led by 6-8 freshman John Mahnken, who averaged 15.4 points a game, the Hoyas were a high-scoring, disciplined team that had beaten the best in the East.

It would be a fitting matchup of geography and style.

It was a one-game, championship setting, East vs. West, with the winner already scheduled to advance to meet the NIT champion later in the week for the Red Cross benefit.

As it had in its previous NCAA games, Wyoming fell behind early, then surged late on the strength of Sailors' floor work, Komenich's scoring, and the rebounding of Jim Weir. But they also got a superb night from substitute Jimmy Collins, who got all eight of his points just when the Hoyas had taken a 28-24 lead and were threatening to break away.

Komenich and Mahnken had been expected to dominate. But they spent so much time neutralizing each other that it was Collins and Sailors who eventually decided the game, 46-34.

Sailors was named winner of the Chuck Taylor medal as the game's outstanding player with 16 points, high for either team. "And he deserved it," wrote Bob Considine. "He's one of the greatest dribblers the yellow Garden court ever saw. He ran through Georgetown's fine defense the other night like a good halfback skirting the steel uprights of the Third Avenue el."

"I learned to dribble, I guess, in grade school," Sailors recalled. "We'd get off the school bus in the morning and go into the gym before class started. We'd get a basketball. The rules were, if you could keep dribbling, you kept the ball."

In an otherwise bleak and somber year, Sailors and Wyoming never seemed to lose it. A month later, almost the whole lineup was wearing other uniforms. But the 1943 trophy remained in the lobby of the Cowboys' athletics building, a shiny memorial to a season as special as the mountains that framed it.

The late Dick Connor was a sports columnist of the Rocky Mountain News and the Denver Post and was named Colorado Sportswriter of the Year 17 times. He was president of both the Pro Football Writers of America and the National Sportswriters and Sportscasters Association.

1944

THE TEAM WITHOUT A HOME

By Lee Benson

It was two in the morning at the Belvedere Hotel in Manhattan and the nine players who made up the 1944 University of Utah basketball team weren't asleep.

Only hours before the Utes had lost their opening game in the NIT in Madison Square Garden, a 46-38 defeat to Kentucky, and now they had been rousted from their beds and summoned to the room of coach Vadal Peterson, who had an offer he thought they might want to refuse.

Officials from the NCAA Basketball tournament had just called, he told his players, and they needed a last-minute replacement for Arkansas, whose team had cancelled because of an automobile accident that had killed an assistant coach and one of the players.

The problem was, the opening-round NCAA game against Missouri was scheduled two nights later in Kansas City. That meant the Utes would have to catch the first train out of New York the next morning. There would be no time for Broadway shows, visiting the Statue of Liberty or riding to the top of the Empire State Building.

"We've made a good showing here, and we've made some money," Peterson told his players. "Now we have a chance to see New York. What do you think?"

The coach's tone implied that he thought it might be a good idea if they called it a season then and there.

In 1944, the Utah basketball team was hardly the most feared in the land and certainly not the best known. The Utes had been the last team invited to the eight-team NIT and now they were getting the last call to the NCAA tournament. They had accumulated a 17-3 regular-season record, but as with most records during the war years, it was suspect.

The Utes didn't have a home gymnasium—their fieldhouse had been converted into an Army barracks. They had played only three college teams all season long—Colorado, Weber State and Idaho State. The rest of their games were against service teams. Their three losses were to Fort Warren, the Salt Lake Air Base and Dow Chemical. Only because Keith Brown, the team's graduate manager, had sent clippings weekly to Ned Irish, president of Madison Square Garden, had they worked their way into the NIT's consciousness and wrangled that tournament's final bid.

When they arrived in New York, they were the epitome of gangly country kids with their hands in their pockets gaping open-mouthed at all them tall buildings.

If somebody had offered, they'd have all bought the Brooklyn Bridge.

This was the makeup of the team: Nine players, seven freshmen, one sophomore and one junior. Their average age was 18½. All were Utahns—the majority Mormons—who had grown up within 35 miles of the University of Utah campus.

They would have all been in the service except for the fact that the seven freshmen weren't 19 yet and therefore not eligible for the draft; the sophomore was center Fred Sheffield, who was in

medical school; and the junior was Wat Misaka, a Japanese-American who, at that stage of the war, couldn't be drafted.

In a year, virtually every member of the team, including Misaka, would be off joining the war effort.

But in March of '44 they had other fronts to conquer.

That's what they told Vadal Peterson, their coach, when he suggested they turn down the NCAA tournament invitation in favor of a sightseeing tour of downtown Manhattan.

In their 2 a.m. meeting they voted unanimously to get right back on the train and accept the NCAA bid. If they got out of Kansas City alive, they could return to New York for the NCAA final game.

With the brashness of teenagers, they told the manager at the Belvedere as much when they asked him not to rent out their rooms because they'd be right back.

At Kansas City, they beat Missouri, 45-35, in their NCAA Western Regional opener and next faced an Iowa State team that had beaten Pepperdine, 44-39.

Iowa State, like all the teams Utah faced in its postseason play, was older and more experienced than the Utes. Utah did not have any armed services programs, like the Navy's V-12 training program, in its curriculum, and consequently did not have servicemen on campus who were still free to play college basketball.

Iowa State was a heavy favorite in the Western Regional tile game. So heavy, in fact, that Reaves Peters, the tournament director, came to Brown, the Utah manager, before the game and tactfully explained that the winner would have to catch a New

York-bound train at midnight and he'd already checked Iowa State's players out of their hotel rooms—and if it was all right with the Utes, they'd be leaving their luggage in Utah's rooms.

As it turned out, after Utah beat Iowa State, 40-31, the Cyclone players stayed that night in Utah's rooms, and the Utes slept in Pullmans—on their way back to the Empire State.

By now, Utah's players were losing their anonymity—in particular, a slender 6-4 blond-haired freshman named Arnie Ferrin. He had scored 12 points against Missouri and another six against Iowa

State and was the heart of Utah's attack—especially so after Sheffield, the defending NCAA high jump champion and the Utes' starting center, sprained an ankle in practice in Kansas City and was rendered ineffective the rest of the way.

In the NCAA championship game in Madison Square Garden—the affair was a Final Two back then—Utah was up against Eastern Regional champ Dartmouth, yet another seasoned squad made up of soldier-athletes. Many of the Dartmouth players had been transferred by the military and hadn't even been

on campus at the beginning of the school year. Among the team's best players were Harry Leggat, a former New York University star sent to Dartmouth by the Marines; Bob Gale, formerly at Cornell; and Dick McGuire, a proven star at St. John's now assigned to Dartmouth by the Navy V-12 program.

The morning of the final, Pete Crouch, Utah's assistant coach, overheard a breakfast conversation among the Dartmouth players. They were suggesting that they should play an intrasquad scrimmage before the game—so the people could get their money's worth.

Thanks to Couch, this information found its way into the pregame locker room. Only a week had passed since their first experience in Madison Square Garden—when they lost to Kentucky in their NIT opener—but the Utes were now adjusted to life in the big city. The 15,000 fans who came to watch the title game—establishing a new single-game NCAA tournament record —did not unnerve them. Indeed, the New Yorkers' penchant for siding with the underdog was an added plus.

Dartmouth could not break loose from the freshmen, and with a minute to play in regulation the Big Green found themselves down by four, 36-32. Gale got a field goal to cut the deficit to two and then, with two seconds on the clock, McGuire made a set shot that sent the game into overtime.

Ferrin, who had scored 18 points in regulation and was on his way to the tourney's Most Outstanding Player award, took charge in the overtime, scoring four points as the teams drew to 40-40. He drove for the game-winner in the closing seconds, but the ball bounced loose near the free throw line, where Utah's Herb Wilkinson picked it up and made an off-balance shot that just beat the buzzer, and Dartmouth, 42-40. Now it was time to see the sights—almost.

The New York newspapers had arranged for the Red Cross benefit game two nights later, also in Madison Square Garden, pitting the champion of the NCAA—Utah—against the NIT champion—St. John's of New York.

No one had to hype this game. A crowd 18,125 strong filled the Garden to raise $35,000 for the war effort. Ferrin scored 17 and

Wilkinson 11 as the Utes, now known in New York newspapers as the "Blitz Kids," won going away, 43-36.

They were the toast of the town. Parties were held in their honor everywhere. Their money was no good in any of New York's finest restaurants and theaters. They saw "Finian's Rainbow" and the Ice Follies. They ate at the Copacabana. They were feted at the Waldorf-Astoria. They were on Kate Smith's CBS radio show and Senator Elbert Thomas invited them to Washington, D.C., to dine.

But that was one invitation they turned down. They caught the train going straight back to Salt Lake. There they were paraded through the city streets in convertibles as they told tales of their trip back East, where not only had they managed to see the sights, but they had been one.

Lee Benson wrote sports for the Salt Lake City Desert News, covering every Final Four from 1978 to 1993 when he left the newspaper to write books. He returned to the Salt Lake City Desert News in 1998 where he is a metro columnist.

1945
THE BIG MAN ENTERS COLLEGE BASKETBALL

By Dan Foster

Hank Iba, whose Oklahoma A&M teams won the seventh and eighth (1945 and 1946) NCAA basketball tournaments ever staged, looked back over four decades one day and concluded that 1945 was an especially sig-

nificant year.

"Those were the years," he said, "which brought the big man into basketball."

And 1945 was special not only because it brought together Bob Kurland and George Mikan, both of whom would grow to legendary status as players, but it also became a reference point in the friendly duel between the NCAA and the NIT for recognition as the No.1 postseason basketball tournament.

Just as Kurland's seven-foot frame and remarkable skills had helped his Oklahoma A&M team win the NCAA championship, Mikan's 6-10 frame and talent were the catalyst in DePaul's capturing the NIT title. Both would later be enshrined in the NBA Hall of Fame.

It was during the last winter of World War II that those two teams emerged as the best in the two college tournaments. In an added climax to the season, they were brought face-to-face in a benefit game for the Red Cross. It was labeled the "Champion of Champions" game.

As Ken Rappoport related it in his 1979 book, "The Classic," early foul trouble for Mikan sent him out of their confrontation game with only nine points. Kurland had 14 in Oklahoma A&M's 52-44 triumph.

Given the unquestioned superiority of the NCAA tournament's stature over the NIT in the 1980s and '90s, it may be difficult to realize that until 1945, when the NCAA's champion was recognized as the "true" national champ, the NCAA had not overtaken the NIT in tournament prestige.

The '45 NCAA triumph was the first of two in succession for Iba's Oklahoma A&M Aggies (later the Oklahoma State Cowboys).

Utah freshman Arnie Ferrin scored 22 points to lead his team through an overtime and to the national championship victory over Dartmouth, 42-40, in Madison Square Garden. It was the Utes' second appearance in as many weeks in New York, having earlier lost their first game in the NIT. But this time, 15,000 fans watched the underdogs win and Ferrin gain the MOP award.

His 1945 team, like the rest of the great teams in his 38 years as the Aggies' coach, was characterized by a strict control offense and a physical man-to-man defense where forwards sometimes turned into linebackers.

Having remained close to the sport since his last coaching season in 1970, it was Iba's opinion that, "in 1945 and '46, we were playing much better defense than they are right now. There was more stress on defense and possession.

"Keeping possession of the ball was the strength of defense in the early days."

As the NCAA tournament format operated from its inception in 1939 through 1951, the starting field included one team from each of the eight NCAA districts.

Although the rule against goaltending was in force by 1945, changing Kurland's earlier style, he was still a dominant figure—on both defense and offense.

With Kurland scoring 28 points in the first round, the Aggies routed Utah, 62-37. Cecil Hankins, described by Iba as "a great outside shooter," scored 22 points, Doyle Parrack 16 and Kurland 15 as the Aggies dispatched Arkansas 68-41 in the semifinals.

Kurland didn't have to wait until he faced Mikan to play against a future NBA Hall of Famer. While Kurland and Mikan would be enshrined there, so would Dolph Schayes, a member of the New York University Violets team in 1945.

Schayes, playing center, scored 13 points as NYU beat Tufts, 59-44, and 14 in NYU's 70-65 overtime conquest of Ohio State in the semifinals. Against the Aggies in the final, Schayes—younger, smaller and less experienced than Kurland—scored six points to Kurland's 22

as Iba's team won the championship game, 49-45.

Iba, whose 767 college coaching victories rank sixth, described in tones worthy of a pulpit the emphasis his teams place on controlling on offense and patrolling on defense.

"We ran our offense with set plays," he recalled. "There was no freelance. We'd run the set, and reset and run it again."

Defensively, "we never did play anything but man-to-man," except for the season before he won the 1945 national title.

They played some zone then, Iba recalled, because Kurland could pin enemy shots to the backboard, or sweep them away around the basket. But after the goaltending rule came in, it was back to man-to-man.

He said an outside shot then was "about where the three-point line is now and we didn't take a whole lot of those. I imagine we were taking better shots. We had to get inside of the free throw line."

The emergence of big Bob Kurland, and the other big men in college basketball, made all that possible.

Dan Foster started with the Piedmont newspapers in 1948, was sports editor of the Greenville Piedmont and the Greenville News. His coverage of Final Fours dates to 1966.

1946

MISTER IBA'S PRIZE PUPIL BOB KURLAND

By Bob Hurt

Some called him Hank and others called him "The Iron Duke" but to those who best

knew Henry P. Iba, he always was Mister Iba.

It was Mister Iba this, Mister Iba that, as if Mister was his given name.

Maybe it was. Maybe Mister was given out of respect to a man who coached basketball for 41 years, and won 767 games. Only five major college coaches have more wins.

Iba, who won so often, ironically is remembered for one he lost. He coached the 1972 U.S. Olympic team, "robbed" in the basketball final in Munich. A Yank victory celebration was interrupted when the secretary general of the basketball federation extended the game by three seconds—three seconds used by the Russians to win, 51-50.

More appropriately, Iba should be remembered for his 1946 Oklahoma A&M team, which became the first to win back-to-back NCAA titles by defeating North Carolina, 43-40, in Madison Square Garden. That team was pure Iba—disciplined, unselfish, deliberate.

It was built around seven-footer Bob "Foothills" Kurland, a basketball Pygmalion brought to life by Iba.

In Kurland's opinion, no Iba team, before or since, came as close to doing what the coach wanted as that one.

"And there were other teams we met that year with more talent," Kurland said. "North Carolina may have been one. I'm talking about physical speed and grace and so forth."

It was not a big Aggie team. The forwards were Weldon Kern 5-10 and Sam Aubrey 6-4 with A.L. Bennett 6-0 as the first sub. The guards were J.L. Parks 6-0 and Blake Williams 6-2.

Kurland chuckled as he looked back on the motley crew.

"We had Sam, who had his butt shot off. We had Kern who was barely 5-10. J.L. Parks had fingers about two inches long and actually hit the ball with his fist when he dribbled it. Blake had a bad heart. More than once, we had to stop a game because his heart was fibrillating. Bennett was a great athlete, but not a great driver. He had been in the Battle of the Bulge. When the chips were down, he just didn't rattle."

Iba's raspy voice, which sounded as if he gargled with sandpaper, took on an edge as he talked about what Kurland had said. He contended he had great athletes, as good as any of that day. In Iba's mind, part of being great was following orders. These players did.

"I'd go to war with those guys," he said.

So would the U.S. of A. Four members of the team, including Aubrey and Bennett, had been in World War II.

They mixed well with Kurland, Kern and Williams, who had been starters on the 1944-45 team which was 27-4 and a 49-45 victor over New York University in the NCAA final.

The soul of the team was to become Sam Aubrey, who in 1970 succeeded Iba as head coach at the school which was by then Oklahoma State.

"That team didn't have any griping," Aubrey said. "We knew what we wanted. The man told us what we wanted."

Aubrey left A&M in 1943 to go to war. In September 1944, Aubrey was shot in the hip while serving in Italy. He spent a year in a hospital, where a doctor warned him his condition would deteriorate and relegate him to a wheelchair at age 35.

In September 1945, Aubrey hobbled onto campus with a cane

and vowed he would play.

"The poor guy; he couldn't make it the length of the floor at first," Iba said. "But he ended up starting every damn ball game. He was a team player—not a lot of flash, but he did his job."

Kurland recalled Sam stumbling to the floor while trying to backpedal in a defensive crouch.

Ironic. Aubrey has a strong recollection of Kurland stumbling over the same Gallagher Hall planks.

Aubrey roomed with Kurland when the shy 17-year-old kid arrived in Stillwater from a St. Louis suburb in 1942. Aubrey recalled that Kurland was "awkward." Kurland called himself "clumsy."

Others were less kind. Phog Allen, the venerable Kansas coach, referred to Kurland as a "glandular mezzanine-peeping goon."

Iba was infuriated at his old coaching friend. Later in Kurland's freshman year, Iba finished a game at Kansas with four players on the floor rather than use his only remaining eligible player, Kurland.

"Hell, Kurland wasn't ready to play," Iba said. "There was no way we could help ourselves, the way the game was being called. I didn't want to embarrass the boy."

Kurland quickly developed from "goon" to "great"—a fact brought to Allen's attention in 1946 when the big redhead scored 28 points as the Aggies beat Kansas, 49-38, to win a playoff for a spot in the NCAA tournament.

Kurland worked at scoring. He once spent an afternoon putting up 600 left-handed hooks as Iba watched. The first 100 did not draw iron. Then he started hitting.

Kurland, however, endeared

himself to his coach by majoring in defense. He became so adept at swatting foes' shots out of nets that Oklahoma coach Bruce Drake built a platform behind the hoop in 1944 and talked a national rules authority into mounting it to observe Kurland's second-story work. That led to the establishment of goaltending rules.

Kurland's scoring average improved each season from 2.5 to 13.5 to 17.1 to 19.5. Only once did he cut loose. On Feb. 22, 1946, he scored 58 against St. Louis and "Easy" Ed Macauley, then a freshman, to erase the national record of 53 set by DePaul's George Mikan.

Kurland vs. Mikan were classic confrontations of the day, hyped-up duels which largely were responsible for opening basketball doors to big men—a fact in which Kurland took pride.

Kurland was sensitive. He always insisted he was 6-11 and three-quarters of an inch, not seven feet.

And he was emotional. Blake Williams said Kurland threw up before each of his games against Mikan. They were standoffs, each team winning twice.

Mikan went to the pros. Kurland went into AAU ball with the Phillips 66ers and wound up as the long-time national sales manager for the oil company.

The Aggies ended the 1945 season by beating DePaul, the NIT champ, 52-44, in a special Red Cross charity classic but lost to the Demons to start the 1946 season in Stillwater.

The Aggies were to lose only one other game. Among their 31 victories was one over DePaul in Chicago.

They breezed through the regional by beating Baylor, 44-29, and California, 52-35.

Ben Carnevale's North Car-

Oklahoma A&M's Bob Kurland became a dominant player as the war years ended in the mid-'40s and America turned to a different style of competition. Kurland and George Mikan were the first big men whose style changed the game. And it was Kurland, the anchor of Henry Iba's back-to-back national championship teams, who brought about the game's first goaltending rule.

olina team posed more of a problem in the final in New York. The
Tar Heels were led by 6-6
Horace "Bones" McKinney, who
vowed to talk the Aggies out of
the title if he couldn't beat them
out of it.

His efforts to needle Kurland
backfired. McKinney was held to
five points. Not until John
"Hook" Dillon moved into the
pivot did the Tar Heels make a
late and futile run at A&M.

Kurland scored 23 points and
fed mates for three more buckets
to earn the tournament's Most
Outstanding Player award for the
second straight year. He also
forced what Carnevale called the
biggest turnover of the game.
Kurland had his back turned to
the ball, which accidentally
bounced off his hand to a
teammate.

The unsung hero, however,
was Bennett. The Tar Heel press,
an unfamiliar weapon in those
days, confused the Aggies until
Bennett invented a new way to
pass the ball into play.

"Not too many guys can play
low to the floor," Aubrey said.
"So A.L. just got down and rolled
the ball in like a bowling ball and
they just froze."

*Bob Hurt has been sports editor
and columnist for The Daily
Oklahoman, The Topeka (Kan.)
Capital-Journal and the Arizona
Republic. He was selected his
state's Sportswriter of the Year
nine times. He's now retired and
lives in Phoenix.*

1947

THE ORPHANS TAKE THEIR PLACE IN HISTORY

By Lesley Visser

It was six months after a radical new bathing suit had been
modeled in Paris, named after
the atomic bomb test on the
island of Bikini. It was the year of
"A Streetcar Named Desire," and
the year Chuck Yeager flew his
experimental Bell X-1 through
the sonic barrier. It was the year
an actor named Ronald Reagan
testified before the House Un-
American Activities Committee
on what he knew about Commu-
nism in Hollywood. It was 1947,
the year Holy Cross won the
NCAA championship.

They were called the
"orphans," a team from a tiny
Catholic school in Worcester,
Mass., that never played a home
game. They practiced in a local
barn, played some games at the
Boston Garden and a few more at
the Boston Arena. The rest of
the time they were away. No team
from the East had ever won the
NCAA championship and Oklahoma A&M had won it two years
in a row. But on March 25, 1947,
more than 18,000 fans at Madison Square Garden saw Holy
Cross beat the Oklahoma Sooners, 58-47, in the championship
game.

It wasn't a big team (only one
player was taller than 6-3) or a
very experienced team (no seniors, two juniors and a handful of
sophomores). But it was, in a
sense, a veteran team. Bob Curran had played for the Navy in
Chicago; Charles Graver had
been a forward at the Victorville

Army Air Base and Andy Laka
played in Greensboro, N.C., for
one of the best service teams in
the country.

Two more Crusader standouts
had been service starts. Sophomore guard Joe Mullaney served
three years as a B-26 Marauder
pilot and was named MVP while
playing at Turner Field in Georgia. Center Frank Oftring spent
three years as an aviation
machinist while leading the
Quonset (R.I.) Naval Base to the
First Service Command title in
1945, the same year Bob McMullan carried Fort Dix to the Second Service Command title.

They were serious players led
by a serious coach named Alvin
"Doggie" Julian. He was 46 years
old, a basketball devotee from
Reading, Pa. In the seventh
grade, Julian used to watch the
Boston Celtics when they came to
play in the old Reading Armory.
He studied the masters of the fast
break and patterned his game
after the Celtics' basic maneu-
vers. His nickname came from an
incident in the 11th grade. While
walking to school with some
friends, Julian stepped aside to
let a woman pass. His friends
continued on, oblivious to
Julian's good manners. When
they discovered he was 20 yards
behind them, one of them called
out, "C'mon little doggie," and
the appellation stuck.

In 1947, Julian was already a
legend in college basketball. He
put together a disciplined team
known as the "Fancy Pants A.C."
because of the intricate way they
played. After losing three straight
games early in the 1946-47 season, Julian directed his team to
23 straight victories, including
three in the NCAA tournament.
Because he had 10 good players,
Julian platooned them. One team
had Dermott O'Connell, George
Kaftan, Joe Mullaney, Ken Hag-

gerty and either Frank Oftring or Bob Curran. The other had Bob McMullan, Charles Bollinger, Andy Laska, either Oftring or Curran and a freshman named Bob Cousy.

Cousy had been the schoolboy star at Andrew Jackson High School in New York City. Even then, he was the stylish scoring guard who could pass quicker than a summer afternoon. In 1947, 30 years before Patrick Ewing, Cousy wore a T-shirt underneath his uniform. His college bio said he liked poetry and playing basketball—"365 days a year."

In March 1947, Holy Cross took the train to New York as the Cinderella squad of the ninth NCAA tournament. In the quarterfinals against Navy, Joe Mullaney dazzled the fans with nine field goals and even some one-handed shooting. Defensively, he went to work on the Middies' scoring ace, Kenny Shugart. Sophomore George Kaftan, the "Great Greek," scored 15 points and Holy Cross rebounded from a 23-16 deficit to win the game, 55-47.

In the semifinals against powerful City College of New York (CCNY), Kaftan scored 30 points, one shy of the Garden record for individual scoring set by George Glamack of North Carolina in 1941. Mullaney's hook shot gave the Crusaders a 27-25 lead, but CCNY evened the score at 36-36. Holy Cross rallied to beat Nat Holman's Lavender, 60-45.

Kaftan, Oftring and O'Connell led the charge against Oklahoma in the final. During the first 18 minutes, the lead changed hands 10 times and the score was tied on nine occasions. The Sooners looked to the great Gerry Tucker (who was called a "giant" at 6-6). Tucker scored 15 points in the

first half and Oklahoma took a 31-28 lead, but Doggie Julian put Bob Curran on Tucker in the second half and the Sooner center scored only seven points.

Kaftan, the 18-year-old forward, was named tournament Most Outstanding Player for his 63 points in three games, including 18 in the championship against Oklahoma.

It was the first time anyone from Massachusetts had ever won

the coveted honor and the only time a team from the Bay State, where Dr. James Naismith invented the game, ever captured the title game.

Back in Worcester, more than 15,000 people jammed Main Street to sing and dance while Holy Cross' deep purple banner was raised to the top of the flagpole at City Hall. The orphans had won the crown.

It was 1947, before multi-year

contracts, million dollar endorsements and high powered agents. George Kaftan went on to become a dentist and Bob Curran became a successful insurance salesman. Joe Mullaney made his name as a coach, Andy Laska became a respected athletic director and Bob Cousy went to the Hall of Fame.

In the old Boston Record, sportswriter Dave Egan summed up their winter of '47. "For Kaftan, Mullaney, Oftring, Cousy and O'Connell, it will always be yesterday," Egan wrote. "We know them and hail them as champions; we place them in a special group of invincible underdogs who will never die as long as New England lives. Stallings and his Braves, Leahy and his Eagles, Julian and his Crusaders. There they will stand, side by side, men and teams of such resolve and character that they could not and would not lose."

Lesley Visser began her career in print journalism. She was a sportswriter for The Boston Globe and then moved to television in the '80s, working for CBS Sports and ABC Sports. She covered and attended Final Fours over her career and she particularly enjoyed the 1985 Final Four won by Villanova.

1948

FABULOUS FIVE: EVEN BETTER ON FILM

By Dave Kindred

One winter day in 1975, the general manager of the ABA Kentucky Colonels, a tall and beefy man named Alex Groza,

flicked on a movie projector and asked a sportswriter to sit down and have a look.

They would see film of a basketball game played in 1948 by the University of Kentucky's "Fabulous Five." Groza had been one of those Kentucky players. He was 6-7 and 220 pounds in his college days. Not as tall as Bob Kurland, not as wide as George Mikan, Alex Groza was a strongman whose bounding, running, shooting and ballhandling foreshadowed the gifted giants of basketball's future.

Only he seemed not to believe that of himself. He said as much to the sportswriter that day in 1975. "We were good for our time," Groza said of his Kentucky teams, "but we couldn't play with these kids today."

He turned on the projector with the idea the movies would confirm his judgment. What Groza saw on the film was a team with one man taller than 6-4. He saw a team without a jump shooter. He saw the year 1948 from the perspective of 1975, and he looked at the "Fabulous Five" as a curiosity of an age long past, a dinosaur bone uncovered in a high-tech age.

The sportswriter saw something different. What the sportswriter saw he will never forget, for in the movies' images he saw the past made real. It had been one thing to hear old-timers speak of the "Fabulous Five." We learned their names by rote: Ralph Beard and Kenny Rollins at guards, Alex Groza at center, Wallace "Wah Wah" Jones and Cliff Barker at forwards. We would nod in deference to the old-timers who insisted on the greatness of those players.

But did we really believe it? Not likely. Young sportswriters think the world was invented five minutes ago. So the sportswriter

was ready to agree with Alex Groza in 1975 that the "Fabulous five" of 1948 wasn't all that good—until he saw the movie, and then he said to Groza, "You're right, Alex. You weren't as good as people say. You were better."

The movie showed Kentucky on the run. It was breathtaking. Groza ripping off a rebound. An outlet pass to Barker on the right side. Quickly across midcourt to Rollins, who tipped it ahead to Jones. And Jones whipped the ball into the middle, there to Beard on the fly down the free throw lane. From end line to end line, Kentucky moved the ball from rebound to layup in five seconds with each man handling the ball and the ball never touching the floor.

As the movie played out on Groza's office wall, Kentucky worked without mercy to win an NCAA tournament game by 20 points. The unforgettable images were of Groza's quickness with a little hook shot and of Beard's magic on the fast break. However self-depreciatory Groza would be on that winter day in 1975, the movie images told the whole truth: the "Fabulous Five" could flat play some ball.

They were a kind of team never before seen. They won the NCAA without a giant in the middle. They didn't play offense in the standard style of walk-it-up-and-make-a-dozen-passes. In an era of cautious, plodding, defensive-minded teams, here came Kentucky on the run. The speed itself was unusual; but here speed was only part of the equation: running, always running, yet Kentucky was beautiful in its ballhandling precision. They were an '80s team in the '40s. They were the future made real.

In Groza, Kentucky had the

requisite strongman in the middle. Working the perimeter, running the break, taking the short jumper, Kentucky had a little guard who was All-American three times, who twice was college player of the year and who would be All-NBA.

He was Ralph Beard, 5-10, 160 pounds, a competitor of such ferocity that he once awoke from a dream to find himself squeezing his pillow in a bear hug and calling out the name of a man he'd guard the next night, "I've got you, Jerrell, you son of a bitch."

Never had there been a better guard in college basketball than Ralph Beard. Not John Wooden in the '20s, not Bob Cousy in the '40s. The great coach Clair Bee said in 1948, "Ralph Beard is what this game is all about." Phillips Oilers coach Bud Browning said, "Beard is absolutely the best." Adolph Rupp, Beard's coach, said, "Ralph's the greatest basketball player I ever saw." For Kentuckians who adored Beard, the photograph that best identified the little guy showed him stern-visaged and hard-muscled, flying—always flying—for another layup at the end of a sudden sprint that left the enemy wondering where he went.

After his freshman year at Kentucky, Beard asked Rupp to write a letter detailing his weaknesses so he could work on them that summer. Rupp advised him to improve his free throw shooting, use his left hand more on the dribble and develop a 15-foot jump shot. "If you can correct those few weaknesses," Rupp wrote to Beard, "you will not only be a greater basketball player, but you will be almost a perfect basketball player."

Beard took Rupp's word as gospel. "Some guys say they hated Rupp. Not me. He was it as far as I was concerned. If he told

me to run through a brick wall, I'd have backed up as far as it would take. I wanted to show him I was the best basketball player who ever came down the pike."

With Beard at guard in 1948 was Rollins, a six-footer with good speed. "He was the catalyst, the unselfish one," Beard said. Rollins put his gifts to the ultimate test in the NCAA tournament semifinal when Rupp assigned him to guard college basketball's newest phenomenon, the Holy Cross guard named Bob Cousy.

Cousy's exploits had prompted a banner-maker to hang a bedsheet in Madison Square Garden: COUSY—THE GREATEST. Going against Kentucky and Rollins, Cousy scored one point. After Kentucky won, 60-52, with Beard and Groza scoring 13 each, someone delivered the Cousy bedsheet to Kenny Rollins.

Kentucky's championship victory over Baylor, 58-42, was anticlimactic. In it Groza scored 14, Beard 12. The 1948 championship was Kentucky's first, earned in a season when the Wildcats won 34 of 36 games. After the season, Rupp's team competed in the Olympic Trials and finished second to the Phillips Oilers. In the 1948 Games in London, the gold medal U.S. team included Rupp as assistant coach and all five Kentucky starters—Groza, Beard, Jones, Rollins and Barker—as team members. Kentucky won the national championship again in '49, Beard's senior season.

In that winter of 1975 when Alex Groza invited a sportswriter to see the past, the writer later told Ralph Beard about the movies. He told Beard he thought Groza was too modest and he asked Beard how good the "Fabulous Five" had been.

"Of all our good years, we

were best in '48," Beard said. He smiled then, warmed by the memory. "You tell Alex to get suited up because I don't care if we're 50 years old or what, I think we can beat these kids today."

Dave Kindred is the back page columnist of The Sporting News after a distinguished career as book writer and lead columnist for The (Louisville) Courier-Journal, The National, The Washington Post and the Atlanta Journal and Constitution.

1949

GROZA FOILED IBA'S STRATEGY

By Tev Laudeman

Hank Iba had a surprise for his Oklahoma A&M basketball players when they went to Seattle to play Kentucky for the 1949 NCAA championship. The Aggies would not use their traditional sagging man-to-man defense, designed to take away the high-percentage shot.

Iba figured Adolph Rupp's Wildcats had too many long-range sharpshooters for the sagging defense to work. So Iba decided to take on Kentucky in a straight man-to-man.

He assigned J.L. Parks to stick with three-time All-American guard Ralph Beard, a deadly long shooter. Jack Shelton, a 6-6 forward, drew another Kentucky All-American, 6-4 Wallace "Wah Wah" Jones. Vernon Yates, a 6-4 forward was to cover 6-2 Jim Line, a junior forward and the only Wildcat starter who was not a senior. Joe Bradley would guard Cliff Barker, Kentucky's ballhandling wizard.

Bob Harris, at 6-7 the same height as Kentucky center Alex Groza, was given the toughest task of all: stopping Groza, the Wildcats' third All-America and arguably the best center in the country.

The defense was 80 percent effective; four of Kentucky's starters were shut down. Beard, Jones and Barker each had one field goal, Line two.

The other 20 percent of A&M's defense was fatally flawed. Harris, whom Iba had called "the best defensive center I've ever coached," couldn't handle Groza.

The smooth, mobile center scored nine field goals and seven free throws for 25 points as Kentucky won, 46-36, before 12,500 spectators in the University of Washington Pavilion.

For the second straight year, Groza was named the NCAA tournament's Most Outstanding Player.

Kentucky became only the second team at that time to win two NCAA championships. Ironically, Oklahoma A&M was the other, winning in 1946 and '47 under Iba.

Yates, a senior in '49 for A&M, remembered that final game

vividly. He didn't doubt that the Wildcats had more talented players, but he wondered if the outcome might have been different, at least closer, if the Aggies had played their standard defense.

"What really won the game (for Kentucky) was the fact that we didn't sink back and help out," Yates said. "In my opinion, that was the key. I think we could have allowed a few more outside shots and sunk in there to help Bob Harris. That was the first time Mr. Iba had changed his defense that I know of. He never did cover strictly tight man-to-man. He always sank and helped. 'Fill the middle, fill the middle,' that's all we were ever told. That night he decided to go strictly tight man-for-man. He thought Harris could cover Groza; that's what he thought."

Yates recalled how, out of force of habit, he lapsed into his old defensive style of sagging inside. A&M was leading, 3-0.

"As soon as the ball came to Jim Line, he took that little left-handed pop shot from the corner and hit it," Yates recalled.

Yates said he was immediately pulled from the game "long enough to get chewed out."

Yates, later a high school teacher and successful coach in Ponca City, Okla., said he and his teammates expected to defeat the Wildcats.

"We thought we could slow 'em down," he said. "That was our game, slowing people down and making them play our way." A&M was able to stop Kentucky's fast break, but Groza was so strong inside that the Wildcats' set offense was effective.

"You might say we beat the Aggies at their own game," Kentucky assistant coach Harry Lancaster said the next day. "We played as near a possession type of game as we have ever played."

The genesis of Iba's defensive planning may have come four nights earlier in New York's Madison Square Garden when Kentucky gave a marvelous performance in whipping Big Ten champion Illinois by 29 points, 76-47, for the NCAA Eastern Regional title and a trip to Seattle. Illinois had gotten by Yale, 71-67, in the first round.

Groza scored 27 points against Illinois, but Iba may have been more impressed by the 15 points of Line, the nine apiece by Jones and Beard and eight by Barker. Jones had spent a good part of the game on the bench.

Or, Iba could have been equally impressed by Kentucky's opening game of the Eastern playoffs when Groza scored 30, Line 21 and Barker 18 in an 85-72 victory over Villanova. The Wildcats' balance was vital in that one because Paul Arizin had also scored 30 to get an even break in a duel in which he and Groza guarded each other.

Kentucky had as much balance as any college coach could want. Groza and Beard had been named to the Associated Press All-America first team. Those two plus Jones had been picked on the United Press International first five.

The Wildcats had an easier time getting to the final game than Oklahoma A&M. The Aggies barely escaped being upset by Wyoming in the opening game of the four-team Western playoffs. Jack Shelton's layup with four seconds to play gave A&M the 40-39 triumph in Kansas City. Oregon State defeated Arkansas, 56-38, in the other Western game, then lost to A&M, 55-30.

No. 1-ranked Kentucky vs. No. 2 Oklahoma A&M. A study in contrasts.

Rupp was a firm believer in the fast break and a perfectionist set offense, based on slashing drives to the basket and taking the outside shot to open up the opposing defense. He also taught an aggressive man-to-man defense. No one ever doubted that Rupp was serious about defense. What he didn't believe in was what Iba taught: slow-down basketball.

But the deliberate offense had worked wonders for Iba and A&M. He wanted to get the good percentage shot and test the patience of the opposing defenses. Rupp and Iba were without question two of the best ever to coach the game.

Kentucky came to Seattle with a 31-2 record, having lost to St. Louis, 42-40, in the Sugar Bowl final and to Loyola of Chicago,

67-56, in the NIT's first round.

Oklahoma A&M was 23-4 with losses to St. Joseph's of Philadelphia, DePaul, Oklahoma and Bradley. A&M had beaten Kentucky's Sugar Bowl conqueror, St. Louis, and had avenged all its losses but the one to St. Joseph's.

Kentucky was a six-point favorite against A&M. Rupp's basic strategy was to go to his top gun, Groza, as much as possible. To that end, Wah Jones was given the job of driving across the lane to draw attention away from Groza— then Jones was to pass off to Groza.

It worked beautifully, a perfect plan considering Iba's decision not to sag into the middle. Five of Groza's field goals were lay-ups, the other four were hook shots.

Groza's most important layup was one he manufactured for himself. With the score tied 5-5, he intercepted a pass and scored to put Kentucky ahead for the first time. The Wildcats never trailed after that.

"We got behind, we had to play the uphill game, which is not our type of play," Iba said after the game.

Groza recalled that A&M "didn't have a lot of speed. We had a lot, and good outside shooting. With Wah's quickness and speed and ability, when he made his move, someone had to get him. It opened the inside for me."

Harris fouled out four minutes into the second half with the Wildcats leading, 31-21.

"I guess that's an answer to those guys who said Harris would stop him," Rupp said after Groza scored a tournament-record 82 points in three games.

Tev Laudeman covered Kentucky basketball for The Louisville Times when Adolph Rupp was coach. He also wrote for the Portsmouth (Ohio) Times and Indianapolis Times. He wrote the book "The Rupp Years."

The decade closed as many pioneering basketball coaches emerged. Oklahoma A&M's Henry Iba continued a collegiate coaching career while taking the helm of America's Olympic teams and crafting a worldwide dominance in the sport. The respect his peers—and today, historians—pay "Mister Iba" is unique among the early day inventors and innovators of the game.

1950-1959

RUSSELL, CHAMBERLAIN, BAYLOR, WEST AND ROBERTSON

In the locker room of Washington's Hec Edmundson Arena, Kansas coach Dr. Forrest C. "Phog" Allen gave his final charge to the Jayhawks before they faced St. John's in the 1952 title game. Listening intently was Dean Smith (center), who would later join Allen as an influential coach.

By the mid-1950s, America was in the midst of an unprecedented social and cultural revolution. The nation was hooked on the new one-eyed monster named television, which overnight changed tastes and habits forever. And while families from coast to coast were glued to the tube, they also had more leisure time and more money to indulge such fads as the Hula-Hoop, the Davy Crockett coonskin cap, and the 3-D movie. In music, the big-band sound of the '40s had been replaced by something called rock 'n' roll, the leading practitioner of which was a snarling, pouting, swivel-hipped ex-truck driver from Memphis, Tenn., by the name of Elvis Presley. He was considered so risque that when he appeared on the Ed Sullivan television program, he was shown only from the waist up.

Sports was enjoying its biggest boom since the so-called "Golden Era" of the 1920s. Through the decade, the New York Yankees, Brooklyn Dodgers and Milwaukee Braves battled for supremacy in major-league baseball. Pro football began to gain credibility and support when TV allowed fans to see first the great Cleveland Browns teams, then the benchmark National Football League championship game between the Baltimore Colts and the New York Giants in 1958. A college football coach named Paul "Bear" Bryant moved from Kentucky to Texas A&M to Alabama on his way to building a legend.

As far as college basketball was concerned, the 1950s will be remembered for the arrival of the black athlete as a dominant force. And surely it wasn't coincidental that as more teams came to have black players, the game's overall level of skill also improved dramatically.

The 1955 championship game boiled down to a duel between La Salle's Tom Gola, a gifted 6-7 white player of the sort who had dominated the game for the previous 10 years, and San Francisco's Bill Russell, a skinny 6-9 black center who became the greatest defensive force the game had ever seen. By either blocking shots or forcing players to alter their trajectory, Russell elevated defense to an art form as he led the Dons to back-to-back championships in 1955 and '56.

The year after Russell departed the college scene for the Boston Celtics, Kansas seemed to have the next dominant center in 7-1 Wilt "The Stilt" Chamberlain. But proving that basketball still was a game where teamwork usually would prevail over a one-man show, North Carolina outlasted Kansas through three overtimes in the 1957 title game, a contest that many still regard as the greatest in NCAA history.

By the end of the decade, the game's dominant players were 6-6 Elgin Baylor of Seattle, 6-5 Oscar Robertson of Cincinnati, and 6-3 Jerry West of West Virginia. Those three probably would be on anybody's all-decade team, along with Chamberlain and Russell. Yet of those five, only Russell played on an NCAA championship team.

As far as college basketball was concerned, the 1950s will be remembered for the arrival of the black athlete as a dominant force.

In 1957 Kansas and North Carolina faced off in an epic Final Four game. The North Carolina defense held Wilt Chamberlain (above), the Kansas sophomore, to 23 points and won the championship.

1950

"ALLAGAROO, GAROO, GARA"

By Malcolm Moran

The institution is known as the City College of New York, but for its students, alumni and fans, there was no need for such formalities. For them, the place is simply known as "City." Anyone who was there around the time of the 12th NCAA basketball championship can remember the pride in going to City, as well as the emotional value of the following words:

"Allagaroo, garoo, gara;
Allagaroo, garoo, gara;
Ee-yah, ee-yah, sis-boom-ba;
Team, Team, Team."

During the brief, remarkable stretch in which the Beavers of City College made basketball history, the words were screamed in the old Madison Square Garden on Eighth Avenue between 49th and 50th Streets; downtown at Times Square, uptown at the main campus building at 139th Street and Convent Avenue; really anyplace in a city where basketball had become a passion.

At that time, the Beavers were the passion. Decades later, the New York Knickerbockers would win an NBA championship with a game reminiscent of the City College style—a game that emphasized movement, the creation of opportunities, and the unselfish, never-ending search for the open man. In the last week of March in 1950, however, the Knicks' involvement in the new league's playoffs was an afterthought. The Beavers were playing for a championship—their second of the month.

City had already defeated Bradley, 69-61, for the champi-

onship of the older National Invitation Tournament (NIT). The victory was part of an eight-game winning streak that sent the Beavers to a rematch with the Braves in the NCAA championship game on the same Garden floor.

In the 1980s, credibility would be achieved with important victories in the presence of network television cameras. But in 1950, national attention was the result of a successful appearance before the 18,000 seats at the old Garden. Those seats were filled late on that Tuesday night, March 28—10 nights after the

NIT final—with fans who had come to see if the Beavers could complete an achievement known as their Grand Slam (NIT and NCAA titles).

Midway through second half, six Braves each had been charged with four fouls, and Bradley trailed by 11 points. But the Braves switched from their zone to a man-to-man defense, gambled with full-court pressure, and reduced the lead to five with two minutes to play. With the rules of the time awarding possession of the ball after a free throw attempt—regardless of whether the foul shot was made

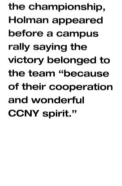

The '50s began in New York, and Madison Square Garden was home to the Beavers of City College of New York and their coach, Nat Holman. After defeating Bradley University for the championship, Holman appeared before a campus rally saying the victory belonged to the team "because of their cooperation and wonderful CCNY spirit."

or missed—a 66-61 lead was usually considered safe.

The City lead was not. Bradley's Gene Melchiorre, the smallest player on the court, stole a pass, dribbled half the length of the floor, and made a layup to cut the lead to three.

The Beavers seemed to end the crisis when Norman Mager made a foul shot and Irwin Dambrot scored for a six-point lead with 57 seconds to play.

But City's continued mistakes frightened the New York crowd. After a foul shot by Bradley's Joe Stowell, Melchiorre made a layup, intercepted a pass, and scored again. Suddenly the Braves were within a point with 40 seconds to play.

A City timeout did not prevent the Beavers from making another mistake. Ten seconds later, the Braves had the ball and a chance to take the lead. Melchiorre drove the lane, into an area occupied by three Beavers.

Years later, a slow-motion look at the films does not produce a clear answer to what happened. Melchiorre's drive took him into a triangle of dark CCNY shirts where he was stripped of the ball. To the outrage of the Bradley fans, a foul was not called.

Dambrot lifted a lead pass to Mager, downcourt at the other foul line. Mager went in alone for the layup that put the Beavers ahead by three points, 71-68— the final margin—with 10 seconds to play.

Nat Holman, in his 31st season as the coach at City College, proclaimed this Beaver team to be his greatest. Their Grand Slam seemed to be just a beginning. Just one starter was a senior, and four important parts of the team were sophomores. The Helsinki Olympic Games, two years away, could have been the final championship step for a his-tory-making group.

Classes were suspended. The buildings on the main campus in upper Manhattan were emptied except for resourceful students who leaned out of windows for a view of the celebration rally.

The bell on the top of the main building was rung for five minutes. The moment was pro-claimed as the proudest in the 102 years of the college. Harry N. Wright, the CCNY president, said: "I want to point out that they are given no scholarships to play ball, and they have not been imported to play basketball. I am particularly proud of their high scholastic rating."

And then it was all over, and a new, sadder history was recorded.

Seven members of the cham-pionship team, and eleven from other colleges, were arrested in the game-fixing scandal that changed the game forever. The Board of Higher Education also reported that high school records of 14 players had been changed to make them eligible for admis-sion to CCNY.

The Board determined that City would no longer play games at the Garden, and that the emphasis would be placed on an intramural program. Hol-man was suspended by the Board, but later won an appeal of the decision.

"I will not at any time say anything about it," he said. "That situation is dead. My heart bleeds for some of those youngsters who made a mistake. They say to err is human, to forgive divine. The thing past ... Those boys have all been on their feet. They're all fine citizens now and the press will never get anything from me. They'll never get it from the coach."

Malcolm Moran began cover-ing the Final Four in 1979 in Salt Lake City and has been a *regular since. He was the lead col-lege writer for the New York Times during many of those years before returning to the Midwest where he now has a similar assignment for USA Today.*

1951

THIRD TITLE'S CHARM ... A CIGARETTE LIGHTER

By Earl Cox

With volatile coaches Adolph Rupp and Paul "Bear" Bryant occupying offices just a few feet apart, the late 1940s and early 1950s were super-charged times at the University of Kentucky.

Rupp's basketball teams won consecutive national champi-onships in 1948 and 1949. Bryant's football Wildcats, after losing the 1950 Orange Bowl to Santa Clara, gained national recognition when he directed them to a tremendous upset vic-tory over Bud Wilkinson's Oklahoma Sooners in the 1951 Sugar Bowl.

Yes, there was competition and rivalry between Rupp and Bryant.

After Bryant left Kentucky for Texas A&M and eventually Alabama, he got a lot of mileage by telling a story about basket-ball-mad Kentucky.

"When Adolph won those national championships, they gave him a Cadillac," said Bryant. "Here's what I got for stopping Oklahoma's winning streak in the Sugar Bowl and then winning the Cotton Bowl." He held up a cigarette lighter!

Three months after Bryant took Kentucky to its first major

bowl (the Orange in 1950), Rupp's third-ranked basketball team was humiliated in the first round of the National Invitation Tournament by City College of New York, 89-50.

Despite the big loss to CCNY, Kentucky was an exciting place to be, recalled Cliff Hagan, who later became the director of athletics there.

"Kentucky was the first team to win more than one NCAA (championship) and also the NIT, and Bryant was winning all those games," said Hagan. "And everyone was excited in the spring of 1950 about mov-

ing into Memorial Coliseum, which was the Taj Mahal of on-campus basketball arenas."

Rupp was more than excited. He was so devastated by the NIT loss that for the second time in his career he scheduled a spring practice.

"The only other time he had done that was in 1948 when his starting team represented the USA in the London Olympics," said Hagan.

Rupp wanted to get an early start with his outstanding freshmen—two of whom were Hagan and Frank Ramsey, both future Hall of Famers.

Hagan, who had graduated from Owensboro, Ky., Senior High School at mid-semester, would not be eligible until after the first semester of 1950-51 and Rupp said that he probably would not use Hagan at all, thus preserving three full seasons for the 6-4 forward-center.

After three weeks of spring practice (it was legal then) Rupp was itching to get started again. The 1950-51 season was his 21st at Kentucky and his record was 410-77. He had the new coliseum. His teams were 72-16 in major tournaments during his first 20 years. His sophomore-studded 1949-50 team was 25-5 and he had all those promising freshmen.

Rupp said, as he began practice for what was to become his third championship season: "Potentially, we have one of the best teams in Kentucky history."

Only one senior starter, Capt. Walt Hirsch, was on the 1950-51 Wildcats. Eight juniors returned, headed by 7-0 All-American center Bill Spivey, who had broken many of Alex Groza's Kentucky records.

Among other Wildcats were Lou Tsioropoulos, C.M. Newton, Guy Strong, Shelby Linville, Bobby Watson and Lucian "Skippy" Whitaker. Rupp had quality and depth at all positions.

Kentucky defeated Purdue, 70-52, in the Memorial Coliseum dedication game, then blitzed Rupp's old coach, Phog Allen, and alma mater Kansas, 68-39, as Spivey outplayed Clyde Lovellette. The Cats took a 6-0 record to New Orleans for the Sugar Bowl Tournament, where they lost a 43-42 overtime game to St. Louis in the first round. Three days later, Bryant's football team ended Oklahoma's 47-game winning streak.

Whether that had anything to do with it or not, Rupp decided to play Hagan at the start of the second semester. Hirsch, having played varsity ball his freshman season, was ineligible for postseason play, and that may have been the reason Rupp decided to use Hagan.

The smooth hook-shooter played his first varsity game on his 19th birthday, Jan. 26, 1951, scoring 13 points against Vanderbilt. He started for Spivey in this first game of the Southeastern Conference Tournament in Louisville and scored 20 points. Hagan scored 25 the next day against Alabama and the Cats

gained a spot in the final against Vanderbilt. The Commodores had lost to Kentucky by 32 points on Feb. 24 in Lexington, but they turned the tables on the Cats in Louisville on March 3, 61-57.

Two tournaments for Kentucky, two losses for Kentucky.

"We turned down a chance to play in the NIT," Hagan said, "but coach Rupp wasn't happy when the NCAA put him against in-state rival Louisville in a first-round game."

Rupp had other reasons to be crotchety besides having to play Louisville.

"Coach Rupp had a bad year with his health," said Hagan. "He had trouble with a cornea, a bad back, his leg was in a cast because of a bad knee and he had a bad stomach."

To prepare for the NCAA, Rupp added a postseason game with Loyola, beating the Chicago team, 97-61. The Cats then beat Louisville, 79-68, at Raleigh, N.C., and it was on to the Eastern Regional at Madison Square Garden and a return engagement with St. John's. The Cats had beaten the Redmen, 43-37, on December 23 at New York City and this time the Kentuckians again prevailed, 59-43. Rupp's team scored 16 in the last five minutes to pull away.

Kentucky won the Eastern championship as Spivey scored 28 points and Linville got 14 to lead the Cats to a 76-74 squeaker over Illinois. Linville got free under the basket to score the decisive goal with 12 seconds left.

So it was on to Minneapolis to meet Western champion Kansas State, coached by Jack Gardner. Hagan had the flu and Whitaker started in his place. Spivey was sick, too, suffering from a cold.

Kentucky trailed, 29-27, at halftime, but the second half was

all Kentucky. The Cats took control early and went on to win Rupp's third national championship by a score of 68-58. Spivey more than lived up to his All-America billing with 22 points and 21 rebounds. Hagan scored 10 points. K-State center Lew Hitch was hot early, scoring 10 points in the first half. But Rupp got on Spivey's case and the big man held Hitch to three the rest of the way.

Hagan turned the final game around. With the Cats trailing, 20-13, midway through the first half, Rupp sent Hagan in. He tipped in a missed free throw then led a Kentucky rally late in the first half and continued to play well throughout. Linville was also an effective player for Kentucky, scoring eight points and rebounding well.

A crowd of 15,428 showed up for the game at Williams Arena on the campus of the University of Minnesota. There was no television. "The only Minneapolis station was not interested," said Hagan.

The Cats had a hard time getting back to Kentucky. Bad weather grounded their plane and they had to take a train to Chicago, a plane to Cincinnati and another on to Lexington.

At the victory banquet, Rupp praised Hagan: "We wouldn't be here if Hagan hadn't played this year."

Earl Cox was executive sports editor and columnist at The Louisville Courier-Journal and Times. He was founder of the Associated Press Sports Editors Association. He is now retired.

One semifinal game in 1952 pitted Santa Clara against Kansas, which won 74-55 to move to the championship game and the title. It was late in that game when a fiery little sub entered the game to steal the ball for the Jayhawks. Years later, that sub, Dean Smith, would have an even bigger impact on 11 Final Fours in which his North Carolina Tar Heels played.

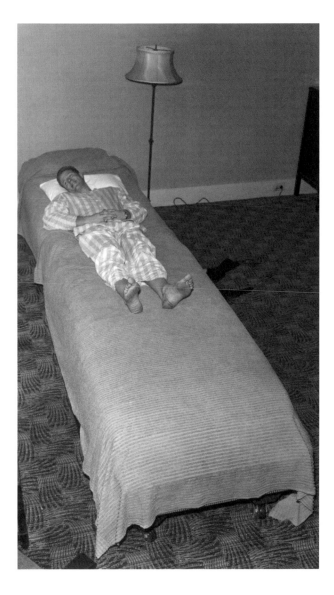

The era of big men began in the '40s and '50s. At the 1952 championship, 6-9 Clyde Lovellette led Kansas. When he requested a longer bed, the hotel manager put together two beds lengthwise.

1952

WHEN LOVELLETTE GOT CAUGHT IN THE PHOG

By Dick Snider

By the time the game ended and the Kansas Jayhawks had defeated St. John's of Brooklyn to win the 1952 NCAA basketball title, a sportswriter was standing on the court next to KU's legendary coach, Dr. Forrest C. "Phog" Allen.

The tournament was in Seattle and it was well past deadline back at the writer's newspaper, the Topeka (Kan.) Daily Capital. He was in a hurry.

"Doc," the sportswriter yelled as the celebration started, "how about a quick quote for the folks back home?"

Allen, 66, who was in his 42nd year as a college head coach, and who had just won his first national championship, hesitated only a second.

"Tell them," he yelled back, "that we were just like Casey at the bat." With that Allen started to move into the crowd. The sportswriter grabbed his arm.

"But Doc," the writer yelled into his ear, "Casey struck out."

"Yeah," Allen thundered, "BUT WE DIDN'T"

That was that.

The sportswriter was hoping he would say something about Clyde Lovellette, his 6-9 senior center, who had played exceptionally well most of the season and who had been phenomenal in the final week and in the NCAA playoffs. The title was a personal triumph for the 245-pound Lovellette as much as it was for the controversial Allen.

In the last two games of the regular season, Clyde scored 33 points as Kansas defeated its top rival, Kansas State, to clinch a tie for the Big Seven title, and then scored 41 in a victory over Colorado that clinched both the title and the NCAA berth.

In regional play in Kansas City, he scored 31 in a 68-64 win over Texas Christian and 44 in a 74-55 bashing of St. Louis. Allen called the latter Clyde's best game ever.

In Seattle, he scored 33 as Kansas whipped Santa Clara, 74-55, in the Western final, and 33 more as the Jayhawks wiped out St. John's, 80-63, in the NCAA championship game.

And remember folks, this was in the days when 30 points was a whole bunch, and 40 was a rare night to remember.

Kansas went on to play in the Olympic Trials and defeated Southwest Missouri State and La Salle before losing to the Peoria Caterpillars of the AAU in the final. Lovellette scored 91 points in the three games but somehow missed a layup that could have been one of the biggest buckets of his career.

With 50 seconds to go against Peoria and the score tied, Lovellette stole the ball and dribbled the length of the court, escorted by two teammates. It was a three-on-nothing break. Incredibly, Clyde missed the layup. Peoria got the rebound and scored with eight seconds left to win, 62-60.

Clyde and four other Jayhawks made the Olympic squad that went to Helsinki and defeated Russia in the final.

Despite all this, Look magazine, headquartered in New York and one of the major sports voices of the day, didn't name Lovellette to its All-American first team. This caused Allen to dust off his old observations that "New Yorkers are taller and fairer than the Chinese, but not nearly as progressive."

Allen had a lot to say and made his usual headlines, as Kansas ran out the season. First, Phog ripped the NCAA playoff system, saying Kansas was going only because the players wanted to go, and calling NCAA tournament officials "as big a bunch of promoters as the AAU's quadrennial transoceanic hitchhikers."

After Kansas won the NCAA title and faced the Olympic Trials in New York's Madison Square Garden, Allen threatened not to go unless he could have at least

one Midwestern official work Jayhawk games. He didn't get the
one he wanted, but he got one.

Phog had no reason to com-
plain about the NCAA Final
Four, particularly after St.
John's upset Kentucky, which
included the likes of Cliff
Hagan and Frank Ramsey, in
the Eastern final in Raleigh,
N.C., and Santa Clara bounced
UCLA in the Western final in
Corvallis, Ore.

Kansas won in Kansas City in
a tournament that is memorable
not only because of Lovellette,
but also because a TCU player
named George McLeod closed

out a remarkable season there. In
24 games, he fouled out of 14
and had four fouls in nine of the
other 10 (in all probability, an
NCAA record that still stands).

Big Ten champ Illinois won in
Chicago to complete the Seattle
field, and Lovellette took care of
the rest. The toughest time
Kansas had came the night
before the tournament when
Clyde went out for the evening
and was missing all night.

It wasn't his fault, and Allen
knew where he was, or at least
thought he did. Lovellette
laughed about it later but admitted it was a matter of some con-

cern at the time. Here's what
happened:

A Sigma Chi fraternity
brother of Clyde's from KU had
become an ensign in the Coast
Guard and was stationed on a
cutter anchored in Puget
Sound. He invited Lovellette
out for dinner and things went
fine until they tried to return to
shore in a small boat.

A dense fog had set in, and
the two couldn't make it. After
wandering around for a while,
they wound up back on the cutter, and Clyde didn't get back to
the hotel until after dawn.

"Phog had something to say to

As the 1952
championship game
wound down, coach
Phog Allen took
Lovellette from the
game with a fond
handshake as
Kansas won, 80-63.

me," Clyde recalled, "but not too much. I think he was as glad to see me as I was to be back on dry land."

An early-rising radio man from Topeka, Gerry Barker, saw Clyde enter the hotel upon his return, but he never said anything and neither did the Jayhawks, so the rest of the media missed the story.

Compared to current Final Fours, the 1952 affair in Edmundson Pavilion on the University of Washington campus didn't amount to much. There was no television, so the teams traveled directly from the regionals to Seattle, and settled it all by playing Tuesday and Wednesday nights.

A few radio stations covered the tournament, but there probably were no more than a dozen newspapers from outside the area represented there. Because it was an Olympic year, the Associated Press sent star writer Will Grimsley out from New York to cover it. It was the first time the Associated Press had invested that heavily in Final Four coverage.

Things were so slow that when the writers covering Santa Clara learned that Midwest writers called Lovellette "The Great White Whale," they looked over their roster and dubbed Kenny Sears, the lean, fair-skinned Santa Clara star, "The Wan Worm from Watsonville."

Members of the Kansas supporting cast also deserved mention. Allen's assistant was Dick Harp, who was said by many to do most of the coaching while Phog did all the talking. Harp never dignified that observation with a reply.

On the squad with Lovellette was a fellow named Dean Smith, who didn't play much but who obviously learned a lot. There was Charlie Hoag, who also played football well enough to be ranked right up there with contemporaries Billy Vessels of Oklahoma and Bobby Reynolds of Nebraska.

There were the Kelley brothers, Dean and Allen; B.H. Born, who would lead the Jayhawks to the 1953 Final Four; Al Squires, the first black player ever at Kansas; and the rest—Kenney, Lienhard, Hougland, Keller, Heitholt and Davenport.

Allen died in 1974 at 88. Lovellette played professional basketball and was in law enforcement for a time before becoming a teacher at White's Institute in Wabash, Ind.

Dick Snider was the sports editor and later managing editor, of The Topeka Daily Capital before joining Bud Wilkinson as assistant director of the President's Council for Physical Fitness in the Kennedy administration. Today, he is retired in Topeka, Kan., where he still writes a weekly column for The Topeka Capital-Journal.

1953

McCRACKEN'S SWEET REVENGE

By Ted O'Leary

Indiana University basketball coach Branch McCracken's deliverance from three years of musing over what might have been came in 1953, appropriately at the expense of coach Forrest C. "Phog" Allen of Kansas.

In the late summer of 1948, one of the nation's most ardently recruited high school centers—Clyde Lovellette of Terre Haute, Ind.—was in Bloomington, having assured McCracken that he would enroll at Indiana. McCracken figured that a big center like Lovellette would provide the missing element that Indiana needed to win its second NCAA championship. The first had been won over Allen's Kansas team in 1940.

McCracken was not unduly alarmed when just before enrolling, Lovellette said he was going home to pick up some belongings. He never returned.

By mid-September he had enrolled at Kansas. Asked how he had landed such a prize, Allen blandly told newsmen that Lovellette had decided to attend Kansas because he suffered from asthma. Although he was an osteopathic physician, Allen did not explain why asthma sufferers would find the Kansas climate more salubrious than that of Indiana.

Many years later, recalling notable recruiting coups, Allen, making no reference to asthma, with a wink told a writer, "There was nothing irregular in my recruiting of Wilt Chamberlain—I sold his mother on Kansas. But Clyde Lovellette—well, that's another story." He did not tell it.

In 1952 McCracken had been forced to watch as Lovellette, who had become one of the most dominant players in collegiate history, led Kansas to one of the most lopsided victories in an NCAA final, over St. John's of New York. Lovellette broke nine tournament records in the process.

Kansas' success with Lovellette substantiated McCracken's belief that college basketball had reached a stage where a big, good-shooting center, of which Lovellette was the prototype, was essential for national dominance.

Believing he had on his squad forwards and guards of national championship caliber,

---

Kansas returned to defend its title in 1953 but Indiana, with Don Schlundt, Bobby Leonard and Charley Kraak, defeated the Jayhawks for the championship, 69-68. Indiana kept Kansas center B.H. Born (25) out of position, which got him into foul trouble. Schlundt led the Hoosiers with 30 points.

McCracken went prospecting for the missing ingredient. He found what he sought in Don Schlundt, 6-6 and still growing. He was playing for Washington-City Township High School in South Bend, Ind. When Schlundt visited Bloomington in the summer of 1951, McCracken, recalling Lovellette's defection, promptly enrolled him in summer school.

Schlundt met expectations. Not only did he grow four inches, as a sophomore he established a Big Ten season scoring record. His addition, plus the switching of excellent long shooter Bob Leonard from forward to guard

after the 1951-52 season, worked wonders. The Hoosiers went to the Final Four in Kansas City (where Indiana had won its 1940 championship) with a Big Ten title and a 21-3 record. The losses—to Notre Dame, Kansas State and Minnesota—were by a total of five points. All three losses came on field goals in the last 30 seconds of play—a memory that returned to haunt some of the Indiana players as their championship game against Kansas reached its final 27 seconds with the result still agonizingly in doubt.

That the defending champion

Jayhawks made it to the NCAA tournament at all, let alone the championship game, was totally unexpected. Four starters from the 1952 championship team, including Lovellette, had been lost. Kansas was picked no higher than third in the Big Eight race and Allen said he doubted Kansas would win more than five games in 1952-53.

However, some factors were overlooked. B.H. Born, painfully thin but tall 6-9, had been completely overshadowed by Lovellette as a sophomore. But two years of daily practice scrimmages against Lovellette had

Indiana coach Branch McCracken joined the late-game debate at the scorer's table, where the number of B.H. Born fouls seemed crucial. The scorer signaled Born's fifth foul, but the Kansas bench and the press row showed only four—which became the argument's result. However, McCracken soon smiled as the team posed for its championship picture.

noisy exhortations and the Kelleys got them from the Kansas City crowd.

Kansas played its semifinal against tournament favorite Washington, which came in at 29-2. The Huskies were led by Bob Houbregs, regarded by many as the top college player of the season. Although obviously outsized, Kansas rushed to an 8-0 lead. Rattled by the Kansas fullcourt press, which somebody said started when the Huskies came through their hotel door, Washington not only failed to score on its first six possessions, it didn't even get the ball to the keyhole area.

Kansas stole the ball 18 times. At the half the Jayhawks were up by 11. If it wasn't all over then, it was when Houbregs, outscored by Born 25-18, fouled out in the third quarter (college games were played in quarters then). Kansas won, 79-53. Indiana players were apprehensive over what they had seen.

Indiana's semifinal against Louisiana State, led by the great Bob Pettit, was a classic example of a basic basketball dilemma— how to defense a team that possesses both a strong inside and a strong outside offense. The Tigers began with a compact defense intended to hold Schlundt in check under the basket. Leonard, finding himself loosely guarded just behind the foul circle, promptly hit six field goals in a row. LSU was forced to go outside after him, thus freeing Schlundt inside. He and Pettit each scored 29, while Leonard added 22, as Indiana won, 80-53.

The pulsating Indiana-Kansas final was a welcome contrast to the two semifinal lulling blowouts. In Indiana, Kansas faced a team with even more speed than it offered and an equally tenacious full-court

taught Born more than he would have learned as a starter matching up against lesser players. Allen added two superior athletes—football stars Harold Patterson and Gil Reich—to his squad. Dean Kelley's brother Al became a starter and the two

5-11 Kelley's became the leaders of a terrorizing full-court press.

Playing in Kansas City's Municipal Auditorium, 40 miles from the Kansas campus, was almost like playing at home for the Jayhawks. Pressing defenses tend to be inspired by

press. Respecting Indiana's speed, Kansas played more cautiously on defense, rarely pressing beyond the center line.

Only once in the game did one team seem to be on the point of breaking away from the other. With Schlundt on the bench in the first half after picking up his third foul, Kansas gained a six-point lead. Hastily, McCracken sent Schlundt back in and he helped pull the Hoosiers into a 41-41 tie at the half, even though Dean Kelley had allowed Leonard only six shots from the field, only one of which was successful.

Indiana led by one at the end of the third quarter, which had been marked by a bitter dispute. When a foul was called on Born, the scorers signaled that it was his fifth, disqualifying him and almost certainly dooming Kansas. The Kansas bench claimed its scorebook showed only four fouls on Born. Writers at the press table said their books bore that out. After rechecking, the official scorers agreed. That sent McCracken into a tirade. He charged that the scorers had eliminated one of Born's fouls. He also questioned their hospitality. "We came out here as your guests," he yelled, "and now you are robbing us."

Later came another eruption, this time by Indiana's Charley Kraak. Angered by a charging foul with 1:21 left to play and Indiana ahead by three, Kraak slammed the ball on the court so hard that, as he recalled years later, it almost bounced up and hit the ceiling. Presumably, McCracken almost did too, as he saw Kansas given three free throw opportunities—one on a technical—and possession of the ball under the rules then in effect. Patterson converted only one of his free throw chances and

Al Kelley missed on the technical. But on the ensuing possession, Dean Kelley hit a layup with 1:05 left. So the game was tied (for the 14th time) at 68-68. With 27 seconds left, Leonard made one of two free throw chances.

During a timeout, Allen instructed his players to hold the ball for 22 seconds, then get it to Al Kelley for a shot that might give Kansas its second straight NCAA championship. The possibility loomed that Indiana was fated to lose for the fourth time on a last half-minute field goal. When Kelley got the ball, he found he had no chance to get off a shot over a thicket of upstretched Indiana's arms. He snapped the ball to little-used substitute Jerry Alberts deep in the corner on the baseline. His desperate shot appeared on line, but it banged against the rim and an Indiana substitute, Dick White, snatched the key rebound of his career to preserve the 69-68 victory. Leonard later confessed he couldn't stand to look at Alberts' shot.

Indiana had suited up at its hotel about a block from the auditorium. After the game ended, Indiana students hoisted their victorious players on their shoulders and carried them back to the hotel. The sight of young men carrying other young men, apparently wearing brightly colored long underwear, through a downtown city street near midnight may have startled the unknowing. But to those caught up in the near hysteria of the moment, nothing could have seemed more appropriate.

The Kansas team took the bus back to Lawrence, arriving after midnight to be greeted by more than 2,500 cheering supporters. Allen told the throng, "I have received more cheer from this

team than any other in my 43 years of coaching."

Ted O'Leary was an All-American basketball player and Phi Beta Kappa at Kansas. He was a writer and book reviewer for 54 years at The Kansas City Star and a regular contributing writer to Sports Illustrated for 25 years. He died in the autumn of 2000.

1954

TOM GOLA AND THE EIGHT GARBAGE MEN

By Dick Weiss

Tom Gola was the Magic Johnson of the 1950s, a gifted 6-7 junior All-American who put his personal signature on La Salle's national championship team. He was the son of a Philadelphia policeman who grew up in the Olney section of the city, just walking distance from the school's campus.

The brightest star in the rugged Catholic League when he played at La Salle High School, Gola was recruited by more than 60 schools. When he accepted a scholarship to play for Kenny Loeffler at La Salle, he only had to travel across the street.

Gola, a quiet neighborhood kid who learned how to play the game in the school yards at Incarnation Parish, gave the tiny Christian Brothers' school a national address during his brilliant career. Gola was the first freshman ever selected MVP in the NIT when he combined with Norm Greckin and Buddy Donnelly to lead La Salle to the 1952 championship.

Two years later, he was the

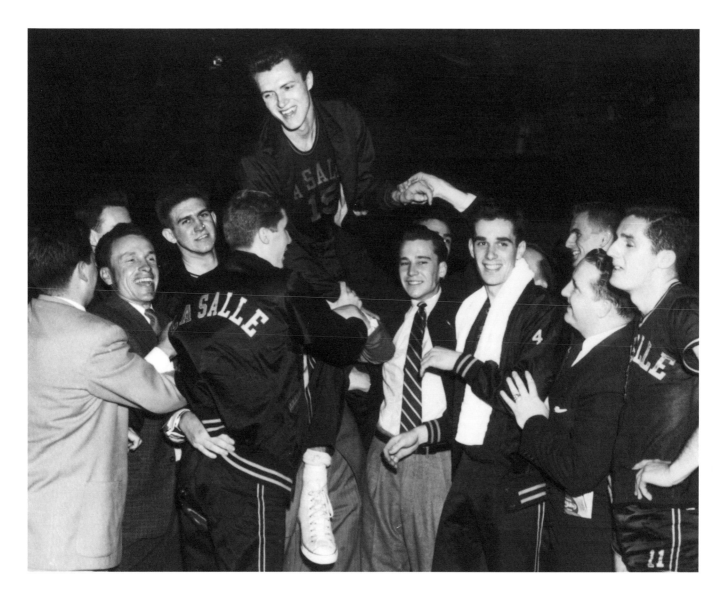

dominant player in the game.

Gola could play all five positions. Loeffler used him at center, but did not limit him to the post in the Explorers' flash pivot offense. Gola was too valuable. He could pass. He could handle the ball. He could rebound. He could play great defense. He could score.

He could score at will, but never did, preferring to enhance the abilities of eight other, more anonymous players.

Gola averaged 22.8 points during the tournament and was an overwhelming choice for Most Outstanding Player when the

Explorers defeated Bradley, 92-76, in the championship game in Kansas City.

Gola only scored 19 in the final, but that did not stop Bradley coach Forddy Anderson from lauding him.

"Gola killed us," he told the writers afterward. "It wasn't his shooting that killed us. It was the way Gola controlled the ball by grabbing those rebounds off the backboards and the way he kept faking our defense out of position, opening up the middle so their other players could drive through for layups.

"Actually, Gola hurt us the

most when he was just faking around out there, working without the ball."

In that respect, Gola might have been light years ahead of his time. He was La Salle's meal ticket throughout the season and did wonders for Loeffler, who had been hospitalized the previous summer for a severe case of ulcers.

Loeffler, who coached the NBA Providence Steamrollers before accepting the head coaching job at La Salle in 1949, was a brilliant man who once served as a federal labor negotiator and was an accomplished pianist. He was a stern disciplinarian who had a reputation for squeezing the most out of his talent.

Loeffler thought he would open the season with talent to spare. But then Jack George, a 6-3 guard, signed to play pro basketball with the Philadelphia Warriors after he was discharged from the Army. Jackie Moore, a 6-7 center who played a pivotal role on the Explorers' 1952 NIT championship team, was declared academically ineligible. Forward Bill Katheder entered the service and guard Eddie Altieri, the best ballhandler on the team, was a victim of the five-year eligibility rule.

"Our team this year is Tom Gola and eight garbage men," Loeffler reportedly told an audience of New York City writers before the Holiday Festival that year.

Loeffler molded his 26-4 team around Gola and senior lead guard Frank "Wacky" O'Hara and used them as the catalysts for a young team that also featured sophomores Fran O'Malley, Bobby Maples, Charlie Singley, Frank Blatcher and Charley Greenberg.

O'Hara and Greenberg both played with Gola in high school. Singley, who played at West Catholic, also had a Catholic League background. Blatcher prepped at South Philadelphia High School and the Navy. O'Malley was from St. Rose of Carbonville in upstate Pennsylvania. The 6-6 Maples was originally from Chicago but was spotted by Loeffler when he played for naval teams in Wilmington.

O'Hara was dependable. The sophomores were talented but erratic. Gola was simply great. The older college fans in Philly still talk in reverent tones about the time Gola overshadowed the

great Frank Selvy when the Explorers defeated Furman, 100-93, before a record crowd of 9,164 at Philadelphia Convention Hall. Selvy scored 40, but Gola had 25 points and 27 rebounds in 32 minutes.

The Explorers, who were distinguishable by their short sleeve jerseys, dominated the East and looked like a lock to return to the NIT, where they had been upset in the semifinals the year before.

But the Explorers created quite a stir locally when they chose to participate in the NCAA tournament instead of going to the Garden for the NIT. It was no secret that players would have preferred to play in New York City, but the Middle Atlantic Conference, a loose organization of smaller colleges in the Philadelphia area that controlled scheduling, reportedly twisted the Explorers' arm to enter the 24-team NCAA tournament.

La Salle, ironically, was almost eliminated in the opening round by Fordham. The Explorers won, 76-74, in overtime but needed a great pass from Gola to O'Malley for a layup to tie the game at 66-66 in the final second of regulation.

Gola got the ball at the foul line, surrounded by three frantic Fordham players. He spun and jumped, ready to take the shot. Then, at the last second, he spied O'Malley underneath the basket.

"Even when he's thinking, 'Gola can kill you,'" said a disappointed Fordham coach Johnny Bach after Gola, who finished with 28 points, destroyed the Rams in overtime.

Gola scored 26 in a more convincing 88-81 second-round win over North Carolina State. Gola dominated the Eastern regional final, scoring 22 points as the Explorers breezed to a 64-48 win over Navy. Charlie Singley added

16 as the Explorers prepared to head for Kansas City.

Before the team left, the Philadelphia Chamber of Commerce presented shamrocks, specially flown in from Ireland, to O'Hara for St. Patrick's Day.

As it turned out, La Salle did not need much luck. Gola and Blatcher, a protégé of NBA great Paul Arizin who learned to shoot in the South Philadelphia church leagues, each scored 19 points during a 69-54 win over upset-minded Penn State in the national semis.

Bradley succeeded in shutting Gola down to some degree in the final, but Blatcher broke loose again, this time scoring 23. Singley added another 23.

When La Salle arrived back in Philadelphia, the Explorers were greeted by more than 10,000 fans, who jammed the corridors and plane aprons at Philadelphia Airport.

The crowd knew just what to say when Gola deplaned.

They started the "Go Gola Go" chant that has since become a big part of La Salle folklore.

Dick Weiss, a Philadelphia native, has covered Final Fours since 1970, including Villanova's Final Four appearance in 1985, for the Philadelphia Daily News.

1955
EAST VS. WEST
GOLA VS.
RUSSELL

By Ted O'Leary

In his preview of the 1952-53 basketball season for the "Official NCAA Basketball Guide," Jim Enright, a knowledgeable

La Salle's Tom Gola was carried from the court by fans and teammates after he led the Explorers to the 1954 championship. The nation's dominant player, Gola took his Philadelphia team to the final two years in a row.

Chicago sportswriter and respected basketball game official, asserted that the time had come to reverse Horace Greeley's famous advice, "Go West, young man."

Enright suggested that if Greeley were alive today and a basketball fan, sound judgment would compel him to proclaim, "Go East, young man, in your desire to find the 1955 national basketball champion." Enright turned out to have been disoriented.

Enright listed two dozen teams he said were the most likely to make it to the 1955 NCAA tour-

nament. He did not name San Francisco. The most likely candidates for national college player of the year, Enright declared, were Tom Gola, defending NCAA champion and La Salle's two-time All-American, and Sihugo Green of Duquesne, who Enright asserted, had the best chance to dethrone La Salle.

This is not to fault Enright. Except for a few insiders on the West Coast, San Francisco was just another aspiring basketball team and Bill Russell was a young guy who went to San Francisco because it was about the only college to offer him a scholarship. Ridiculed at Oakland's McClymonds High School for his awkwardness, Russell worked long hours to improve his play. As a 6-6 senior center, he had played well enough to interest San Francisco, which at the time didn't even have its own court.

In Russell's first year on the varsity, the Dons went 14-7. By the beginning of the 1954-55 season, Russell had reached an announced six feet, 10 inches. Russell dissented, complaining. "I'm only 6-9 and five-eighth of an inch. Don't call me 6-10. I'm enough of a goon already!"

The skills that were to make him probably the best defensive player in basketball history, both college and professional, made Russell the ideal player for San Francisco coach Phil Woolpert. Woolpert was convinced that defense was the basis of basketball success, a belief mostly borne out by college results in the decade of the 1950s. "We figure to have the ball only about half the time in a game," said Woolpert, "so in practice, we work on defense half the time."

San Francisco first began to attract national attention as a result of its performance in the All-College Invitational Tourna-

ment in Oklahoma City, one of the first and most prestigious of the Christmas holiday tournaments. San Francisco trounced tournament favorite Wichita State, 94-75, and the following week made the wire service Top 20 polls for the first time that season.

San Francisco had lost its third game of the season, to UCLA, but it never lost again that season, or the next either. No other team came closer than 10 points except Oregon State, which in the NCAA West Regional challenged the Dons to the end, losing 57-56 in the final.

Joining San Francisco (26-1) in the Final Four at Kansas City were La Salle (25-4), Iowa (19-5) and Colorado (18-5). Almost everyone predicted a final between San Francisco and La Salle. Few confrontations in college basketball history had been more eagerly awaited than that between Gola, who had recently been named to a five-man all-time college team, and Russell. A similar individual matchup would make headlines years later when Magic Johnson of Michigan State faced off against Larry Bird of Indiana State in 1979.

What happened in the semifinal games only whetted the interest of basketball followers everywhere. La Salle beat Iowa, 76-73, with Gola scoring 23 points and San Francisco defeated Colorado, 65-50, as Russell scored 24 points. Wrote Bob Busby in the Kansas City Times:

"A packed crowd of 10,500 at Municipal Auditorium probably never before saw such a display of talent as was presented by two centers in one evening. Gola was perfection personified in all departments, as usual.

"Russell showed great all-around ability. The 6-10 San Francisco junior swept rebounds

from levels halfway up the backboard and he made one two-handed dunk shot over his head with his back to the basket."

Now the Gola-Russell matchup seemed assured. Russell downplayed the individual angle, saying, "I'm not worrying about Gola. I'm just going to try to help my team win." Russell granted, however, that "Gola could really give Coach (Woolpert) an ulcer."

A startling strategic move by Woolpert turned the Gola versus Russell buildup into an excitement-dampening letdown. To the astonishment of his players,

Woolpert informed them at their pregame meal that he had decided to assign 6-1 K.C. Jones to guard Gola, who was six inches taller. Woolpert figured that with Jones dogging Gola wherever he went, Russell could lurk under the basket, congesting the middle, blocking La Salle drives for layups and picking up rebounds.

The strategy proved inspired. Russell ended with 25 rebounds to go with 23 points. During one 21-minute period Jones held Gola scoreless. His point total for the game was 16.

La Salle coach Ken Loeffler's

scouting report on Jones proved only too accurate. On the locker room blackboard he had scribbled, "Jones, No. 4. Can hit from outside." So he did, adding 21 points to San Francisco's total in a 77-63 victory. The outcome was never really in doubt.

One of the most graphic descriptions of Russell's play was included in the report on the final in Sports Illustrated, then a fledgling magazine. After noting that La Salle was not able to deny Russell the ball, the report went on: "Particularly deadly were Russell's tap-ins. Timing his leaps perfectly, he would soar

It was Bill Russell's moment in 1955 as he jumped in the air and clicked his heels. An almost unknown San Francisco team held off Tom Gola and La Salle for the championship in Kansas City. Russell, the Final Four MOP, and teammate K.C. Jones dominated the game. Russell scored 23 points and grabbed 25 rebounds.

into the air just as a shot by a colleague floated in toward the basket and tip the ball in the basket while La Salle defenders impotently stretched and strained beneath. It was not Gola's night to give an ulcer to Phil Woolpert but Russell was no help for Ken Loeffler's duodenal condition."

It is a measure of how interest in the Final Four has increased through the years. Sports Illustrated, which would later cover the event like a World Series or Super Bowl, devoted only three columns to its report and did not give the author of its story a byline.

The 1955 Final Four set off repercussions that went beyond the crowning of one more NCAA champion. The performances of Russell and Jones, plus the presence of four other blacks on the San Francisco squad, accelerated the liberation of black college basketball players from the restrictions that racial prejudice had imposed upon them for far too long. By 1958, four of the five consensus All-America players were black.

In March 1956, after Russell had led the Dons to their second consecutive NCAA championship, the basketball rules committee outlawed offensive goaltending. No longer would a player be allowed to do what Russell had elevated to a physical art form. After watching him guide and tap teammates' shots into the basket, voluble Kansas coach Phog Allen, who had campaigned for raising the height of the baskets from 10 to 12 feet, raised the ante to 20 feet!

Appropriately the new anti-goaltending rule was called "the Russell rule," part of Bill Russell's legacy to college basketball.

1956

THE NCAA CROWNS FIRST UNDEFEATED CHAMPION

By Art Spander

Bill Russell, gray in mustache and mellow in mood, squinted into a spotlight and attempted to peer into the past.

"Who are all those old people sitting next to me?" he asked in mock surprise. A muffled laugh carried through the hotel ballroom. Sweet nostalgia carries with it frightening realizations.

Thirty years had flown since that first championship season. Yesterday these men had carried the University of San Francisco to consecutive NCAA basketball titles. Now there were baldheads, pot bellies and delicious memories.

Their accomplishments continued after graduation. "One judge and several lawyers," noted Phil Woolpert, who had coached those San Francisco teams. "These men have been successful."

No more successful than Woolpert himself. When great college basketball coaches are discussed, we hear the names of Wooden and Rupp, and Smith and Allen. But rarely Woolpert. Which is wrong.

He was man ahead of times. He was also a man who preferred remaining behind the scenes.

Woolpert died at age 71 in May 1987 in the deep forest of Washington's Olympic Peninsula, figuratively hiding from the spotlight and pressure of a sport he helped shape but in the end came to disparage. "The tail is wagging the dog," he contended,

alluding to an imbalance between academics and athletics. His final job had been as a school bus driver over dirt roads. And that's the way his world ended ... with a whimper.

The bang came earlier. NCAA championships in 1955 and 1956. Sixty consecutive victories. Coach of the Year awards. But if there's anything worse than losing all the time it is winning all the time. He retired from San Francisco in 1959, talking about the strain of his nerves.

There would be other seasons on the floor, a brief period in control of the San Francisco Saints, a franchise in the American Basketball League, and then some time formulating a program at the University of San Diego.

In the early 1970s, the man who brought together Bill Russell and K.C. Jones for the first time would flee from the ills of recruiting and the shouts of the fans by moving to Sequim, Wash. It was there he spent the final 15 years of his life, far from the maddening crowd.

Once in a while he would return to the past. The journey was always pleasant. "Isn't it great to be back together on an occasion like this?" he asked those who had come to the 30th reunion. The response was thunderous applause, as he knew it would be.

"I may sound immodest," he said, "but I firmly believe those two teams were as great as any in college basketball. In 1956 we beat everyone by seven points or more."

Everyone. The Dons were the first undefeated team in history to win the NCAA tournament. They went 29-0, extending the streak that had started the previous season to 55 straight victories. Five more would accrue the following season before that historic defeat.

Credit Russell, who revolutionized the game. Credit Jones, who could handle the ball and, as seen from his achievements coaching the Boston Celtics, could also handle men. Credit Phil Woolpert, who turned out to be a crusader for civil liberties as well as an instructor in zone defense.

"Phil was so far ahead of other coaches in recruiting black players it was scary," said Pete Newell. "There were a lot of rednecks then."

Newell was the man who Woolpert replaced as San Francisco coach in 1949. Newell was the man who would coach the University of California to an NCAA championship in 1959. Irony: That was the last team without a black player to win the title.

America was different in the 1950s. Phil Woolpert was different from many Americans. The only color he cared about was that of a man's uniform.

In later years, Bill Russell would complain of Woolpert's insensitivity toward blacks, and toward Bill Russell in particular. Eventually, those feelings were soothed.

"I have thrown down some of my psychological baggage," Russell said in what amounted to an apology. "Phil Woolpert saw something in me nobody else did. He gave me my chance."

We know what Russell did with the opportunity. NCAA championships at San Francisco in 1955 and 1956. An Olympic gold medal. And, as the Boston Celtics center, a domination of the NBA that would never exist again.

During the 1954 season, when Russell was a sophomore and awkward rather than arrogant, San Francisco started three whites and two blacks. The next

season the lineup was the same, and the blacks were indignant. Russell and Jones knew Hal Perry belonged in the lineup instead of Carl Lawson.

Tension was noticeable. "The Junior Globetrotters," someone wrote when the Dons went to three black players. Convention worked against Woolpert. Perception worked for him. The hell with the old ways. Perry would start. So would the winning streak. And many years in the future Hal Perry, then an attorney, would confess: "I owe Phil Woolpert everything."

Woolpert would explain he

owed his wife, Mary, everything. The day he was named San Francisco's coach in 1949, Phil sat down at a desk stacked with telegrams and letters and began to peruse the roster and the schedule. He couldn't balance one against the other.

"I went home," he recalled on more than one occasion, "and told Mary I was quitting, for the athletic director to get another guy. I wasn't going to coach USF. I wasn't ready for the job.

"She called me a coward and a quitter and names that are censored. What could I do? I put my hat back on, went back to the

The game that seemed to go on forever pitted Wilt Chamberlain against a talented North Carolina team. Going into a third overtime, Chamberlain yelled from the bench before returning to play. Teammates Lew Johnson (foreground) and Bob Billings watched what many experts call the finest Final Four championship game, won 54-53 by North Carolina.

office and dug into the debris. Mary was the inspiration for everything I have accomplished."

What Russell accomplished was literally to change the rules of basketball. After the Dons' first championship, in 1955, the rest of the college coaches, facing the specter of another year of Bill's greatness, widened the three-second lane from six feet to 12 feet.

Russell used everything he had against Iowa in the championship game at Northwestern University's fieldhouse. So did Woolpert.

Jones had played in one game two years earlier before an appendectomy ended his season. Although permitted to play the regular schedule in 1955-56, K.C. was ruled ineligible for the tournament.

In the opening minutes of the final game, the Dons trailed, 15-4, their biggest deficit of the season. But Woolpert switched guard Gene Brown on Iowa's Carl Cain, who would have been K.C.'s man.

Cain stopped scoring. Russell started rebounding. The Dons beat the Hawkeyes, 83-71. "I can't say how much I contributed to our success," advised a humble Woolpert.

His contribution was enormous. Phil Woolpert was unique.

Art Spander has all sides of the Bay Area covered, writing columns for the San Francisco Examiner, the Chronicle and the Oakland Tribune as well as for an Internet site. A frequent award winner, he began his career at United Press International.

1957
WHEN THE FINAL FOUR CAME OF AGE

By Frank Deford

The 1957 championship made a watershed year for the NCAAs and was, indisputably, one of the two or three most important tournaments. It was not just that North Carolina won in perhaps the most exciting final—before or since—in triple overtime; North Carolina also won its semifinal in triple overtime. North Carolina finished undefeated and became the first team from the old Confederacy to take the title.

In a sense, that was the last step in making college basketball truly national, for before that champions had come from the East, West, Midwest and the Southwest. Perhaps even more significant was where the personnel came from. Carolina, an essentially regional university in a Protestant state, fielded a team of Irish Catholic Yankees (and a Jew), while the team it beat in the final, Kansas, a rural state of down-home whites, featured a black sophomore seven-footer from Philadelphia, the fabled Wilt Chamberlain. College basketball was never the same again.

In point of fact, though, the '57 championship did not have the immediate effect all of the foregoing would suggest. For purposes of comparison, recall that about a year and a half later the National Football League finally went on the map with a similar equivalent showcase—the overtime championship between the Baltimore Colts and the New York Giants. That changed the stature of the NFL literally overnight. But the greatest game ever played in college basketball, Carolina's 54-53 over Kansas in triple overtime, was only the beginning of the process which made college basketball big time.

There were simple reasons for this. In 1957, even though everyone in college basketball recognized that the NCAA tournament had replaced the NIT as the official championship, the parochial New York Press—and its first cousins, the National Press in New York—still looked down on the NCAAs as a bush-town rival imitation. Even the presence of Chamberlain, who, it is safe to say, was the most ballyhooed athlete ever to enter college, wasn't enough to attract genuine national television coverage.

A few years ago, in searching for photographs to go with an article on the game, Sports Illustrated discovered, to its amazement, no more than three or four photographers on the floor. Sports Illustrated itself gave the game exactly one page—and no photograph—buried deep in the magazine back where there used to be bridge and food articles. Jerry Tax, who covered basketball for the magazine then, managed to get the article in only by pleading that it was, after all, three overtimes, Wilt The Stilt had been upset and the kids who wore Carolina blue all came from New York.

Ironically, even though almost nobody saw the game—there was, evidently, only one television feed, back to North Carolina—the Kansas loss appears to be what is responsible for Chamberlain being tagged with a loser label. Chamberlain himself was convinced that was so. But in fact, he played a terrific game, and Carolina had to be almost picture-perfect to win by a point. In fact, in the last five seconds, Carolina botched defense on Chamberlain and the teammate passing the ball to Chamberlain botched the pass. Chamberlain was the only one who did it right, but he didn't get the ball, and he got forever jacketed as a loser.

Actually, Carolina had no business even being in the final. Chamberlain had scored 32 to lead Kansas past San Francisco, 80-56, in its semi, but the only reason the Tar Heels got past Michigan State was because Bob Cunningham, the fifth man and a defensive specialist, scored a career-high 21 when the others went cold. Michigan State led, 64-62, and had Jumpin' Johnny Green on the free-throw line with six seconds left in the first overtime. But Green missed, and Pete Brennan took the rebound, drib-

bled the court and fired up a 20-footer at the buzzer to stay alive. As Chamberlain told Tommy Kearns, the Carolina playmaker, years later after the old rivals became best friends: "Tommy, you were blessed."

Frank McGuire, the Tar Heel coach, sent Kearns to jump against Chamberlain at the tip-off. He wanted to rattle the giant;

North Carolina's Lennie Rosenbluth (top) fouled out and a distraught Chamberlain (above) was consoled by coach Dick Harp. Chamberlain blamed himself for the loss and Harp soon retired from coaching.

Kearns was the smallest Tar Heel, short of six feet. Chamberlain won the jump, of course, but Carolina won the rest of the half, going to the locker room on top, 29-22. Kansas coach Dick Harp elected to play a box-and-one, dogging the Carolina high scorer, Lennie Rosenbluth. It was not, it turned out, wise strategy. Carolina did better, sagging everybody onto Chamberlain.

But in the second half, Chamberlain brought Kansas back. Thirty-one minutes into the game, the Jayhawks finally took the lead, 36-35, and second-guessers still think they could

have blown it open then—especially with two Carolina starters in deep foul trouble—but Harp elected to sit on the ball.

Still, it almost worked. Kansas led, 44-41, with 1:45 left, and when Chamberlain, moving up to high post, made a beautiful pass down into Gene Elstun, Rosenbluth had to foul Elstun—his fifth. When Elstun moved to the line, Chamberlain clearly remembers spotting a buddy in the stands and smiling at him, sure of victory. But Elstun missed and the moment was gone, and with seconds to go in regulation, Kearns tied it at 46-46 from the

free-throw line.

In the first overtime, each team scored one basket. In the second, nobody scored at all. The Tar Heels especially were exhausted, for their bench was thin, their high scorer was out of the game, and they were entering their sixth overtime— 110 minutes of action—in barely 24 hours.

Kearns made a basket and then a one-and-one, but Chamberlain came back with a three-point play, and when Elstun sank two free throws Kansas was up, 53-52. There were 10 seconds left when Joe Quigg, the center who had been playing with four fouls for almost half an hour's playing time, got the ball at the top of the key. Quigg pump-faked and drove against Chamberlain, but Maurice King reached in as Quigg put up the shot, and the foul was called. Six seconds remained on the clock.

Carolina called timeout, not Kansas. McGuire was renowned for knowing when to call time. Quigg was a 72 percent free-throw shooter on the year, but he had missed his only foul shot in this game, so McGuire wanted to reassure him. "Now, Joe," he said, "as soon as you make 'em ..." and then McGuire went on to discuss the defense.

Quigg swished twice, 54-53.

When Kansas threw in to Chamberlain, Quigg was also the one who batted the ball. Kearns picked it up, dribbled once and then heaved the ball high in the air. He had seen "Hot Rod" Hundley do that once. By the time the ball came back down, North Carolina was the undefeated NCAA champion.

McGuire threw a victory party that night for all the Carolina people in Kansas City. The tab was $1,500, which the athletic director considered far too exces-

During the 1959 regular season, Cincinnati's Oscar Robertson dominated play throughout the Midwest. In the tournament, he led the Bearcats up to the semifinal game against eventual champion California. Bob Dalton held Robertson to 19 points in that game, well under his season average of 35. All Dalton had to do for two nights in a row was to contain the two finest players of the year, and he did.

1960-1969

THE OHIO CONNECTION AND LEW ALCINDOR

UCLA coach John Wooden (above) watched the final minutes of the 1964 championship when the Bruins defeated Duke for their first title. Players Fred Slaughter, Gail Goodrich and assistant coach Jerry Norman were part of Wooden's 10 national championship teams. The year 1964 also marked the ninth and final championship played in Kansas City's Municipal Auditorium.

The world changed on November 22, 1963, never to be the same again. An assassin's bullet cut down John F. Kennedy, the charismatic young American president, during a motorcade in Dallas. It marked the end of the postwar era that had been relatively happy and carefree and the beginning of a long, dark, troublesome period in which the nation became involved in a faraway war it didn't understand.

Suddenly young people, more than in any previous generation, came to challenge and question all the old rules, standards and values. As the decade unfolded, the nation seemed on the brink of being torn apart. In the magnolia-infested backwoods of the Deep South and the teeming asphalt jungles of the big city ghettos, blacks and their supporters fought for racial equality. On the college campuses, kids protested the Vietnam war by chanting, "Hell, no, we won't go." And in places such as Los Angeles, Memphis, Chicago and Kent State, puddles of blood marked the death of our dreams, our hopes, our innocence.

But from all the turmoil, strife and conflict came some bursts of creativity that were as frightening as they were exciting. In music, movies and the arts, performers began probing the limits of their minds and their talents. The Beatles led a revolution in music, changing tastes forever. The decade also gave us actor Dustin Hoffman in "The Graduate," a brilliant new TV show called "60 Minutes," the shocking Broadway play "Hair," and the scandalous female fashion known as the mini-skirt.

Sports hardly lived in a vacuum during the 1960s. A young black man named Cassius Clay won the heavyweight title, became a Muslim, changed his name to Muhammad Ali, and was stripped of the title for refusing to be drafted on religious grounds. Sports novels such as "The Long Season," "Ball Four," and "Instant Replay" revealed that our heroes often had feet of clay. In college sports, many athletes indicated sympathy with their fellow students by wearing longer hair, questioning their coaches more often and speaking out on the issues of the day.

In college basketball, the decade's early years were dominated by Midwestern teams. For four straight years from 1960-63, at least one team from Ohio played in the final game every year. The torch was passed from center Jerry Lucas and Ohio State in 1960 to coach Ed Jucker and his Cincinnati champions of '61 and '62 to Loyola of Chicago in 1963. But when the greatest dynasty in the game's history arrived, it materialized on the West Coast, of all places.

Of the six NCAA tournaments held from 1964-69, the UCLA Bruins won five, enabling coach John Wooden to surpass Kentucky's Adolph Rupp as the coach with the most titles. His best player was Lew Alcindor, a 7-1 center from New York City who was so conscious of his roots that he eventually became a Muslim and changed his name to Kareem Abdul-Jabbar.

If he was the dominant player in the decade, perhaps the most interesting was Bill Bradley, a cerebral kid from Princeton who was good enough to score 58 against Wichita State in the 1965 NCAA consolation game. He went on to become a Rhodes Scholar, a pro star with the New York Knicks, a U.S. Senator from New Jersey and a presidential candidate.

In college basketball, the decade's early years were dominated by Midwestern teams. . . But when the greatest dynasty in the game's history arrived, it materialized on the West Coast.

As Texas Western walked from the floor of Maryland's Cole Fieldhouse in 1973 (above), a milestone in the evolution of the college game was reached. An unknown Southwestern school with a starting lineup of all black players defeated the heavily favored, all-white Kentucky Wildcats.

1960

HOMEGROWN AND OHIO PROUD

Jerry Lucas led Ohio State into the 1960, 1961 and 1962 finals with a team that included John Havlicek, Larry Siegfried and Bob Knight. The Buckeyes defeated California in 1960 but lost to Cincinnati in 1961 and 1962.

By Dick Fenlon

They had come to Ohio State from the hamlets and cities of Ohio.

Center Jerry Lucas was from Middletown, near Cincinnati.

Forward John Havlicek was from Lansing, the eastern Ohio mill town where a buddy named Phil Niekro learned to throw a knuckleball.

Guard Larry Siegfried was from Shelby.

Reserve forward Bobby Knight was from Orrville, Mrs. Smuckers' place, famous for its jams and preserves.

Guard Mel Nowell and forwards Joe Roberts and Dick Furry were from cross-city Columbus.

They were all basketball players—two of such immense talent that it would land them in the Hall of Fame. And on the night of March 19, 1960, in the Cow Palace in San Francisco, they stood a victory away from bringing the school its first national title.

Defending champion California barred the door—coached by Pete Newell, led by All-American center Darrall Imhoff. The night before, the Golden Bears, noted for their defense, had put the clamps on Oscar Robertson, holding him to four field goals, and beaten Cincinnati, 77-69. Playing one of his best games, the 6-10 Imhoff had scored 25 points, grabbed 11 rebounds, and clogged the middle on defense.

On the morning of the final, Fred Taylor, the young coach of the Buckeyes, happened into a

Sports Illustrated reporter.

The magazine, the reporter said, had just completed a poll of coaches on who would win the final game.

"I've got news for you, you're not the favorite, by far," he said.

Fred Taylor wasn't surprised. When it's youth against experience, go with the experience. Cal (29-1) had been there before, and it would be playing before a home-state crowd. The 24-3 Buckeyes were on a roll, but they started three sophomores in their

first year of varsity basketball.

But Taylor also had some news of his own.

"I think we may be a little bit better than anybody thinks," he said.

It was the understatement of the season. Taylor was only 34, and in his second season as a head coach. A sophomore, in effect—just as were starters Lucas, Havlicek, Nowell and Knight, a substitute. But the coach knew what his team could do, and he knew what he was going to have his team do.

"We gambled on defense in a couple of areas," he remembered. "And it worked out. On offense, I suppose we thought we were good enough to take the ball to them. Everybody said you couldn't take it to Imhoff."

Wrong.

Ohio State worked the middle. Roberts scored on a driving layup, and Nowell on another. The Buckeyes led 11-6 before Lucas made his first basket. It was also a layup.

Ohio State ran when it could, and worked when it couldn't, and by halftime the Buckeyes led, 37-19. They had tried 19 shots, made 16, and were on their way to a 75-55 victory that would be regarded as one of best final-game exhibitions ever given by an NCAA champion.

Fred Taylor, more than a quarter of a century later, would not argue with that, but he would dismiss the acclaim that Ohio State's 84 percent shooting in the first half got. "Everybody talks about the shooting percentage," he said. "Lord, only one shot came from outside the paint."

Ohio State in 1960 was that good.

Ohio State in 1960 could, when the time came to do it, do just about anything it wanted to.

It was a team of such diverse and exquisite talents, skillfully meshed, that it seemed to transcend eras and time warps. Four decades later, you could still suppose that this team, in its youth, could play any team from any time anywhere.

"I know they believe it," Taylor said.

"They believe it to this very day. Because they really could do a little bit of everything. They could run. They could set up. They could defend. And their passing was something to watch."

And, yes, that word: chemistry.

"Taking team goals and individual goals and seeing that they mesh toward a total winning season is one of the most difficult things in coaching," Taylor said.

"I'll guarantee you they didn't all like each other equally, but they sure as heck had respect for one another. And that was a very important facet. I kid them now. I say, 'You were playing roles when none of us were smart enough to call it role-playing.'"

It was a team conceived in confusion. Floyd Stahl had resigned as Ohio State coach in April 1958, just as Lucas, Havlicek, Nowell and Knight were approaching graduation from high school. Taylor, his former assistant, remained, and did the recruiting.

Taylor wondered, under the circumstances, if he could convince the prize prospects to come. And if he could, would he be there to coach them? He was the last man to be interviewed for the head coaching job—on June 5, 1958. He was named the next day.

The Buckeyes went 11-11 his first season. The freshmen, ineligible for varsity, played six practice games with the upper classmen, losing the first four, winning the last two. Taylor, meantime, began to set up Ohio State's scheme with the next season in mind.

When it arrived, the Buckeyes rolled to six straight victories before losing, 97-92, at Utah. Two games later they were outscored at Kentucky, 96-93. They would lose only once more—99-83 at Indiana after they had wrapped up the Big Ten title and a tournament berth.

"The biggest problem early was getting the idea over that

we'd have to shut people down," Taylor said. "After the losses at Utah and Kentucky it became obvious to them that they had to do a better job on defense. That's when they really started to play."

Jerry Lucas was a consensus All-American for the first of three straight years.

John Havlicek played with the grit that would later make him an all-time NBA great with the Boston Celtics. "You had to tear the uniform off him to get him out of a game," Taylor said.

Knight came off the bench and hit two 20-foot baskets to help put away Western Kentucky in the regionals.

For him, enduring fame would come later as a coach.

But for Taylor—who beat Knight into the Hall of Fame as a coach—the best night of all would be that night in the Cow Palace when the homegrown Buckeyes answered not only the bell, but every question.

There was one question that Taylor never had.

"I always believed there was such good basketball played in this state that you didn't have to recruit the world," he said.

Dick Fenlon covered Final Fours first when at the Louisville Times and later after joining the Columbus Dispatch, where he became the sports columnist. Today, he is retired and living in Columbus.

1961

TEAM EFFORT COACHES DREAM ABOUT

By Pat Harmon

The championship game in 1961 was the 23rd in the NCAA series and the eighth played in Kansas City. It was supposed to be a routine demonstration by an all-time super team.

It didn't turn out that way.

One year earlier, the Ohio State Buckeyes had won the championship and their margin over California, 20 points, was a record for the final game. The Buckeye starting lineup—three sophomores, one junior, one senior—had "dynasty" written all over it.

Ohio State started the season with four returning regulars—Jerry Lucas and John Havlicek (future all-pros), Larry Siegfried and Mel Nowell. They represented 74 percent of the Buckeye scoring power from the year before.

The fifth position on the team

was taken by Richie Hoyt. And there was valuable sixth man Bobby Knight, who later would leave his imprint on the NCAA as the coach of three Indiana champions.

Cincinnati opened the season with two veteran starters—Paul Hogue and Carl Bouldin. The Bearcats had lost 63 percent of their point-maker to graduation—chiefly in the person of Oscar Robertson, who had led the nation in scoring for three straight years.

After some early experimenting, the Cincinnati lineup was

completed with Bob Wiesenhahn, Tony Yates and Tom Thacker.

At the start of the season Ohio State was magnificent. Cincinnati was awful. The Buckeyes went unbeaten in all their scheduled games, the first time a Big Ten team had done so since 1915. They won the games by an average margin of 22 points and reached the Final Four riding a 32-game winning streak.

Cincinnati lost early games by margins of 19, 17 and eight points. Then the Bearcats won some close ones—by five points, three points and one point. They had a 21-game winning streak of their own going into the championship.

If the result was a bombshell to most observers, it was no surprise to the winning coach. Ed Jucker had coached in the East and his philosophy was formed around the concepts of Clair Bee, Joe Lapchick and Bill Rinehart, three brainy basketball leaders. He had come to Cincinnati as assistant basketball coach and head coach for baseball. (In the latter job, he had Sandy Koufax as his pitcher for one year.)

This was Jucker's first year as Cincinnati's head coach. He told his players: "We have lost Oscar Robertson, the most complete basketball player of all time. But among you there are some who shoot well, some who pass well, some who play great defense. Put them all together, and the product will be an Oscar Robertson—as a team."

Jucker's formula for beating Ohio State had five points:

1. Match them in rebounds or close to it. (Cincinnati outrebounded Ohio State, 36-32.)

2. Put on defensive pressure to delay their fast break. (The Buckeyes made only one fast-break basket.)

3. Play Jerry Lucas loose; too often the other center fouls out against him. (Lucas scored 20 of Ohio State's first 41 points and 27 all told. But his counterpart, Hogue, stayed in the game.)

4. Play Havlicek tight. (Wiesenhahn held Havlicek to four points and scored 17 himself.)

5. Play our own game of short, sharp passes, working for the close-in shot. (Cincinnati committed only three turnovers, Ohio State had eight.)

The final was a match between Ohio State's run-and-shoot offense and Cincinnati's careful artistry. Rarely has there been a closer contest. (The score was tied 14 times.)

Ohio State got off to a 20-13 lead, but Cincinnati caught up at 20-20. At the half Ohio State led, 39-38.

Early in the second half, Bouldin put in five jump shots as Cincinnati rolled to a 52-46 lead. Ohio State made 10 straight points—four by Nowell, two each by Siegfried, Hoyt and Lucas—to go up 56-52. Cincinnati got in front, 61-59. Then Knight made a layup, tying it 61-61 and sending the game into overtime.

Cincinnati got the tip in the extra period, worked the ball carefully and passed to Hogue, who tried a layup. He was fouled by Lucas. Hogue made two free throws, Cincinnati went ahead, 63-61, and never trailed again. With Ohio State forced into foul trouble, Yates made three free throws in crucial spots and Wiesenhahn socked in a layup. The Bearcats won, 70-65.

Lucas was the game's high scorer with 27 points, but Cincinnati showed balance. Wiesenhahn had 17 points, followed by Bouldin with 16, Thacker 15, Yates 13 and Hogue nine.

Jucker said in his postgame interview, "Not any All-American players, just an All-American team."

It was the first time two schools from the same state had met in the NCAA final. And it was an Ohio show in most ways. The Buckeyes' starting five plus their sixth man, Knight, were from Ohio high schools. The Bearcats had Hogue, the son of a Knoxville, Tenn., school principal, but the other four kids were from Cincinnati. All four lived within 12 miles of the college campus.

Of the five Cincinnati starters, each had at least one game in which he led the team in scoring. Wiesenhahn was the season's leading scorer, Hogue the leader in free throw percentage, Bouldin the best in field goal percentage, Thacker tops in assists and Yates the man with the fewest fouls.

Five departments—five leaders. A true team triumph.

Pat Harmon covered Final Fours for newspapers in Champaign, Ill., Cedar Rapids, Iowa, and Cincinnati, Ohio. He was sports editor of the Cincinnati Post before becoming public relations director for the College Football Hall of Fame in South Bend, Ind. Today, he serves as curator and historian for the Hall.

Ohio State's young coach, Fred Taylor, gathered his team around him in a timeout during the 1961 championship game. The strategies and methods of Taylor were studied carefully by a substitute player, No. 24. That player, Bob Knight, would go on to win three national championships as a coach and credit Taylor and other great coaches for his own success.

1962
A BRAND NEW BREED OF CAT

By Hubert Mizell

In one of its periodical pontifications, Sports Illustrated took a deep, frosty whiff of February 1961 air and editorially anointed Jerry Lucas, John Havlicek, a crewcut scrub named Bob Knight and their fellow Ohio State Buckeyes as "the best college basket-

Cincinnati coach Ed Jucker was carried from the court after the Bearcats' victory in the 1961 championship—the first of Jucker's two championship titles.

ball team of all time."

Lew Alcindor was 14, still playing junior high school basketball in New York, and UCLA did not romp among the NCAA elite. Ohio State had mutilated California, 75-55, in the 1960 national finals and the redshirts from Columbus were lollygagging along on a 32-game winning streak.

But as America wondered if anybody could stand up to coach Fred Taylor's bullies, a threat was festering in the Bucks' own neighborhood. Downstate, a new-look team from the University of Cincinnati dared—amid the narrowmindedness of the early '60s—to start three, and eventually four, black players. The Bearcats were, in the Buckeye dictionary, about to become the meaning of the word "nemesis."

Cincinnati had achieved the Final Fours of 1959 and 1960 but wilted in the national semifinals. And now Oscar Robertson,

the Magic Johnson of the day, had gone off to the pros. If Cincinnati hadn't won it with Oscar, how could it …

But Ed Jucker, destined to be a short-lived colossus in the coaching profession, put a quick and disciplined team on the floor that could defense Ohio State into oblivion. It became an all-Ohio NCAA final in 1961 and the Bearcats strangled the giant, 70-65. Rather than an aberration, it would be a harbinger.

The 1962 Final Four was at Freedom Hall in Louisville. Ohio State made the championship game for a third consecutive time. Lucas, Havlicek and their crowd were still around and the Bucks (25-1) were ranked No. 1 in the polls. But, again, there stood Cincinnati.

At that time, newspapers weren't sold that the NCAA Final Four was that big of a deal. After all, it was only college basketball and no major television network thought enough of the Final Four to put it on the air. Some sportswriters had to talk their newspapers into letting them cover it—at personal expense.

It was worth it.

Speaking of harbinger.

One of the 1962 national semifinalists was UCLA, the first time John Wooden coached the Bruins as far as the Final Four. UCLA was eliminated by Cincinnati and then dropped the third-place game to Wake Forest, both by two points, but it would be a Westwood preamble to a UCLA run of 10 NCAA championships in 12 seasons (1964-75), a record that was not made to be broken.

That fourth-place Bruin squad, the tablesetter for the UCLA unstoppables of the Alcindor (Kareem Abdul-Jabbar) and Bill Walton eras, has become a trivia question that only the most devout Final Four disciple can

handle. Just who were Wooden's five starters in 1962? You got it right if you said Fred Slaughter, 6-5 at center, Pete Blackman, 6-5 and Gary Cunningham, 6-6 at forward with John Green, 6-2, alongside Walt Hazzard, 6-2 at guard.

Since Wake Forest did make that Final Four, the Deacons deserve at least some mention in this retrospection. Wake was a dying powerhouse breed, an all-white major college basketball squad. Horace "Bones" McKinney, an ordained Baptist minister, coached them to 12 straight victories to make it to Louisville. The Deacons (22-9) were led by a muscular 6-8 center, Len Chappell, and a 5-9 guard who, at the time, had a full head of hair and a killer jump shot—Billy Packer.

But it was the main event, the second coming of Cincinnati-Ohio State in the NCAA finals, that made 1962 one of the more glistening charms on a Final Four bracelet.

It takes a little less trivia expertise to recall the lineups of those Bucks and Bearcats. Ohio State's supporting cast for the 6-8 Lucas and the 6-5 Havlicek included Doug McDonald at forward and 6-2 Mel Nowell and 6-0 Dick Reasback at guard. Bobby Knight, a senior, sat well down the Buckeye bench. Cincinnati's main men were 6-9 Paul Hogue, 6-8 George Wilson, 6-5 Ron Bonham, 6-2 Tom Thacker and 6-1 Tony Yates.

Lucas was struggling on a gimpy knee. From the opening tip, he would be physically blitzed by the 235-pound Hogue. Cincinnati's beating of Ohio State in the 1961 finals had been no fluke. That would become immediately and painfully evident to the Bucks.

Ohio State did lead, 23-22, but then the Bearcats ripped away on an 11-2 run. Cincinnati

As the 1963 game reached a last minute climax, Loyola's Jerry Harkness goes for and hits a jumper from the baseline as Cincinnati's foul-plagued Ron Bonham held his position and tries to avoid his fifth foul. The Ramblers designated Harkness for the final shot, but it was a rebound layup by Vic Rouse in overtime that iced the 60-58 upset for Loyola.

was ahead, 37-29, at halftime and was never threatened in the closing 20 minutes, coasting to a 71-59 win. Hogue outscored Lucas, 22-11, and Thacker buried Havlicek, 21-11.

Jucker, at 45, was finally acclaimed as one of the slickest minds in the coaching racket. Defense was the heart of his scheme, with the aggressive, quick-handed Yates as the Bearcat catalyst. Jucker called Yates "the best defensive player in the country." When the 1962 NCAA tournament ended, nobody argued; especially nobody from a twice-thrashed Ohio State University.

The following season, Cincinnati threatened for an unprecedented third straight NCAA Championship. But Loyola of Chicago ended the dream in the 1963 Final.

Hubert Mizell has covered Final Fours for 35 years for the Florida Times-Union, the Associated Press and most recently as a writer and columnist for the St. Petersburg Times.

1963
THAWING THE CINCINNATI FREEZE

By Ron Rapoport

The all-tournament team for the 1963 NCAA basketball championships spoke volumes about the nature of the outcome.

The team contained Tom Thacker, George Wilson and Ron Bonham of Cincinnati, whose team did not win the title, and the tournament's Most Outstanding Player, Art Heyman of Duke, whose team did not even play in the championship game.

Only Les Hunter was there to represent the team that did take home the trophy that year, which seemed to be proof enough that even when the final buzzer had sounded, nobody could really believe that Loyola of Chicago had actually pulled it off.

Maybe it's not fair to torment the selectors of the all-tournament team this way. They did, after all, have a perfect excuse for their embarrassment. In order for the squad to be announced immediately after the game was over, the balloting was conducted with about 10 minutes left. And with 10 minutes left, Cincinnati was murdering Loyola.

Cincinnati had also gone through the season undefeated and ranked a unanimous No. 1 in the polls. So what if Oscar Robertson wasn't in school anymore? If any team knew what it took to win a big basketball game, it was Cincinnati.

Loyola, on the other hand, had been a relatively unknown quantity when the season started. Sparked by the playmaking of scrappy Chicago-born Johnny Egan, the Ramblers had been through a lot in the few years they had been together. Egan was the only white starter and Loyola was the first nationally prominent college team to start four black players. Loyola had, in that era of heightened racial passions, undergone the indignities of hate mail, separate housing arrangements in the South and even threats of arrest before a game in New Orleans.

But despite the fact that experiences like these had served to harden and bring the Loyola team together, nobody figured it to be a match for Cincinnati. And when Ed Jucker's squad stretched a 29-21 halftime lead to 45-30, the game seemed as good as over.

Cincinnati was the top defensive team in the nation, after all, having allowed an average of only 52.6 points per game. Loyola, the national scoring leaders with 92.9 points, seemed finally to have met a team that knew how to shut it down.

It might have been about this time, when Loyola's chances seemed so desperate, that one of the most famous photographs of that tournament was taken. It was of a Rambler cheerleader on her knees at courtside, praying for deliverance from the Cincinnati onslaught. The cheerleader was Kathy Ireland, daughter of the Loyola coach.

For his part, George Ireland was engaged with more worldly concerns. He was trying to figure out a way to stop the Bearcats and to get his own team's lagging offense to produce before it was too late. Fortunately for him, he was given some unexpected help from the Cincinnati side of the court.

Jucker sent his team into a stall, trying to burn some time off the clock by employing the understandable philosophy that if Loyola didn't have the ball it couldn't score. Ireland responded by having his team press Cincinnati all over the court.

"I think they passed up too many good shots when they went into that freeze with 10 minutes to go," said Jerry Harkness, Loyola's scoring leader and a player many thought should have been named to the all-tournament team.

Given this reprieve, Loyola made the most of it. Playing with a poise that was supposed to be one of the chief assets of the tournament-hardened Bearcats, the Ramblers slowly began chipping away at their big deficit. Cincinnati, in the mean-

time, surprisingly and irretrievably began to fall apart.

Error followed error and foul followed foul as Loyola crept within striking distance. By the time the clock wound down to the final few moments, three Cincinnati starters—George Wilson, Tony Yates and Tom Thacker—had four fouls and the whole team seemed to be playing nervous, tentative basketball. With 12 seconds left, Loyola trailed by a single point and, frantic to get the ball back, Harkness fouled Cincinnati's Larry Shingleton.

Shingleton made the first free throw but missed the second.

Hunter snatched the rebound and flung it to Harkness who drove for a layup that tied the game at 54-54. The buzzer sounded. Against all probability, Loyola had forced the game into overtime.

Both teams managed two baskets to tie the game at 58-58 and then, with barely two minutes remaining, it was Loyola's turn to gamble on a change of style and strategy. The hard-running, shoot-from-the-hip Ramblers slowed the game down and held onto the ball in an attempt to take the last shot.

The idea was to let Harkness, the team's leading scorer who was

averaging 21.2 points during Loyola's five postseason games, take the last shot. And, indeed, the Ramblers got him the ball with a few seconds left. But Cincinnati's Ron Bonham surrounded Harkness in a flurry of waving arms, and Harkness, unable to get a shot off, passed to Hunter.

Hunter shot; the ball rolled off the rim directly into the eager grasp of Rambler forward Vic Rouse. His rebound layup that ended the game with two seconds left may have been the easiest part of the Ramblers' long and improbable season. Loyola, with

Loyola coach George Ireland (above) took his Ramblers to the finals in Louisville's Freedom Hall, where he instructed players Vic Rouse, Johnny Egan and Jerry Harkness before the tipoff. Their upset win ended Cincinnati's quest for a third title in a row.

Walt Hazzard cut and drove through the Duke defense in 1964 to lead UCLA to its first of 11 Final Four championships. Making two key steals in the second half, Hazzard was named MOP. One more item of Final Four history: This photograph of Hazzard was the first from the tournament ever published on the cover of Sports Illustrated.

a stunning 60-58 upset, reigned as the national champion.

Ron Rapoport has covered Final Fours for several newspapers throughout his career, which ended as a sports columnist at The Chicago Sun-Times. He is known throughout the nation for his sports commentaries on National Public Radio's Weekend Edition.

1964

A DYNASTY BEGINS

By Bob Hentzen

As the celebrating UCLA Bruins were cutting down the nets in Kansas City's Municipal Auditorium, Kansas State coach Tex Winter watched and observed to a writer, "I still think we could have beat 'em."

Shucks, Winter wasn't the only coach to express that opinion during the 1963-64 season. How could any coach not believe there was a way to handle a ballclub with no starter standing taller than 6-5?

But UCLA was perfect, 30-0, after downing Kansas State, 90-84, in the semifinals and Duke, 98-83, in the final.

This was a memorable Final Four in that it was the start of UCLA's dynasty—the remarkable 12-year stretch in which John Wooden coached the Bruins to 10 national titles.

Wooden agreed that his first NCAA championship team didn't intimidate anybody. "They watch us warm up and can't see how we beat anyone," he said before the 1964 Final Four. "Teams don't get scared when they look at us, but we cause a little fright when we play. Our strength is real good

quickness and unity."

UCLA didn't go into that season with much respect. Sports Illustrated's preview called the Bruins "too short" and labeled 6-3 guard Walt Hazzard "the poorest defender on the coast."

But Hazzard, who came to Westwood from Philadelphia on a one-year, make-good basis, was to change some opinions. "He passes through holes you couldn't throw a golf ball," Sports Illustrated later wrote.

Despite its unbeaten record, an average victory margin of 19.4 and the No. 1 national ranking, UCLA arrived in Kansas City for the national showdown as anything but an overwhelming favorite. No. 2 Michigan (22-4) also qualified, eliminating defending champion Loyola of Chicago, 84-80, en route in the Mideast semifinals. No. 3 Duke (25-4) also was present, scoring one-sided victories over Villanova and Connecticut in the East Regionals.

Kansas State (22-5) was unranked, but had plenty going for it. The Wildcats were fresh off a 94-86 upset of fifth-ranked Wichita State in Wichita in the Midwest final. They had come close to UCLA, losing 78-75, in a December neutral-court game. They would be playing on the Municipal Auditorium boards where they had won the Big Eight's Christmas tourney. They would be the crowd favorites.

UCLA didn't have a cakewalk in the West Regional, having to rally twice. After squeezing Seattle, 95-90, the Bruins fell behind San Francisco by 13 points in the first half before overhauling the Dons, 76-72, and breaking their 19-game winning streak.

Enthusiasm ran high for the 1964 Final Four, although it was tame by today's standards. For the Friday-Saturday night dou-

bleheaders, all 10,800 seats were sold out a month in advance. Tickets cost $7 per session and scalpers were asking $50 by game night. A 16-station television network had been established.

The first semifinal matched Michigan against Duke. They were not strangers when they met because of a December game won by the Wolverines, 83-67, on their home court.

Dave Strack's team was respected for both beef—it averaged 201 pounds—and talent. Guard Cazzie Russell, 6-5 and 218, was the star with a 24.6 scoring average, but he came to Kansas City with a bad ankle. The supporting cast included 6-7 center Bill Buntin and forwards Oliver Darden, 6-7 and Larry Tregoning, 6-5.

Vic Bubas' Blue Devils had the reputation of being a brainy team—four players were on the dean's list—and featured 6-4 Jeff Mullins with a 24.4 average. Big guys Jay Buckley and Hack Tison, both 6-10, also were double-figure scorers.

Duke's chartered plane had swerved into the mud while braking on landing in Kansas City. Nobody was hurt and the Blue Devils proceeded to put the hurt on Michigan in a 91-80 triumph. Buzzy Harrison's four long jumpers in the first half lit Duke's fire, and Buckley finished with 25 points and Mullins 24 to more than offset Russell's 31 for Michigan.

Then Kansas State, led by 6-6 senior Willie Murrell and with 7-0 Roger Suttner in the lineup, took on Wooden's diminutive but quick-as-a-hiccup Bruins. Their "big man" was 6-5 Fred Slaughter from nearby Topeka, who had gone unrecruited by the area teams coming out of high school.

UCLA had started the same five every game—the 6-3 Hazzard and 6-1 scoring machine Gail Goodrich at the guards, Slaughter at center, and 6-5

Keith Erickson and 6-3 Jack Hirsch at forwards. The first subs off the bench were Kenny Washington and Doug McIntosh.

Despite the lack of size, the

Bruins seldom were outrebounded, averaging eight more per game than their opponents.

The partisan crowd was roaring as the Wildcats inched

A contemplative Hazzard held the championship trophy in the locker room after the final (above). In the game itself, the strategies of coaches John Wooden of UCLA (above, left) and Vic Bubas of Duke (above, right) formed the texture of the championship.

ahead, 75-70, with 7:28 left, but poised UCLA never blinked (K-State did, hitting but 10 of 21 free throws) in pulling out a 90-84 victory.

Erickson, averaging 10.1 points, tallied 28 in the semifinals while Hazzard contributed 19 points and nine assists. The 6-3 Washington came off the pines to score a career-high 13. But Washington was just getting warmed up as Duke found out less than 24 hours later in the championship game.

Washington, who came to Kansas City with a five-point average, scored 26 and hauled down 12 rebounds as UCLA blew away the Blue Devils, 98-83. The result was all but determined when the Bruins rattled off 16 straight points—eight by

Goodrich—in a two-minute, 34-second blitz late in the first half to open a 43-30 lead.

Duke missed 10 straight shots and committed three turnovers (two on steals by Hazzard) against UCLA's vaunted full-court press in that fatal span. The only problem the Bruins experienced in the second half was spark-plug Hazzard fouling out for the first time all season with 6:04 left. No sweat—UCLA led, 86-70, at the time and coasted in.

Goodrich, the southpaw who led the Bruins in scoring that season, finished with 25 while Mullins paced Duke with 22.

The all-tourney team consisted of Hazzard, the Most Outstanding Player, and Goodrich, Mullins, Murrell and Buntin. The latter was a stallion—33 points

and 14 rebounds in Michigan's 100-90 win over Kansas State in the third-place contest.

"This team has come as close to reaching maximum potential as any team I've ever had," Wooden said when it was over, adding, "It's most unlikely that I or anyone else will have it (a perfect season) again."

Wooden was wrong on the last part. Three more of his championship teams (1967, 1972, 1973) were unbeaten and Indiana duplicated the feat in 1976.

Bob Hentzen came to the Topeka (Kan.) Capital-Journal from the Daily Oklahoman and was named sports editor and columnist in 1968. He covered Final Fours regularly until his retirement in 1997. He was the former president of the U.S. Bas-

ketball Writers Association. He died in 2000.

1965
THE BEST SECOND FIDDLE EVER

By Mark Purdy

There are trivia questions, and there are trivia questions. And then there is Gail Goodrich, UCLA Class of '65. He shouldn't be the subject of a trivia question. But he is.

In fact, Goodrich may be the most famous trivia question—or at least the most famous name to be a famous answer to a famous Final Four trivia question—in history.

The Question: Which player scored 42 points in the NCAA championship game while leading his team to the Final Four title, but was not named the tournament's most outstanding player?

The Answer: You already know the answer.

In the long-playing record album of UCLA Basketball's Greatest Hits, Goodrich always is the guy who gets the last cut on side two—the 90-second outtake thrown in as an afterthought. His is the forgotten song on an album of blockbusters by Hazzard and Alcindor and Walton and the rest. Always.

In much the same way, when the 1965 Final Four is remembered, Goodrich often is considered more of a backup singer than a headliner.

It's hardly fair. When you examine the evidence, you will find that Goodrich was one of the NCAA tournament's most spectacular performers. He averaged 35 points per game in the West

Regional at Provo. He then did the same thing in Portland while orchestrating UCLA's rush to its second straight championship.

So what about the most outstanding player award, then? What happened?

Bill Bradley. That's what happened.

Among the four teams competing that year at the Portland Memorial Coliseum—UCLA, Michigan, Wichita State and Princeton—there were basically three players who the average American basketball lover knew by reputation.

There was Cazzie Russell of Michigan, who was powerful but stylish.

There was Goodrich of UCLA, who was gritty but quick.

And there was Bradley of Princeton, who was perfect.

Before he even set foot in Oregon, Bradley had been all but canonized by the nation's sports press. It wasn't his fault. The guy truly did seem to leap off a Wheaties box onto a basketball floor. Bradley, a native of the Missouri heartland, was a two-time All-American. He had served as captain of the 1964 U.S. Olympic Team in Tokyo. Plus, as a quintessential Ivy Leaguer, he had earned a Rhodes Scholarship to Oxford University in England.

If the world really were a Wheaties box, Bradley would have swept Princeton to glorious victory. Instead, in the semifinal against Michigan, Bradley picked up his fourth foul one minute into the second half. That smothered his game like a wet blanket. Princeton lost, 83-76. Russell had 28 points for Michigan.

Meanwhile, in the other semifinal, UCLA quickly vaporized Wichita State, 108-89. Goodrich played barely two-thirds of the game but still scored 28 points.

Compared to Bradley's lean Ivy style, however, Goodrich was a blue-collar runt. As a 5-2 high school freshman, he plaintively had said to his mother, "I don't understand why God gave me all this ability and not the height to go with it." As a 6-1 college senior, he still felt like the picked-on underdog.

"When coach Wooden made me play forward during my sophomore year, I couldn't understand it," Goodrich said once of his UCLA experience. "But looking back, it gave me the confidence to go to the basket against bigger men."

This would come in handy the following night, against the beefy Wolverines of Michigan. Little did Goodrich realize that he would be following the toughest act in college basketball.

It was Bradley, of course. In the consolation game, with absolutely no marbles at stake, Princeton coach Butch van Breda Kolff turned loose his Oxford scholar. Bradley wound up with 58 points, a Final Four record.

"He didn't want to shoot," said van Breda Kolff. "But I told him to."

With Princeton's Tigers on their way to scoring 118 points in a 36-point rout of Wichita State, there was no reason for Bradley to worry about being selfish—although there were eyewitnesses who insist Bradley could have had 70 points that night if he had been less altruistic and had taken more of his classic 20-foot jump shots instead of passing the ball inside to teammates.

As it was, Bradley made 22 of 29 field goal attempts and 14 of 15 free throws. When he left the game with 35 seconds remaining, he was given a standing ovation from the 13,000 customers. It lasted a full minute.

The concentration and shooting eye of Princeton's Bill Bradley—a Rhodes Scholar, captain of the 1964 U.S. Olympic basketball team and a two-time All-American—brought a special intrigue to the tournament. But Bradley's skills weren't enough to lead the Tigers past Michigan, and they had to play Wichita State in the consolation game. Some consolation for Bradley, who scored 58 points for an NCAA single-game Final Four record.

tinually driving past the Bruins' Keith Erickson, who had pulled a leg muscle the previous night. Wooden fixed the glitch in a flash. He substituted Kenny Washington for Erickson, made an adjustment in the UCLA press to cut off a passing lane to Russell, and told Goodrich to start taking the ball to the basket.

The results were immediate. The Bruins outscored Michigan, 34-14, to take a 47-34 halftime lead. In the second half, Goodrich put on a clinic. He alternately dribbled away time on the clock, double-pumped in the air to draw fouls, and sailed past the Michigan men to the basket. Three Wolverine starters—Bill Buntin, Larry Tregoning and Oliver Darden—committed their fifth fouls trying to stop Goodrich. During the last 10 minutes of the game, he seemed to set up camp at the free-throw line.

Final score: UCLA 91, Michigan 80.

"It gave me the satisfaction," he said, "that a little man can win in a big man's game."

His 42 points also gave UCLA a new school scoring record. Goodrich was 18 of 20 from the free throw line, 12 of 22 from the field. Russell of Michigan had 28 points, but was not a factor after the first 15 minutes.

And shortly after the final buzzer, Bradley was given the Outstanding Player trophy. Goodrich professed then—and professes now—not to care, figuring his team got the trophy that mattered.

And all three of them know who the real Most Outstanding Player in 1965 was. There was a lot of bad information floating around Portland that year. The hottest tournament rumor, for example, concerned a 7-1 high school senior from New York named Lew Alcindor. Suppos-

"I didn't realize I had a personal record," Bradley said. "I thought they were telling me to shoot because we had a chance at the team scoring record."

Minutes later, Goodrich and UCLA jogged onto the floor for warm-ups. It was a little like being on "The Ed Sullivan Show" and following the Beatles. The crowd already had made up its

mind that the best part of the show was over.

Wrong. The smallest Bruins were about to give Michigan's bruisers a lesson in finesse. Goodrich was about to play what he later would call "his best game" at UCLA.

It didn't begin auspiciously, however. The Wolverines went ahead, 20-13, with Russell con-

edly, after sizing up 100 scholar-ship offers, the kid had decided he would enroll at Boston College to play for its legendary coach, Bob Cousy.

That's another good trivia question.

Mark Purdy has been a sports columnist for the San Jose Mer-cury-News since 1984, after stints at the Dayton Journal-Herald, the Cincinnati Enquirer, the Chicago Tribune and the Los Angeles Times. Winner of many awards, he has covered 22 Final Fours.

1966

A CASE OF BLACK AND WHITE

By Dave Kindred

In his classic history of col-lege basketball, "All the Moves," Neil D. Isaacs returns to the 1920s to remember the New York Rens, a touring team of black players whose success begot the Harlem Globetrotters. These great pro teams, working in a sep-arate and unequal milieu, were the foundation stones of black development in basketball through the mid-'40s. "When Don Barksdale was an All-Amer-ica at UCLA in 1947," Isaacs wrote, "he was as much of a freak as Kurland and Mikan had been in 1944."

In 1950 the Boston Celtics of the NBA drafted the league's first black player, Chuck Cooper of Duquesne. Washington fol-lowed by choosing Earl Lloyd of West Virginia State. The New York Knicks went to the Globe-trotters to acquire Nat "Sweet-water" Clifton. Those events opened the line of ascension for blacks all the way to the top

levels of the game.

Or did they? After having won the 1956 NCAA championship at San Francisco as a teammate of K.C. Jones, the great center Bill Russell declared that the NBA had a "quota system" which lim-ited the number of blacks on each team. The NBA's use of blacks seemed limited to those who could be stars. Seldom did a team use five black players even though the All-American lists of the mid-'50s were domi-nated by Wilt Chamberlain, Elgin Baylor, Willie Naulls, Sihugo Green and Oscar Robertson. America's black colleges were largely untapped sources of bas-ketball talent.

As late as 1962, Southeastern Conference champion Missis-sippi State refused an invitation to the NCAA tournament because it would have to play integrated teams. This was eight years after the U.S. Supreme Court's ruling in Brown vs. Board of Education. The court declared public schools open to all students, black as well as white.

This Mississippi State boycott of 1962 was the dying breath of segregation in college basketball. Cincinnati won the NCAA title that year using four black starters. In 1963, with the gover-nor's de facto approval, Missis-sippi State coach Babe McCarthy spirited his team out of Missis-sippi to play in the NCAA tour-nament. Mississippi State lost in the first round to the eventual champions, Loyola of Chicago, a team with four black starters.

The game was changing in the early '60s, thanks to the influence of black players. Russell's shot-blocking ability showed the pos-sibilities of defense. Baylor's magical body control and Robert-son's mastery of the ball expanded the boundaries of offense. It wouldn't be long

before an event came along which said the game belonged as much to black players as to whites. There would come a time when the issue was settled on a basketball court.

That time was March of 1966. The game: Texas Western against Kentucky. Out of the farthest reaches of Texas, coach Don Haskins created as unlikely a basketball team as ever had won the NCAA championship. "Haskins had brought more blacks to El Paso than they were used to seeing in the whole stu-dent body," Isaacs wrote, "including Dave 'Big Daddy' Lat-tin, Bobby Joe Hill, Willie Cager, Orsten Artis, Neville Shed and Willie Worsley."

Texas Western began the sea-son little-known, but entered the NCAA tournament ranked third in the country with a 23-1 record. Lattin was the biggest Texas Western player, only 6-7 at that. Haskins' team won not because of overwhelming athletic ability; it won with pure, fundamental basketball. It could run and shoot, and the Miners played an unnerving man-to-man defense that allowed no breathing room.

Still, No. 1-ranked Kentucky was the overwhelming favorite in the championship game. These were "Rupp's Runts," the old coach's favorite team, no man taller than 6-5, a team like all of Rupp's: unselfish, good ball-handlers, good shooters, good on the run—the very model of great Kentucky teams, beaten only once in 28 games. The Kentucky stars were Louie Dampier, an All-America guard, and forward Pat Riley, later a successful NBA coach.

Kentucky's semifinal victory over second-ranked Duke, 83-79, seemed to wrap up Rupp's fifth NCAA championship. Texas Western had a matching 27-1

Against a beefy and physical Michigan team, UCLA's Gail Goodrich set a school scoring record of 42 points in the 1965 championship game. Three Wolverines fouled out trying to stop the diminutive senior, who played the game of his Bruin career.

As Kentucky players scrambled to stop the Miners' attack, Texas Western's Willie Cager drove for a second-half basket. Failing to stop Cager were Kentucky stalwarts Pat Riley (42), Louie Dampier (10) and Cliff Berger (45).

record and had survived successive games against seventh-ranked Cincinnati, fourth-ranked Kansas and, in the semifinal, a Utah team that hadn't been pressed in the tournament. Still, who do you expect to win an NCAA championship game—the lords of basketball from the Bluegrass or the upstart commoners from a forlorn corner of football country?

The question was answered quickly. The game's signature moments came barely five minutes into play. Kentucky, perhaps drained by the Duke game, perhaps hurried by good defenders, shot poorly.

Then Bobby Joe Hill made successive midcourt steals from Dampier and Tommy Kron for easy layups. Suddenly, in contrast to Texas Western's quickness, Kentucky was seen as slow afoot.

Don Haskins' five black starters would defeat Kentucky's all-white team, 72-65, and nothing would be the same after that. Rupp would recruit his first black player three years later. All black players would be recruited by all schools, not only the primarily black universities. The Southeastern Conference and Atlantic Coast Conference became powerful leagues built on black talent. George Wallace once promised that the University of Alabama would never accept black students. A decade later, five black players started for Alabama's basketball team and played in a beautiful 15,000-seat arena on campus.

Texas Western's victory over Kentucky was a landmark. Sportswriter David Israel recognized the significance of the game. Writing about the game a decade later, Israel called it "the Brown vs. Board of Education of college basketball."

1967
LET THE ALCINDOR ERA BEGIN

By Gary Nuhn

This was the start of an age—The UCLA Age—as surely as the first flake of snow 3.5 million years ago signaled the start of the Ice Age. What was it, anyway? Nov. 16, 3.498 million B.C.?

The UCLA titles in 1964 and '65 were nice, but they weren't harbingers. Without the import of a King Kong center, UCLA would have become, like San Francisco in 1955-56 and Cincinnati in 1961-62, just a good program that won back-to-back titles, not one that was primed to dominate college basketball for a decade.

UCLA didn't get Kong—he was under contract to RKO stu-

Texas Western's Bobby Joe Hill broke the game open in the second half with two steals and full court drives to score key baskets. When the final scoreboard read 72-65, the Miners' Willie Worsley had an elevated seat to cut the championship game nets.

Wooden sent Bunche a thank-you note, he mentioned that UCLA had a chance to land Alcindor and asked if he could help in any way.

Bunche dropped Alcindor's parents a note. Several days later Wooden received a call that Alcindor would like to visit.

Alcindor visited UCLA not unlike a mail-order bride.

Then Wooden returned the visit to Alcindor's parents.

And Lewie was a Bruin. No huffing, no puffing, no begging and pleading. No dozen trips back and forth across the continent. It was just "Sign here, please, and let's see if we have a uniform to fit you."

It wasn't enough just to have Alcindor, however.

There had been teams in the past with giants—good giants, able giants, athletic giants—that didn't win NCAA titles: DePaul with George Mikan; Kansas with Wilt Chamberlain.

Wooden surrounded Alcindor with brilliant players. It was like the first cast of "Saturday Night Live," a stunning array of talent, each of the pieces making the others better. The other members of Alcindor's freshman class were shooting forward Lynn Shackelford, defensive forward Ken Heitz and guard Lucius Allen, who with junior Mike Warren (later of Hill Street Blues fame), reminded Bruin fans of the Gail Goodrich-Walt Hazzard tag team.

Wooden took that unit and went 26-0 in the regular season. UCLA was scared only once, in a third meeting with Southern Cal, which put on an Ice Age freeze that took the Bruins into overtime before UCLA won, 40-35.

UCLA swept through the West Regional, 109-60 over Wyoming and 80-64 over Pacific, and came to Louisville 28-0 but curiously, not complacent, not bigheaded,

dios and was thus considered a professional—but it did get a towering center: Ferdinand Lewis Alcindor Jr.

In the absence of Kong, Lew would do just fine.

The recruitment of Alcindor is an interesting story, especially viewed from 30 years later when recruiting is sometimes cloaked in used-car-lot, hard-sell hypocrisy.

As UCLA coach John Wooden told it, Alcindor, the nation's most

prized recruit that year, just sort of fell onto the UCLA campus.

Wooden said Alcindor's coach at Power Memorial Academy, Jack Donohue, notified Wooden that UCLA was one of five schools Alcindor was considering, but that Donohue didn't want UCLA bothering Alcindor or his parents.

UCLA alumnus Dr. Ralph Bunche, the diplomat, stood in for Wooden at an awards ceremony in New York. Later, when

Texas Western coach Don Haskins hugged players in an emotional celebration on the Cole Fieldhouse court. A one-time player at Oklahoma A&M, Haskins used the lessons he learned from mentor-coach Henry Iba—his Miners team was well-versed in the fundamentals of the game.

not ripe for the upsetting.

The teams waiting for the Bruins in The 'Ville were Houston (26-3), North Carolina (26-4) and Dayton (24-5), the first two expected, the latter an unranked surprise.

Houston, ranked No. 7, was the first. The Cougars of coach Guy Lewis were a team of excesses—led in points, rebounding and verbiage by Elvin Hayes, "The Big E," and led in fact by guard Don Chaney. Hayes billed the game as a matchup between him and Alcindor. "I don't think Lew can stay with me when he's on defense," The Big E crowed.

Replied Alcindor, "We play a team. We don't play one man."

Houston collapsed a three-man sewing circle around Alcindor, so the Bruin sharp-shooters took over. Shackelford zapped in 22, Allen 17 and Warren 14. The Big E was high-scorer with 25 and high-rebounder with 24, but he couldn't carry the Cougars alone. UCLA won, 73-58, after which Hayes accused his teammates of choking, and bellowed how Alcindor (19 points, 20

rebounds) wasn't such hot stuff after all. He said Jimmy Walker of Providence was the best player in the country.

In the other semifinal, No. 4 Carolina was supposed to slide past Dayton without drawing a deep breath. This was the first of coach Dean Smith's Final Four teams, and it seemed perfectly balanced with bookend forwards Larry Miller and Bob Lewis and a good big man in 6-10 Rusty Clark. The game plan: Take off the warm-ups, run up and down a couple of times, get a lead, go "four corners" and start planning for UCLA. That's what most people thought.

But the Tar Heels ran into a little team of overachievers in Dayton, and they ran into a player, Don May, having the game of his dreams (except, even he wouldn't have dreamed he could make 13 straight shots in his own personal game of Around the World). When May was finished, he had 16 baskets in all, 34 points, and the Flyers had won, 76-62.

The championship game, though, went according to the book.

Dayton and UCLA were staying in the same hotel, The Kentucky. One of the Flyer managers, Dave Borchers, remembers seeing Alcindor in the lobby before the game. "He sank down into a chair and all you could see were these knees," Borchers said.

As the teams warmed up, Dayton was further psyched. "He walked past our bench," said Dayton assistant manager Joe Emmrich, "and he was the biggest s.o.b. I ever saw. I thought to myself, 'God, he's 7-foot-13!' "

The Flyers' single moment of glory came early. Center Dan Obrovac won the tip. That was one of Alcindor's few weak areas—he had difficulty with his timing on jump balls.

You can count the number of minutes Dayton was in the game on one hand. The Flyers missed its first eight shots and 16 of their first 18. It was quickly 20-4, UCLA, and things got worse from there. It was like a forest fire after the wind comes up. Dayton spent the night searching for trenches that weren't there.

Wooden could have named his score, and he did. He pulled his horses early, then watched quietly as a 76-47 lead was reduced to 79-64 final.

"Wooden was a man of tremendous class," said Dayton guard Bobby Joe Hooper. "We'll never forget him for it."

Alcindor led the Bruins with 20 points; Allen added 19, Warren 17 and Shackelford 10. May's 21 topped the Flyers.

Wooden still forbade player interviews in those days, but an enterprising Dayton reporter grabbed a ball, stuck it under his arm and walked into the UCLA dressing room past the guard, posing as a UCLA manager. The reporter told Alcindor he didn't seem very excited for someone who had just won a national championship. "I've always been that way," the big man said. "People think I don't care. I guess I just don't show my feelings like others do."

On the way home, a Dayton fan told Flyer assistant coach Chuck Grigsby that Alcindor didn't impress him very much. "Yeah," said Grigsby, "all he did was take us out of our offense and take us out of our defense. Other than that, he didn't impress us much."

Three days after the finals, the NCAA rules committee, in honor of Alcindor, outlawed the dunk. If it was supposed to end the UCLA Age, it fell a bit short. Ferdinand Lewis Alcindor Jr. just kept getting better.

Gary Nuhn is a sports columnist at the Dayton Daily News. A graduate of Ohio State, he specialized in covering golf and basketball before becoming a columnist. He is a past president of the U.S. Basketball Writers Association.

1968

PAYBACK FOR THE BRUINS

By Joe Jares

Anticipation of the UCLA-Houston/Lew Alcindor-Elvin Hayes rematch in March of 1968 was so delicious, and the game itself so startling, that even those who were there tend to remember it incorrectly as the grand finale of the season.

It wasn't. It was merely the NCAA semifinal—if "merely" can be associated with a UCLA performance that Houston coach Guy V. Lewis described afterward as "the greatest exhibition of basketball I've ever seen."

The Bruins and Cougars had battled at the Houston Astrodome earlier in the season before 52,693 people, the largest crowd ever to see a basketball game in the U.S. up to that time.

In that historic game, forward Hayes had hit 68 percent of his shots, scored 39 points, taken down 15 rebounds and made two deciding free throws in a 71-69 victory that stopped UCLA's winning streak at 47. The Astrodome scoreboard had flashed a gigantic "E" over and over again at game's end.

Alcindor, later called by UCLA coach John Wooden "the finest truly big man ever to play basketball up to his time," had made only four of 18 shots and finished with 15 points and 12 rebounds. His relatively poor performance probably had been caused by a scratched eyeball suffered three games earlier.

"Alcindor was just half of himself because of his injured eye," Wooden recalled. "He had been in a dark room and had not practiced in over a week."

The subsequent Sports Illustrated cover showed Hayes shooting a jumper over Alcindor. The 7-1 UCLA junior pinned up that cover in his locker, where he had to see it before and after every practice. Kentucky coach Adolph Rupp called the Bruins "complacent kids." Wooden pinned that quote up in his memory.

The rematch was in the Los Angeles Memorial Sports Arena, which had loaned its floor to the Astrodome for the earlier meeting. Almost nothing but the floor was the same the second time around. Certainly the crowd was smaller: 15,742 plus closed-circuit television audiences in six L.A. locations.

The event started inauspiciously for Houston—the Cougars' student manager was

This scene was to become a familiar one: UCLA players celebrating with the player of the decade, Lew Alcindor. In 1967, Lucius Allen (42, above) joined the celebration as the sometimes withdrawn Alcindor stood in the back row.

arrested outside the arena and booked on charges of scalping tickets. Things didn't get much better after that. Whoever was wearing Hayes' uniform should have been arrested for imitating the man who had been voted college player of the year.

Wooden and assistant coach Jerry Norman were determined not to let Hayes kill the Bruins again, so they devised a diamond-and-one defense—basically a four-man, diamond-shaped zone, plus the "one," forward Lynn Shackelford, whose job was to adhere to "The Big E" like tape.

"We worked all week on the diamond-and-one," said Shackelford. "This was the one time I felt Wooden and Norman were really trying to get me up for a game. Even during the game, they were screaming and yelling at me not to let Hayes get the ball. When he finally did hit a basket—and we were way ahead—I thought Wooden and Norman were gonna just go crazy. I thought they were gonna come out there on the court and kill me for letting him score."

UCLA got off to a 12-4 lead but saw it slip to 20-19. Then, as Sports Illustrated recalled the shift in momentum, "In the next four minutes and 17 seconds, UCLA outscored Houston 17-5 and generally behaved as if it were playing against five blind-folded Campfire Girls."

Wooden was to remember it as: "probably the greatest blitz any of my teams has ever put together." The Bruins led by 22 at halftime.

Lewis' halftime talk to his undefeated team concerned "pride, not quitting, hanging tough—those good ol' American principles we'll need if we ever fight the Russians or the Chinese or some of those folks." It did no good. UCLA's lead reached 44 before Wooden sent in his subs. The Bruins won, 101-69.

Hayes finished with 10 points and planted himself on the Houston bench with a towel over his head.

"That was the night Lynn Shackelford rose to the occasion," Wooden said. "It was a tremendous individual defensive effort by a player who was not normally a good defender."

Alcindor, Lucius Allen and Mike Lynn had 19 apiece, Shack-elford 17 and never-off-balance guard Mike Warren had 14.

Wooden said the margin of victory perhaps could be attrib-uted to a feeling that, "We knew we were better than some of the

Houston players thought we were, and not as complacent as some coaching peers of mine thought we were."

"We haven't really said any-thing publicly, but we're a vindictive team," said Warren. "We've been looking forward to this game for a long time and we're not looking past North Car-olina. We'll run them back down South, too."

Which the Bruins did 24 hours later; beating the Tar Heels by 23 points, 78-55, then the biggest margin in NCAA champi-onship game history.

Carolina coach Dean Smith had his team, which had beaten Ohio State, 80-66, in the semis, play a slow-down offense and a man-to-man defense. Neither worked well, especially the man defense. Alcindor scored 34 points. Larry Miller of the Tar Heels could manage just 14.

Afterward, Smith called UCLA "the best college basket-ball team ever."

"This game counted a whole lot," said Alcindor, "but the win over Houston was our most satis-fying victory. They'd had a lot to say about us. I don't think they were correct. We wanted to teach those people some manners."

"Our victory over Houston in the semifinals was one of the most gratifying I've ever had as a coach," Wooden said. "But our play against North Carolina in the finals was superior from a technical point of view. I have always felt that neither the excel-lent North Carolina team nor our fine execution against them in the championship game received proper attention or due credit because of the factors that made it anticlimactic in the eyes of so many."

The sub-capacity crowd of 14,438 for the final game reflected that anticlimactic feeling.

1969

EXIT OF A CHAMPION

By Bill Brill

The '69 final was held in Louisville's Freedom Hall, the sixth time in a dozen years the event had been there, and, ironically, the last time.

There was no question who would win. After all, UCLA not only was going for its fifth championship in six years and third in a row, but it was to be the finale for the greatest collegiate player ever, Lew Alcindor.

Since UCLA had begun what would be its decade of domination in 1964 at Kansas City, the Bruins had been virtually without challenge. This time the road to the Final Four was easier than ever.

UCLA never had to leave home. In the 25-team field, the Bruins were an overwhelming favorite. They would have been so under any other circumstances, but in '69, the West Regional was played in Pauley Pavilion.

Ironically, the Bruins entered the tournament with a losing streak—one game. It was the only one Alcindor ever lost in Pauley and one of only two defeats for UCLA during the career of the 7-1 center who was to become Kareem Abdul-Jabbar. UCLA was 90-2 during the Alcindor era. The first loss had been at Houston, where Alcindor's eye problems proved beneficial to the Cougars in a 71-69 upset orchestrated by "The Big E," Elvin Hayes.

Later, in the '68 Final Four at Los Angeles, the Bruins proved that was a legitimate fluke. UCLA 101, Houston 69.

They never were challenged again until the final two games of the regular season. Then, in back-to-back meetings with crosstown rival Southern California, UCLA had to go two overtimes on Southern Cal's court before falling to the Trojans' slow-down, 46-44, at Pauley.

That stunning upset snapped a 41-game winning streak for the Bruins, who also had 52 straight at Pauley. John Wooden was not concerned after the Trojan stall and a collapsing defense limited Alcindor to 10 points. "We haven't been as hungry lately," he said. "Maybe this will wake us up."

The Bruins handled New Mexico State's version of the stall effectively, 53-38. But in the West Regional final, UCLA demonstrated the difference between first and everybody else. Santa Clara, once-beaten and ranked No. 3, was dismantled, 90-52. It was the greatest rout in NCAA West Regional history.

So the Bruins were headed to Louisville, where they were greeted by North Carolina, Purdue and Drake. The Tar Heels were rated No. 4 in their third straight Final Four. Purdue was No. 6; Drake in its first NCAA appearance, was No. 11.

It was supposed to be a rematch of '68, with UCLA playing North Carolina. The Bruins had breezed in that first meeting, 78-55.

But there were warning signs that the Tar Heels weren't on top of their game. They had struggled in the ACC Tournament final against Duke. They had rallied to win both East Regional games. For too long, they had depended on Charlie Scott. He bailed them out in the ACC final, and in the East championship game, it was his jumper with two seconds left that beat Davidson, 87-85. That

As the substitutes played out the remaining minutes of the championship game, UCLA guard Mike Warren cheered his teammates on as the Bruins took the 1968 crown. Later, Warren became a star of the TV series, "Hill Street Blues."

Carolina's Miller made the all-tournament team. The other four were Bruins: Alcindor, Allen, Shackelford and Warren. To demonstrate how strong that UCLA team was, the starter who didn't make the all-tourney team, Mike Lynn, made eight of 10 shots against Houston.

Joe Jares is a sports columnist for the Los Angeles Daily News after spending many years as a staff writer for Sports Illustrated, where he covered Final Fours, among other sports.

North Carolina's Dean Smith raised his hands in frustration as UCLA dominated the Tar Heels by 23 points to win the 1968 championship. The Tar Heels used their famed four-corner offense in the final to no avail.

would be as close as Lefty Driesell, then the Wildcats' coach, would come to the Final Four.

The Tar Heels showed up in Louisville without star guard Dick Grubar. The 6-4 senior injured a knee in the ACC finals and was lost for the season. It was a sign of things to come for Dean Smith, who, over the years, had more players missing at Final Four time than any other coach.

Without Grubar, the Tar Heels were without anybody to guard the opposing shooting guard, and Purdue, winners in the Mideast, had All-American Rick Mount. "He's the greatest shooter in college basketball," gushed Purdue coach George King.

King expected Scott, a 6-5 forward, to guard Mount in Grubar's absence. "If Scott can stop him, he'll have done some defensive job," he said.

Dean Smith didn't put his All-American against the Purdue star. Instead, he called upon senior Gerald Tuttle, a native of London, Ky., who got the rare start because of Grubar's injury.

Tuttle wasn't the answer. Neither was anybody else.

Following the opening basket, Mount and guard running mate Billy Keller scored 24 consecutive points for the Boilermakers. Purdue never looked back, running away from a four-point halftime lead to a shocking 92-65 thumping.

Mount (14-28, 36 points) and Keller made life miserable for the Tar Heels. They outscored the Carolina guards 56-6. Keller wasn't bothered by the press, and while Tuttle and Eddie Fogler couldn't shoot, they couldn't pass, either. North Carolina finished with 22 turnovers, a dozen by its starting guards.

"The boys are embarrassed, and I'm embarrassed for them and the conference," Smith said.

"I don't think there's any fella like my man Keller," said a delighted King.

Then he went courtside for the anticipated slaughter as UCLA went against a Drake team that was 6-8, 6-5 and 6-5 up front. Nobody, obviously, could guard Alcindor, and the Bruins had plenty of help with Lynn Shackelford, Curtis Rowe and junior college transfer John Vallely.

Drake wasn't impressed with UCLA's press or its media hype, for that matter.

Alcindor scored 25 points and grabbed 21 rebounds, but he played only in spurts, even to the point of appearing somewhat disinterested. Meanwhile, the underdogs were scrapping and hustling, and beating UCLA to every loose ball.

It took 56 percent shooting by UCLA to survive, 85-82. By dint of their desire, the Bulldogs forced 22 turnovers and they wound up with 33 more shots (83-50). "That's never happened to one of my teams before," Wooden said, " and I've been coaching a long time."

The Bruins had survived, but barely. One scare was enough for UCLA. Alcindor wasn't about to lose the final game of his career. He had 37 points, 20 rebounds and numerous intimidations. Purdue, which needed to shoot well to stand a chance, misfired often. The Boilermakers were 12 of 51 in the first half, with Mount going 3 for 18. They finished at 29.3 percent.

UCLA breezed, 92-72.

Mount made his first two, then missed his next 14. "I haven't been that bad since a game I played against Wisconsin my sophomore year," said the senior guard. "UCLA has a way of making everybody miss."

"A lot of teams have said after playing us that it might have

been different had they shot better," Wooden said. "But our history has been that they don't shoot well against us. Alcindor forces them to do things differently."

Alcindor admitted he was ready, especially after two Louisville writers picked Purdue to win. "This is my greatest thrill," he said. "Nobody has ever won three straight before. That makes this something special."

What was special, of course, was Lew Alcindor. Twenty years later, Kareem Abdul-Jabbar (he became a Muslim and changed his name) was still scoring points playing basketball. Nobody, ever,

has played so long and so well.

"I don't think I'd go through it again," he said that evening in Louisville. "There have been many times when I wondered if it was worth it. But perhaps it would have been the same no matter where I'd been."

Perhaps.

Bill Brill was the executive sports editor of the Roanoke (Va.) Times & World-News and retired in 1991. A former president of the U.S. Basketball Writers Association and the author of the book, "The History of Duke Basketball," he continues to write, time-to-time, for Basketball America.

In 1969, Alcindor (left) was joined by his father for the post-game celebration. After a narrow win over a surprising Drake team in the semis, the Bruins easily beat Purdue in the championship game.

An Indiana schoolboy hero (far left) who went up the road to Purdue, Rick Mount was the most important part of the Boilermakers' game. However, even his driving layups were not enough to win.

1970-1979

BILL WALTON, AL McGUIRE, MAGIC AND BIRD

With a wink and a nod to the '70s, Bill Walton moved into the key where Lew Alcindor had stood, and the UCLA streak continued. In an era where American youth protested a war, experimented with drugs and grew hair long, Walton put aside some of those thoughts to subscribe to the discipline of team as taught by coach John Wooden.

After the turbulent '60s, the next decade was a time that tested America's national resolve and fiber. The end of the Vietnam war was followed closely by the agonies of Watergate. There was an oil crisis early in the decade, a hostage crisis at the end of it, and an identity crisis throughout.

But it wasn't all gloom and doom. History will remember the 1970s as the decade that gave the world such oddities as Billy Carter, the leisure suit, the designated hitter, Clifford Irving, and serial movies with Roman numerals in their titles ("The Godfather," "Jaws," "Rocky," etc.)

With the end of the draft and the country finally at peace, young people stepped back from the horrors of the '60s and became so introspective as to become selfish. The "Me" generation, it was called. As the divorce rate soared, the traditional family became almost as outmoded as high-button shoes. But even as almost everyone seemed to be redefining their roles and values in this changing society, the sports and entertainment industries continued to grow—and no sport experienced quite the explosion in popularity that belonged to college basketball.

As crowds grew, television ratings soared, new arenas were opened everywhere, and the UCLA dynasty reached its peak before finally fading away. When Lew Alcindor left UCLA in 1969, a collective sigh of relief passed through the sport. So all coach John Wooden did was win the 1970 and '71 championships with teams lacking a dominant center. Then, in 1972, came the word that Wooden had found a big man as dominant as Alcindor, maybe even more so. Nobody could believe it at first, yet 6-11 Bill Walton proved to be every bit as good as his advance billing.

After UCLA's title string was stopped at seven in a row in Walton's senior year, Wooden finally was written off. But the man known as "The Wizard" had one more title left in him before he strolled off into the Hollywood sunset. His legacy to college basketball was a record of achievement that figures to still be standing in 2039, when the championship celebrates its 100th birthday.

Perhaps the decade's most compelling figure was Al McGuire, the flamboyant, controversial, street-wise refugee from New York City who built a mini-dynasty at Marquette. He retired tearfully after his 1977 team won the championship, then reappeared as the color man on an NBC announcing team that also included Dick Enberg and Billy Packer.

So good that it often tended to overshadow the games it called, the McGuire-Packer-Enberg triumvirate was at mikeside in 1979 for perhaps the greatest individual confrontation in championship game history—Michigan State's 6-8 Earvin "Magic" Johnson against Indiana State's 6-9 Larry Bird. Never had the game seen a big man who could pass and handle the ball like Johnson. Even so, he wasn't as complete a player as Bird, who could beat a team with his outside shooting, rebounding, passing or great court sense.

It was a perfect way to end the dramatic 1970s and lead into a glorious future in which the game's popularity became so huge that arenas such as Salt Lake City's 17,000-seat Salt Palace would be deemed too small for the Final Four.

But even as almost everyone seemed to be redefining their roles and values in this changing society, the sports and entertainment industries continued to grow . . .

Earvin Johnson was truly magic, and the classic game of the decade came when Michigan State played Indiana State and Larry Bird for the 1979 title. The game lived up to its advance billing for a while, but in the end Michigan State won decisively, 75-64.

1970

WHO FILLED LEW'S SHOES? EVERYBODY

Artis Gilmore was the heart of the Jacksonville offense, and his aggressive play moved the Dolphins into an early lead in the 1970 NCAA final. That was before UCLA coach John Wooden moved Sidney Wicks into the way.

By Dwight Chapin

The other teams in college basketball were supposed to have a chance again in the 1969-70 season. Lew Alcindor—yes, he was still called that then—was gone after three seasons of incredible domination and a mere mortal named Steve Patterson was in his place.

"No one is going to fill Lew's shoes," said Patterson, a sagacious young man. "It's going to

take all of us, working together, to do that."

Work together they did, directed by Wizard of Westwood John Wooden at his most wizardly. Nearly all of the load, as usual with Wooden teams, was carried by an iron-man five: Sidney Wicks and Curtis Rowe, the brilliant forwards; guards Henry Bibby and John Vallely; and Patterson, who never got the credit he deserved because of the stature of the man who came before him and the man (Bill Walton) who came after him.

There had been one loss in the regular season to Oregon on the road but it seemed to weld the Bruins together, and they had no trouble in the West Regional, beating Jerry Tarkanian's Long Beach State team by 23 points and Utah State by 22.

It looked as if things might be different in the NCAA semifinals at College Park, Md., where New Mexico State was waiting. The Aggies, who had lost to UCLA in the regionals in both of the preceding seasons, saw it as a grudge match they could win. "I feel we've got the momentum going now," said Jimmy Collins, the Aggies' fine guard.

Collins did. He scored 28 points. But his teammates couldn't match the Bruins' quickness, and New Mexico State exited a one-sided loser, 93-77.

That set the Cole Field House stage for one of the most intriguing matchups in NCAA history: a clash of cultures and lifestyles as much as basketball teams. UCLA and Jacksonville; the Establishment vs. the Age of Aquarius; an old, tested coach against one 23 years his junior.

Early in the tournament week, Wooden took his Bruins on a three-hour tour of Washington, D.C.'s, historical sites. Attendance was not optional.

In contrast, Jacksonville's Joe Williams, who wore a lucky suit the color of vanilla ice cream, took his players on a White House tour, but there were no restrictions. "They do what they want to do," Williams said.

Jacksonville was a team that had come out of nowhere to post a 23-1 record, had beaten Western Kentucky, Iowa and Kentucky in the regionals and then topped a St. Bonaventure squad that was without injured Bob Lanier in the semifinals. If the Dolphins were nervous about facing UCLA for the championship, it didn't show. They put on a Harlem Globetrotters-style routine at one practice, while the Bruins watched in quiet amusement, and star center Artis Gilmore fell asleep in a motel armchair before another workout.

Jacksonville not only had "Batman" (Gilmore) and "Robin" (guard Rex Morgan) but two other huge front liners, 6-10 Rod McIntyre and 7-0 Pembrook Burrows III, who, when asked about his name, said, "It's not unusual; my father was named that and so was my grandfather."

For the first few minutes of the final, the Dolphins played as big as they stood, taking a 14-6 lead as Gilmore got free for three easy baskets inside off Wicks, who had been surprised just before game time to learn that he was going to guard the giant. But UCLA called a timeout, and Wooden and Wicks, who many thought was then the most intimidating player in college basketball (at only 6-8) took over.

Wicks, who had been playing to the side of Gilmore, moved behind him, with Patterson and other Bruins sagging in to help out when they could. Wicks didn't require much assistance. The next time Gilmore went up for what he thought would be an easy

shot, Wicks rose above him, whacking the ball away. It was one of those classic NCAA moments now frozen in time. It changed the course of the game, and saved a dynasty.

While Wicks—who acquired the nickname Super Sidney after this performance—was eliminat-

ing Gilmore, Rowe and Vallely shot UCLA into a 41-36 halftime advantage. It wasn't much of a cushion but it was enough, the Bruins figured, if they could make a run in the first few minutes of the second half, which they did as Gilmore missed five straight shots. The lead went

from 8 to 11 to 16 points and Jacksonville could do little about it. With just under two minutes to play, Gilmore fouled out, and Jacksonville fans began taking off their "J.U. Can Do" badges. UCLA won with relative ease, 80-69.

"Everybody was looking for-

The UCLA machine caught fire and its team effort dominated Jacksonville. Above, Henry Bibby (45) scored as Steve Patterson (32) waited, should a putback shot be needed.

Bruin Sidney Wicks could be an intimidating player, but so could Villanova's Howard Porter. Their contest became an amazing sidebar to the 1971 championship game. Porter scored 25 points and was named Most Outstanding Player, but Wicks played for the championship team.

ward to playing without Lew," Rowe said in the locker room "Right now, if Alcindor was on the team, who would the reporters be talking to? Look around you. The reporters are with five people and that's beautiful. Every time somebody mentions three titles in a row, they say Lew did it. Now we just proved that four other men on the team could play basketball— with the best of them."

In the background, John Wooden, who had always seen basketball as a team game, was beaming.

He was already looking

ahead to the next season. "I don't anticipate a letdown," he said. "I think we will always have pride in ourselves and when you have that, you are going to be all right."

And it didn't hurt that the only starter he would lose was Vallely.

Dwight Chapin is a senior sportswriter at the San Francisco Chronicle. He previously was a sports columnist at the San Francisco Examiner. He covered UCLA basketball during the Wooden years for the Los Angeles Times.

1971
PATTERSON GRABS THE SPOTLIGHT

By Dwight Chapin

The blue-and-gold uniforms were the same and so was the aura of invincibility, but this wasn't the same ol' UCLA team that showed up at the Houston Astrodome for the 1971 NCAA tournament.

Of all the teams in the Bruins' amazing 10-time championship run, this one was the shakiest. Maybe it was the chemistry. Several players clashed with coach John Wooden and bickered among themselves. Or maybe it was the fact that teams were lying in wait for the sometimes-arrogant Bruins, particularly on the road. UCLA lost to Notre Dame and Austin Carr in South Bend, and had close calls all along the way—none closer than in the West Regional against Long Beach State.

The Bruins trailed by 11 points in the second half, All-America forward Sidney Wicks was on the bench with four fouls, and Wooden was thinking, "Maybe my wife and I can leave for Houston a day early next week and just have a good time as spectators at the national tournament."

But UCLA came back, escaped with a two-point win on a pair of Wicks free throws, and prepared to meet bullish Kansas in the NCAA semifinals. Not before a bit more testing of authority, however, in an era in which authority was being tested everywhere. As the Bruins got off their plane, a reporter noticed that Wicks had a stubble of beard, and asked him if he planned to keep it for the game. "Yep," Wicks said.

The beard was gone by game time. The coach was still in control.

UCLA hadn't shot well against zone defenses all season, but it blistered the Jayhawk zone in the first half, with the clean-shaven Wicks doing most of the damage. As usual, Wicks played intimidator. In the first half, he yelled at Kansas' ace forward Dave Robisch, "Look out, here I come!" and later he screamed "Halt!" at Robisch, who knew better than to argue with a man whose glare was so intense it probably could have cut diamonds.

Kansas made things interesting for awhile in the second half, getting a tie at 39-39, but then the Bruin defense took the Jayhawks out of what they were trying to do. The result was something that could have been plucked from Wooden's "Pyramid of Success." The Bruins bolted to a 68-53 lead, called in the reserves and won with more ease than the 68-60 final score indicated.

In the process, they survived a brouhaha on the bench. Early in the game, assistant coach Denny Crum—who would move on to the head job at Louisville the next season—told Terry Schofield to go in at guard for Kenny Booker. Wooden ordered Schofield to stay put. Schofield eventually did enter the game, but not before Wooden had railed at Crum, "I'm the coach of this team, and don't tell me how to coach my team!" Guard Henry Bibby had to step in as a peacemaker.

The sidelines were calmer in the title game against Villanova, but the game turned out to be tense.

Villanova had six losses, but it also had destroyed Pennsylvania by 43 points in the East Regional and had beaten a good Western Kentucky team in double overtime in the semifinals. It was coached by university division coach of the year Jack Kraft, and featured marvelous forward

Howard Porter and underrated Hank Siemiontkowski, who had burned Jim McDaniels for 31 points in the semis.

Opening in a 2-3 zone defense much like the one that Long Beach State had used so effectively against UCLA in the regionals, the Wildcats shackled Wicks and Rowe. But that left Steve Patterson free, outside first and then inside, and he broke a long shooting slump with 20 first-half points.

It was the most dramatic half of Patterson's career, and it might never have happened, because early in the season he'd had a disagreement with Wooden over the length of his sideburns and almost quit the team. But he decided not to, saying later, "I've never been a famous entity, but if I'd quit and UCLA lost a champi-

Opposing coaches who faced John Wooden's Bruins found the task frustrating. In a 1971 semifinal game, a talented Kansas team watched the game get away in the second half. Guard Bob Kivisto, coach Ted Owens and assistants Sam Miranda and Bob Hill all showed the strain.

The championship's first experiment with a domed arena taught many lessons. Fans in Houston's Astrodome needed binoculars. Those seated on the floor (no elevated stands were used) had to stand on their chairs to see.

onship, I'd have been infamous."

Late in the first half against Villanova, UCLA went into a stall, hoping to bring the Wildcats out of their zone, Wooden opted to continue that strategy in the second half. That enraged a good portion of the vast Astrodome crowd, along with the Villanova players, who jeered, "You're the national champions. Play ball!"

Wooden would admit that the slow-down was at least partially motivated by his desire to convince rulemakers that college basketball needed a time clock. But his move nearly backfired. The Bruins lost their momentum when they held the ball, and the Wildcats proved surprisingly adept with a man-to-man defense when they came out of their zone. Playing brilliantly down the stretch, they cut UCLA's lead to four points with just under five minutes left, as Porter intimidated Wicks with fadeaway jump shots. With 2:38 remaining, the Bruins' lead was down to three, 61-58. But Bibby, one of UCLA's best tournament players, and Patterson held steady, and when Patterson hit a lay-in with 38 seconds left, UCLA was ahead by six and stayed there, winning 68-62.

Porter, who scored 25 points, was voted Most Outstanding Player, an honor that would lose its luster when it was revealed he had signed a professional contract before the tournament, forcing Villanova to forfeit its season's accomplishments.

But Patterson, who had scored 29, was the man of the moment, and somebody wanted to know what was responsible for his remarkable performance. Maybe, he said, it was the trout he'd had at dinner with his parents the night before at a Houston restaurant. Or maybe—and he looked

over at teetotaler Wooden—it was that glass or two of *vin rose*.

1972
WALTON GANG

By Joe Jares

Being a passionate team man, UCLA coach John Wooden didn't particularly care for the "Walton Gang" nickname dreamed up by the media. Being a conservative Hoosier by upbringing, he didn't care for some of the gang's student-revolutionary dietary attitudes.

(Bob Hope kidded Wooden a few years later: "Who else would grow alfalfa in his garden so Bill Walton could have a decent lunch?")

But he certainly liked the gang's performance on the court in 1971-72, when four of its members—Walton, Keith Wilkes, Greg Lee and Tommy Curtis—were mere sophomores. Wooden was to remember that first Walton Gang as "probably the most versatile of all my teams."

Those Bruins could run in the finest, fleetest Wooden fast-break tradition or, with the 6-11 Walton dominating the middle, play a set offense. They could press or play a set defense. They could shoot—senior guard Henry Bibby had games when he could regularly have tossed a tennis ball into a drainpipe at 20 paces. They could pass and rebound.

And they had a fine bench, so fine that second-string center Swen Nater, who never started a game for them, became a first-round NBA draft choice. So fine that two dazzling, if sometimes erratic, guards—Curtis and Larry Hollyfield—were always ready to spell Bibby and Lee.

Wooden also felt the 1971-72 Bruins "had more academic brilliance than any team I have ever had."

The team surprised Wooden by entering the NCAA tournament undefeated. Each year he predicted the Bruins' regular-season record and sealed it in an envelope kept in his desk. That year the talent level might have warranted a forecast of perfection, but his pick, because of "their extreme youth, their inexperience," was 24-2.

Walton Gang I reached the NCAA Final Four with no losses, but it did come burdened with some controversy. In the final of the West Regional at Provo, Utah, UCLA beat Long Beach State, 73-57. It was a game that sometimes resembled a rumble on the docks.

"Every year we play Long Beach we get slugged," said Bibby.

"There wasn't much basketball being played out there," said Wooden. "What there was, we played it."

Long Beach players complained that Walton was a "crybaby" and that UCLA got the majority of the calls.

Some of this spilled over into the semifinals of the Final Four at the Los Angeles Sports Arena, when UCLA (28-0) played Louisville (24-3), coached by ex-Bruin assistant coach and player Denny Crum.

It was an easy victory. No Cardinal or combination of Cardinals could handle the young, red-haired giant from La Mesa, Calif. Walton, who scored eight straight points in an early three-minute stretch to put his team ahead, 20-14, finished with 33 points, 21 rebounds and six blocked shots.

"Walton is strong, but you can't touch him," said Cardinal center Al Vilchek afterward (he

had fouled out with 12 minutes left). "The officials put him in a cage. He cries a lot. I just don't think a man of his ability should cry so much. He wasn't hurt when he went to the floor in the first half. He was just resting."

"We lost and I'll make no excuses," said Louisville guard Jim Price, who had 30 points.

"UCLA played better and it won, so it is the better team."

"I think this is the best UCLA team I've seen," said Crum.

UCLA's opponent in the final, Florida State, arrived in L.A. with the same sort of outlaw reputation that had been stuck on Texas Western back in 1966. The Seminoles, coached by Hugh

Durham, had just gotten off three years of probation for recruiting violations, and some coaches (not including Wooden) were outraged by their presence.

"We've paid the price," said Durham. "We accepted it. We didn't debate it in the press or in public."

Florida State had beaten

Bill Walton's domination of the game began in 1972 and the crowd in the Los Angeles Sports Arena watched the Bruins' new center lead UCLA to an 81-76 championship game victory over Florida State.

At 6-11 Bill Walton could see more of the game and used his height to pass outside, here to Henry Bibby (45). Florida State gave UCLA its toughest battle of the season, but John Wooden earned his eighth NCAA title.

North Carolina, 79-75, in the semis, a surprise. Seminole guard Otto Perry thought his team was ready.

"No one knew us before. Now they know. We can play with anyone. They have the greatest coach in the world in Wooden and the greatest player in the world with Walton, but we just might upset them."

They almost did. Florida State gave the young Bruins their closest and toughest game of the season. It had a good outside shooter in Ron King and a good inside man in 6-11 Lawrence McCray.

The Seminoles broke ahead, 21-14, but, young or not, UCLA refused to crack and regained the lead, even spurting ahead by 11

at halftime. Florida State won the second half, 37-31, but it wasn't enough. Wooden sent Lee in for the last five minutes to run a keep-away, slow-down game.

Costly turnovers prevented Florida State from catching up and UCLA won, 81-76.

King was high-point man with 27. Walton led UCLA with 24, followed by the silky Wilkes with 23 and 18 for Bibby, who made up for his lousy shooting versus Louisville.

"I'm not that elated because we didn't play that well," Walton said. "Florida State is an excellent team, but we didn't dominate the game the way we know we can. If we had played our game the way we can, it would have been different."

"No excuses, but I don't like to back into things. I like to win convincingly."

Bibby, the senior, wasn't so fussy.

"We made mistakes we shouldn't have made, but any team would like to be in our position right now."

Wooden, a tough taskmaster and a severe critic, also didn't agree with Walton.

"I understand why Walton and some others aren't satisfied," he said. "Bill, for example, sets high standards for himself and is displeased when he doesn't reach them. But I don't think we played as poorly as the players do. Very few championship games I've seen or been in have been exceptionally well played. There's too much emotion and too much at stake for that," Wooden said.

"I was especially pleased when we fell behind but didn't lose our poise. I was not so pleased when we got cautious and started to stand around near the finish, which is why I went to a slower game, to protect our advantage."

"I'm satisfied."

One would hope the Wizard of Westwood was satisfied. UCLA had a sixth straight NCAA title, its eighth overall, 45 wins in a row (the third-longest streak in college basketball annals) and a 30-0 season.

But the dissatisfaction of that stellar sophomore class only served to motivate the Bruins toward their goal of perfection. And as Walton would prove one year later, perfection was an attainable goal.

1973
BILL WALTON'S NEAR PERFECT PERFORMANCE

By George Lapides

Gold was struck at St. Louis in 1973. This was the first NCAA Final Four that was sold out in advance.

Before 1973, the tournament played before sellout crowds, but only because of the game day walk-up at the ticket booths. After 1973, the NCAA went to a lottery system to determine who could buy Final Four tickets.

The 1973 ticket demand was intense because followers from two of the participating teams— Indiana and Memphis State— lived within convenient driving distance of St. Louis.

Indiana loyalists were growing enchanted with their 32-year-old, second-year coach—brash Bobby Knight. About 3,000 of them went to St. Louis to see if Knight and his Hoosiers could deliver a championship.

Memphis State fans created traffic jams on Interstate 55 as they flocked to St. Louis to pull for the Tigers. Almost 6,000 of them—ecstatic over the way Memphis State pounded its opponents in the Midwest Regional and just plain wild about head coach Gene Bartow—made the 275-mile trip.

Otherwise, it was business as usual.

Providence, was the East Regional representative and, as usual, UCLA arrived from the West.

By now, the event had become known as the "UCLA Invitational." The Bruins seemed to own the sport. When they arrived in St. Louis, they were winners of 73 consecutive games over a three-season span and seven of the past eight NCAA championships, including six in a row.

This also was the first Final Four split over a weekend, with the semifinal games on Saturday and the championship on Monday night.

An individual performance that many observers still consider the most extraordinary of all time would be seen in this Final Four.

A hint of Bob Knight's genius also would be seen in the first semifinal game, even though his Hoosiers would lose, 70-59, to UCLA.

"Anytime you go into a basketball game, you don't know what your team is going to do over the course of the entire game," he said the day before the semifinals. "I think you have to wait and see what you can do."

But Knight understood what had to be done. He knew that in order to whip the Bruins, he'd have to figure a way to stop Bill Walton, UCLA's 6-11 junior center and already the Associated Press Player of the Year.

Knight's strategy was simple. He put his strongest player—6-8, 231-pound Steve Downing —on Walton. Downing would lean on Walton, use his muscles, push

and shove, try to intimidate—do whatever it would take to get Walton in foul trouble.

Knight's strategy worked … sort of.

Downing got Walton into foul trouble.

But Downing got Downing into foul trouble, too.

Midway through the second half, Indiana had chopped a big Bruin lead to 54-51. The Hoosiers seemed to have the momentum. Walton, already saddled with four fouls, took a pass in heavy traffic inside, wheeled and drove for the basket. Downing appeared to cut him off. Both tumbled to the floor.

The whistles blew and when they did it became so quiet in the jam-packed arena that you almost could hear John Wooden's scorecard hit the floor.

The refs said foul—on Downing. It was his fourth. Only 97 seconds later he was whistled for his fifth. The Indiana rally abruptly ended.

Knight was more understanding then of the call than he might have been later in his career.

"What the hell difference does one individual make?" he said. "UCLA had what it took to come back and win the game. Anything I could say about it wouldn't make any difference anyway. All that counts is that UCLA won the game by 11 points."

The second game that Saturday matched Dave Gavitt's Providence Friars against Bartow's unheralded Memphis State team.

There were a few Providence fans in the seats behind the South goal. Other than that, it seemed like the entire arena was a sea of Memphis blue.

In the opening minutes, Ernie DiGregorio threw dazzling, half-court, behind-the-back passes to the Friars' big men—especially

to Marvin Barnes—and Providence jumped to an early lead. Memphis State floundered. A Providence zone kept the Tigers playing around the perimeter although their best game was to jam it in the middle to either Ronnie Robinson or Larry Kenon.

The Friars led, 18-12, and then 22-14. But Barnes was felled by a knee injury and the complexion suddenly changed. Larry Finch began hitting from outside, Providence extended its zone and Memphis State then countered by going inside.

Ernie D. scored 32 points, but Kenon had 28, Robinson 24 and Finch 21. Barnes limped back into the game in the second half,

In the St. Louis Arena Bill Walton dominated the night with a near-perfect game. He hit 21 of 22 field goal attempts and scored 44 points to lead UCLA over Memphis State, 87-66. The Bruins controlled the backboards, 40-21.

It ended 87-66, but the margin was somewhat misleading. It would have been a little closer if Memphis State had allowed the clock to run out instead of fouling late in a vain attempt to catch up.

Walton injured his ankle in the game's waning moments. Two Memphis State players, Finch and Billy Buford, carried him to the Bruin bench. You could see the respect in their eyes. The crowd—including the Memphis State throng—gave the UCLA redhead a rousing standing ovation. They realized they had just witnessed one of the greatest championship performances ever in any sport.

Wooden admitted after it was over that this was his best UCLA team ever. "I've never had a greater team both offensively and defensively," said the Wizard of Westwood.

There was no argument from the Memphis State camp.

George Lapides was the sports editor of the Memphis Press-Scimitar. He once was president of a Memphis class-AA baseball team, and he has been a longtime sports broadcaster and radio-show host.

Bill Walton sat on the UCLA bench with an injured ankle and accepted congratulations from celebrating players and coaches in St. Louis. Two impressed Memphis State players helped carry him to the bench after the injury.

but it didn't matter. Memphis State won going away, 98-85.

It would be just another championship game for the Bruins, but in Memphis, the basketball Tigers were bigger heroes than Elvis. Even more fans poured up I-55 on Sunday and Monday, hopeful of acquiring tickets from departing Indiana and Providence followers. Some were fortunate; others milled around the parking lot hoping to join the postgame victory celebration.

But UCLA would rule again. The Bruins' victory party was a quiet one. Their players went for dessert at the Chase Park Plaza Hotel.

Oh, it was interesting and close for a while. Memphis State led early at 12-10, kept within striking distance most of the first half and went to the intermission even at 39-39.

The huge Memphis State following in the crowd of 19,301 was practically hysterical. The

largest national television audience ever to watch a championship game—42 million—may have wondered if this finally would be the time the Bruins would lose.

It wasn't.

Bill Walton wouldn't allow it.

He missed only one of his field goal attempts in the first half, but improved to perfection in the second. For the night he was an astonishing 21 of 22 from the field. He scored 44 points, then and still a record in a championship game.

His coach would joke after it was over that he would speak with Walton about that lone miss at the first practice the following autumn.

The last time the Tigers were close was at 49-47 with 13:48 remaining. Walton scored the next eight points. UCLA connected on 21 of its 30 second-half field goal attempts. The Bruins won the backboard battle, 40-21.

1974
THE HORIZON OF A NEW ERA

By Smith Barrier

The end of the 1974 season marked the beginning of a new era in college basketball. Coach John Wooden and the absolutely amazing UCLA Bruins did not win. That in itself was a phenomenon. UCLA had 38 consecutive NCAA tournament victories, leading to an unprecedented seven straight national championships. But coach Norm

Sloan's N.C. State Wolfpack ended UCLA's run in the national semifinals and then defeated coach Al McGuire's Marquette Warriors for the title.

All of this excitement, and novelty, took place in a basket-ball-crazed section of the U.S. which had never hosted the NCAA Final Four. Louisville, Ky. and College Park, Md. had staged the finals in its formative years, before it was called the Final Four, but that is border South. The civic leaders of Greensboro, N.C., had sold the NCAA basketball committee on coming to "real basketball coun-try" ... to North Carolina, to Greensboro, not a populous metropolis.

It was the first sale of Final Four tickets a year in advance. Louisville and St. Louis had been sellouts several months in advance, but April 1, 1973, was the deadline for ordering tickets in Greensboro. Of Greensboro's 15,400 tickets, 8,800 went to public sale. There were 15,840 pieces of mail with the April 1 postmark, a total of 42,500 orders within two days, averaging 3.2 tickets per order, or 136,000.

Also, it was the first year for pairings rotation, eliminating the previous East-West finals and making it possible for top-ranked N.C. State to play No. 2 UCLA in the semifinals, one of the most eagerly awaited showdowns in tournament history.

When the Bruins stubbed their toes during a late-season swing through the Pac-8, N.C. State replaced the perennial champions atop the polls. The Wolfpack's star player was the splendid 6-4 leaper David Thompson, also known as TWA (Teeny Weeny Afro) because of a brush with disaster that shall be mentioned momentarily.

In the final of the Atlantic Coast Conference tournament, playing on the same Greensboro floor that was to be home of the Final Four, N.C. State outlasted Maryland, 103-100, in what some veteran ACC observers ranked as the greatest game they had ever seen. This was still the era, remember, when only the league champion went to the NCAA, meaning poor Lefty Driesell had to take his Maryland team home.

For the East Regional, the Wolfpack had only to move from Greensboro to its home-court, Reynolds Coliseum on the cam-pus in Raleigh. The Wolfpack whipped Providence and Pitts-burgh to earn a return trip to Greensboro, but got a huge scare when Thompson fell from the sky and landed right on his head. When physicians severely cropped his Afro, Thompson became known as TWA.

When UCLA arrived in Greensboro, its star, 6-11 center Bill Walton, two-time college player of the year, was carrying a paper bag full of California oranges as he got off the transcontinental charter. While UCLA and the other semifinal-ists—Kansas and Marquette—worked out privately on Thursday, a cheering crowd of 5,000 watched the Wolfpack go through their final drills, then sent TWA & Co. off on the two-hour bus ride to Greensboro with a pep rally at which 2,500 fans heard every player say a few words.

Until 1974, only some of the coaches, skipping clinics at the coaches convention, and a few diehard fans turned out for the Friday afternoon practice ses-sions at the Final Four site. But with tickets so scarce in Greens-boro—N.C. State allotted only 100 for students out of its 1,000, and 2,740 students applied—the

only chance to see the teams was in the Friday afternoon practice. Unofficially, since it was free, 6,000 fans attended.

Finally all the hoopla ended and it was time for the big one—UCLA and N.C. State. They met the opening Saturday afternoon, right after Marquette beat Kansas, 64-51. Nobody needed to be reminded that UCLA had soundly defeated the Wolfpack, 84-66, in a made-for-television matchup in St. Louis in December.

For most of the early going, it looked as if the Bruins were des-tined to win again. In the second half, UCLA was up by as many as 11. But the Wolfpack kept chip-ping until it gained a tie and had a chance to win in regulation, only to have Tim Stoddard, later a Major League Baseball pitcher, bounce a side shot off the rim.

The same thing happened in the first overtime, when N.C. State's chance to win ended with 7-4 Tom Burleson bumping a

Most people expected a UCLA celebration in 1974, but North Carolina State, with David Thompson at the helm, got to wear the nets. Upsetting UCLA in the semifinals, the Wolfpack went on to defeat Marquette, 76-64, in the final.

North Carolina State's David Thompson took the ball repeatedly to the basket over a towering Bill Walton. In one of the greatest games in Final Four history, the Wolfpack defeated UCLA 80-77 in double overtime en route to its first championship.

close shot off the back rim.

In the second overtime, UCLA went up seven behind the strength of Walton and Keith Wilkes. Then Thompson put the Wolfpack ahead to stay, 76-75, and he and Monte Towe converted free throws for the 80-77 final.

Wooden has reviewed that afternoon many times since, and he said, "I thought we had the game in hand two times. In the second half, up 11, we took three shots you just don't take when you have the lead. Then in over-

time, up seven, we made a crucial mistake or two, but, that's to the credit of North Carolina State.

But, the Wolfpack still had Marquette to play.

North Carolina Gov. James Holshouser, writing a daily "guest" column in the Greensboro Daily News for the tournament, spoke for everybody: "It somehow seems a shame that Saturday's N.C. State-UCLA game had to be the semifinals. The way it turned out, it would have been a perfect finale. When the No. 1 team in the nation defeats the No. 2 team in two overtimes, it's sort of hard to imaging a fitting encore."

But all of the 15,829 ticketholders showed up Monday night, along with 27 million or so television watchers. The Wolfpack, as predicted, outscored Marquette, 76-64, with Thompson getting 21 points and Burleson 11 rebounds. Two technical fouls on McGuire provided the impetus for the Wolfpack's working margin late in the first half and helped Sloan's team to a 39-30 halftime lead. "The technicals sure gave us a lift," Thompson would say later, while McGuire manfully admitted that his strategy had backfired. That would haunt McGuire until he won his own national title three years later.

When it came time to hand out awards, Thompson was the Most Outstanding Player, Burleson and Towe also made the all-tournament team, along with Maurice Lucas of Marquette and Walton.

The Wolfpack, in their tournament run, had beaten teams ranked Nos. 2, 3, 4 and 6 in the country. Sloan, years later, reviewed "Those Three Weeks" as they became known in his household.

"What happened in 1974 is almost like you're half awake and

half asleep. When you get to this point, everything moves so quickly. You have so many things to take care of, there's no such thing as pressure. I never felt one bit of pressure, we were too busy.

"The enthusiasm of the basketball fans in North Carolina, no question about that … I don't know that we could have won the thing if we played anywhere else. We were good, don't misunderstand, but shoot, if we had been playing out in Los Angeles, I don't know that we could have beaten UCLA. They won three of theirs at home. It makes a difference.

"Everybody you bump into on the street … the intensity is greater … more people able to be at the game, more for us than for UCLA. Of course, UCLA had won so much. They had put themselves in that unenviable position. Everybody wanted to see them fall."

Smith Barrier was publisher of Greensboro Publications and former executive sports editor of the Greensboro News & Record. He is a member of the North Carolina Sports Hall of Fame.

1975
ONE LAST HURRAH FOR THE WIZARD

By Mike Sullivan

The 1974-75 college basketball season was a good one for quips. It was even better for tradition.

Asked in a preseason interview if he thought UCLA could come back, John Wooden, the Bruins' 64-year-old coach, replied puckishly that he "didn't

know we had been gone."

The man had a point. Only a double-overtime semifinal loss to the 1974 champion, N.C. State, had kept UCLA from making an eighth straight appearance in the title game.

With the 1975 championship encounter less that 24 hours away, Joe B. Hall, Kentucky's third-year head coach and the successor to Adolph Rupp, joined in the speculation about a replacement for Wooden, who had just announced his retirement.

"I'm the obvious choice," Hall cracked. "Why ruin two lives?"

No lives were ruined in the San Diego Sports Arena on March 31, 1975, when UCLA used quickness and poise to befuddle Kentucky's bruisers, 92-85, and send Wooden into retirement with what is arguably, the greatest coaching achievement in team sports—10 national championships in a span of 12 years.

But if lives were spared, nerves were liberally abused.

In the semifinals two days earlier, Louisville had played the Bruins off their feet, leading most of the way by five to nine points under Wooden's protégé, Denny Crum.

UCLA won, 75-74, in overtime—its only lead during the extra period—on Richard Washington's seven-footer with two seconds left. With 20 seconds to go and the Bruins trailing, 74-73, Washington had rebounded the missed first attempt in a one-and-one free throw situation by Louisville guard Terry Howard, who had stepped to the line with a 28-for-28 mark on the season.

In the other semi, Hall's Wildcats—who had come rumbling back from the ruins of a 13-13 record the year before—pum-

meled Syracuse, 95-79, getting 24 points and 11 rebounds from freshman reserve Jack Givens. Kentucky used 14 players in a game in which 61 fouls were called.

Columnist Dave Kindred, comparing the two contests, likened the Louisville-UCLA thriller to a Michaelangelo. On that basis he said Kentucky vs. Syracuse was "a Roto-Rooter sign on a panel truck."

Still, many observers in San Diego felt that Kentucky would keep on truckin' past UCLA, despite the inspiration generated by Wooden's locker room retirement announcement.

The Wildcats had four NCAA titles, a total that Wooden had matched in 1968 and surpassed in 1969. They had been runners-up to Texas Western in 1966, one of only two years since 1963 that UCLA did not appear in the championship game.

Kentucky had depth, size and strength to go with its tradition. And it was on a ferocious roll, having stunned top-ranked and previously unbeaten Indiana, 92-90, in a rock-'em, sock-'em Mideast Regional final that avenged a 98-74 loss at Indiana in December.

Looking back, forward Kevin Grevey, who exploded for 34 point in the loss to UCLA, felt that Kentucky left some of its hunger on the floor at Dayton after the triumph over the Hoosiers.

"I think we kind of showed up in San Diego with our chest stuck out because we had beaten No. 1," Grevey said. "It was a case of being satisfied to get there. That experience helped Kentucky win the title in 1978, when the freshmen from our San Diego team were seniors. I still believe we were better than UCLA, but we gave a flat performance."

The 1975 title game was John Wooden's final appearance. After surviving against Louisville in overtime in the semifinals, the Bruins faced a talented and formidable Kentucky team for the title. Wooden fought for every call in the final. A charging Wildcat team saw Kevin Grevey dance down the press tables for a loose ball; Bob Guyette (45, right) powered his way for a shot.

Wooden, meanwhile, did his part to flatten the opposition by surprising his players again, this time with a secret, walk-through practice on the morning of the game. He installed a trap play to free guard Pete Trgovich, whose five baskets late in the first half helped turn the game around, and he ran a brief refresher course of high-post plays for center Washington after relying more on low-post series throughout the season. Washington, the tournament's Most Outstanding Player, scored 28 points.

Emotion wasn't a problem. Not for a team that Wooden freely described as one of his favorites, a team without a superstar.

"We were at the right emotional level," Trgovich said. "We were ready to win for The Man, not emotionally yelling and screaming, but feeling it inside. I knew we were ready for the big one."

When it came time to prove it, though, emotions were spread all over the court, along with the trashing bodies of Grevey and David Meyers, and the crowd of 15,513 was wilder than it had been during the UCLA-Louisville classic, if that was possible.

As the game moved inside the 6:30 mark, Grevey's 20-footer capped a Kentucky run that chopped a 66-56 UCLA lead to 76-75. Then Grevey bellied up to Meyers as the Bruin forward misfired on one of his patented leaning-forward jump shots. Both players went down in a heap. Meyers, slapping the floor with his hand when he was called for a charging foul, drew a technical.

"As an offensive-minded player, I always believed there wasn't any such thing as a charging foul," Grevey said. "Even 12 years later, in a YMCA game, I got mad if a guy doesn't let me come down after I take a shot. There's no question I moved under Dave."

With the one-and-one, the technical shot and an inbounds play, Kentucky had a chance to score five points before the Bruins saw the ball again. But Grevey drew a blank at the free-throw line and freshman James Lee committed a player control foul on the baseline.

Two free throws by Meyers, who scored 24 points, made it 78-75. A bank shot by Bob Guyette, who scored 14 of his 16 points in the second half, drew Kentucky within a single point one final

time. But the Bruins, who got 14 assists from Trgovich's backcourt mate Andre McCarter, were in total control down the stretch.

"I was eight for 10 on free throws in that game and I'd take that any time," Grevey said.

But Hall wasn't used to taking 38 percent shooting from the field, and he was even less accustomed to being outplayed from buzzer to buzzer by a club that employed only six players.

The lone substitute Wooden inserted, 7-1 Ralph Drollinger, delivered 10 points and a game-high 13 rebounds in 16 minutes. UCLA, outrebounded 49-36 by Louisville, beat Kentucky on the boards, 55-49.

"Drollinger's baskets off the offensive board in the first half really killed us," said Hall, whose 6-10 freshman centers, Rick Robey and Mike Phillips, combined for only six points.

It was a magnificent last hurrah for the man they called the Wizard of Westwood. The victory gave Wooden's final UCLA team a 28-3 record and fixed his career mark at the school at 620-147 for 27 seasons. After an uncharacteristic tantrum when the technical was called on Meyers, he was, in the afterglow, his calm, professorial self.

"This was a team victory in the strictest sense of the word," Wooden said. "When I had a Jabbar or a Walton, I approached this tournament with a little more confidence. This team didn't have anyone like that."

What it had was John Wooden. As the records show, no other school ever had anyone like him.

The late Mike Sullivan covered many Final Fours, first as an Associated Press writer in the Louisville bureau, later on the staff of The (Louisville) Courier-Journal. He closed his career at the Columbus Dispatch.

1976
A LAST LOOK AT PERFECTION

By Bob Hammel

It was a special team that came along so suddenly in the Indiana coaching era of young Bob Knight.

It was a haughtiness that said, "You won't beat us," and a ferocity that backed up the words. It had muscle and strength, more of both than the sinewy quickness usually associated with great basketball teams. All five starters weighed 200 pounds or more.

Those five begrudged every opponent every basket.

Knight, as intense a coach as the game has seen, always sent out teams that played in reflection of his demands, his teachings and his refusal to accept less than the best. But in the 1975-76 season, he was given the perfect personnel match for his insis-

Indiana's Quinn Buckner (above and top right) was the floor general of the 1976 team that defeated Michigan for the title. President Gerald Ford hosted the winning team at the White House, and Buckner got to sit in the presidential chair in the oval office. Mixed emotions overflowed at the game's end for coach Bob Knight (lower right), who stood drained and misty-eyed on the victory stand with Kent Benson, Buckner and Scott May.

tences, a team as smart and full of basketball savvy as it was physically powerful. It was a team with an offense called "The Passing Game," and five better passers may never have played together on a college team.

The result was a perfect year—the last of those college basketball has seen.

Much went into the forging of the steel-tough Indiana team that completed a 32-0 season by pulling away from Big Ten rival Michigan, 86-68, in a historic championship game at The Spectrum in Philadelphia, in the nation's bicentennial year.

With no disrespect to John Wooden—or to the psychological magic generated by his Final Four retirement announcement, or to the outstanding team that won him his 10th and final NCAA championship at UCLA—the 1975 title, too, probably should have been Indiana's.

Knight put together a powerful blend of shooters and defenders and laid waste to the Big Ten as no team had before. The 1974-75 Hoosiers won their 18 league games by a record average of 22.5 points per game, and they were an unchallenged No. 1 nationally until the late February day when they lost first-team All-American forward Scott May to a broken arm. Exactly one month later, the 31-0 Hoosiers were beaten in the NCAA Mideast Regional final at Dayton, 92-90, by the Kentucky team that ultimately lost to UCLA in the national championship game.

From the 1975 team, Knight lost shooters Steve Green and "super sub" John Laskowski, and they were missed. He gained on defense, fitting Tom Abernethy into the forward spot that Green left.

Not enough offense, appraisers said in looking at a lineup that suddenly had three players

considered "non-shooters"— guards Quinn Buckner and Bobby Wilkerson, plus Abernethy.

They weren't especially wrong. There was a day when the three combined to shoot 2 for 22, and the opponent was the Michigan team the Hoosiers met in the national final. Still, Indiana found a way to win.

"We call it offense without the ball," Knight said.

Abernethy paired with May to give the Hoosiers two 6-7 forwards who could play defense almost as well as the devastating guard combination that keyed everything: Buckner and Wilkerson.

Buckner, the 6-3 floor general, was a two-year starter at Indiana as a football safety as well as a basketball star-rugged, strong, quick, street-tough and class-room-smart, the consummate basketball leader.

Wilkerson, at 6-7, was remarkably athletic, quicker than Buckner and such a jumper that he—not 6-10 All-American center Kent Benson—handled tipoffs. "You think it isn't intimidating for a guard who's going to be playing against him to see him jumping center?" Minnesota coach Bill Musselman said. "He really complements Buckner. Those two take a team right out of its offense."

Years later, Knight was defining "greatness in a team" when his first NCAA championship team came to mind.

"Greatness in 1976 was Buckner and Wilkerson not letting anybody come across mid-court. Greatness was May being a tremendous defensive player and the second-best defensive forward on our team—Abernethy being the best. Greatness was Benson playing in the middle.

"That was a team almost impossible to beat," professed

Knight, "because of its toughness, its strength, its size."

The 1976 NCAA tournament marked the second year in which the field was opened to non-champions of major conferences, but there were restrictions. Only the runner-up was eligible; no team was sent more than one geographical region away. For extra teams in the East (that is, the ACC—the Big East hadn't formed yet), that meant an assignment in the Mideast, already clogged with powerful teams.

So No. 1 Indiana looked at a regional that included No. 2 Marquette, No. 6 Alabama and No. 8 North Carolina. It was a circumstance that changed the tournament forever. The very next year, seeding was introduced.

But on they came, like Ruth, Gehrig, Foxx, Simmons and Cronin for Carl Hubbell in all-star baseball lore: St. John's (90-70), Alabama (74-69), Marquette (65-56), UCLA (65-51) and Michigan (86-68).

Coach C.M. Newton's Alabama team led in the regional semifinals, 69-68, with two minutes to go when May—college basketball's player of the year—came off a typical Indiana pick and sank a 17-footer that wasn't an especially high percentage shot. "May's got a little more latitude than the other guys," Knight said.

Indiana vs. Marquette pitted No. 1 vs. No. 2, Knight vs. Al McGuire, in the Mideast Regional final at Baton Rouge, La. McGuire later referred to it as the game that matched two lineups in which all five starters on both teams went on to the NBA.

And so it was, just as the next one was: Indiana vs. UCLA in a rematch of the season opener. All 15 Indiana, Marquette and UCLA starters became pros. Indeed, 19 months after the night in Philadelphia when their quest reached the national championship goal, all five Indiana starters were in starting lineups of pro teams on opening night of the NBA season.

Michigan did not have five future pros, but the Wolverines had fought their way through the Midwest Regional, past Adrian Dantley and Notre Dame (80-76), and Missouri with a hot hand named Willie Smith (95-88, despite 43 points by Smith). In the Final Four, the Wolverines took on another unbeaten team, Rutgers, and ran to an 86-70 victory.

And the Wolverines had a 35-29 lead at halftime of the final game. Indiana was wobbling. Wilkerson hit his head on the floor during a play in the first two minutes of the game and went to a hospital with a concussion. The backcourt demolition team was broken up. Memories of the 1975 title that got away with May's injury inevitably floated through Hoosier heads.

The game went into its last 10 minutes tied, 51-51. Down the stretch, with sophomore Jimmy Wisman filling in for Wilkerson but All-Americans May and Benson and captain Buckner doing the heavy work, Indiana was flawless. May scored a game-high 26 points, 20 in the second half, and fouled out stout-hearted Waymon Britt, a 6-2 forward whose defensive tenacity was crucial to coach Johnny Orr's team.

Benson scored 25 points (15 in the second half) and—for the third straight time—fouled out Michigan's freshman star, Phil Hubbard (the only college freshman to make the gold medal U.S. Olympic team that year).

Buckner, whose career average was slightly under 10 points per game, scored 16 points (12 in the second half) and took over Wilkerson's scheduled defensive

assignment on swift Michigan standout Rickey Green. A devotee of basketball statistics wrote to Sports Illustrated to say in the second half of the game Indiana had the best "OER" (offensive efficiency rating) he had ever charted: more than 1.5 points per possession—with the national championship at stake.

By then, they had been well-schooled in defense of their right to that championship. That stamp of No. 1 they wore all year long, most of the time by unanimous vote, had trained them well.

Lute Olson, the coach at Iowa, said, "The number one problem is, although they are very good offensively, they win with their defense. They take you out of your offense and you wind up having to free-lance."

Minnesota coach Jim Dutcher said: "I don't think they're as overpowering as they were last year. I said at the time that was the best college team I'd ever seen."

Down deep, Knight agreed, and he felt for the seniors of that 1975 team who had joined him in the opening days of his coaching era and done so much to carry the program to the top—with no national championship ring to testify their role.

On the steps of The Spectrum, heading out into the night that was his own hour of crowning achievement, Knight fielded one more handshake of congratulations and said wistfully, "Thanks. But it should have been two."

Bob Hammel covered Indiana basketball for some 30 years and has authored several books on Indiana sports. He was longtime sports editor of the Bloomington (Ind.) Herald-Times, and remains on the editorial management staff there. He currently is writing a new book about the Bob Knight years.

Center Kent Benson scored 25 points to lead the Hoosiers' second-half charge to the 1976 championship. Indiana, which trailed Michigan by six at halftime, became the last team to complete a perfect season.

1977
SEASHELLS, BALLOONS AND AL McGUIRE'S MOMENT

By Edgar Allen

He stood amid the deafening roar of Atlanta's Omni, his ecstatic followers hoarsely shouting their appreciation and approval. This was it for Al McGuire, the moment wrapping up a colorful career of coaching. Something special for the New York City kid who grew up helping his mom and dad run a corner bar—who captained a good St. John's team in 1951 and who spent some time playing with the Knicks in the NBA.

It was one of the sport's more dramatic moments.

The 1977 NCAA championship only a few clock-ticks away, McGuire pulled away from a hug by long-time assistant Hank Raymonds, stood up, and with tears coursing down his cheeks, left the bench and made his way to the silence of the Marquette locker room.

"I want to be alone," he said as he entered the empty room, a towel to his eyes. "I'm not afraid to cry."

Seashells and balloons, as Al liked to call such occasions in his Big Apple terminology. College basketball 1977 had a fitting climax in The Al McGuire Story. It was in midseason that he had announced he would join Medalist Industries in Milwaukee as vice president. The 67-59 tingler over North Carolina in the final at Atlanta made for the perfect ending.

Emotions more under control as he met the press 30 minutes later, McGuire said huskily, "I feel washed out, but I'm very pleased. Normally, street fighters like me don't end up like this; but the numbers came up, and it's nice."

Thus did one of basketball's most absorbing figures wrap up a 20-year career, the last 13 at Marquette, where he was 295-80 and went to 11 consecutive post-season tournaments. Twenty years of haranguing officials. Taunting hostile crowds. Kicking tables. Knocking over chairs. Throwing towels. But still a favorite of fellow coaches and a tremendous contributor to the game. One who continued in the limelight as a network college basketball analyst.

"All I could think about at the end was—why me?" McGuire told writer Steve Guback later. "After all the jocks and socks, driving the car at Belmont Abbey, freshman coach at Dartmouth, all the PALs (Police Athletic League) and CYOs (Catholic Youth Organization). And to have it end like this …" The reminiscing trailed off.

Soap opera television couldn't have done it up better than the Final Four in Atlanta.

Downcourt from the Warriors' bench was Dean Smith. Smith was already in "the big time" at Chapel Hill when McGuire was toiling at nearby Belmont Abbey, beating the bushes for Atlantic Coast Conference hand-me-down prospects and busing over rural North Carolina roads for games on homey little campuses.

Smith had won a world championship with his 1976 U.S. Olympic team but never the NCAA's top prize.

It would elude him again this time.

Perfecter of the four-corners offense, Smith may have used it once too often against Marquette—or at least too soon. Fiercely battling back with an 18-4 rampage after trailing, 39-27, at halftime, Carolina electrified its supporters, predominant in the close-to-home Omni, by taking a 45-43 lead. Shortly after, with more than 12 minutes still left to play, Smith opted for the spread pattern. The Tar Heels had won all season with the four-corners, but this time it led to their downfall.

"We were glad to see it," said Warrior Butch Lee, who scored 19 points and was voted the tournament's Most Outstanding Player. "They had a good streak going. It gave us a chance to catch our breath."

The break came when Bo Ellis blocked Bruce Buckley's attempted shot with just under 10 minutes left. Marquette scored on Jim Boylan's reverse layup and was never again headed.

The 67-59 final score was somewhat deceiving. It was 51-49 with 1:56 to play, but the Warriors expanded the margin on free throws. Willis, Boylan and Gary Rosenberger each hit four-of-four from the line to wrap it up.

"They went into their own delay game and killed us by making all their free throws," said Smith.

Walter Davis, playing with a broken finger sustained during the regular season, led the Tar Heels with 20 points, but Phil Ford, recovering from a hyperextended elbow, was noticeably slowed and managed only six. The ACC champs also played without Tom LaGarde, who went out late in the season with a knee injury.

Carolina fought doggedly to reach the Final Four after winning the ACC regular season and tournament titles. The Tar Heels squeaked by Purdue (69-66), Notre Dame (79-77) and Kentucky (79-72) to qualify for the Omni trip.

In Atlanta, after Midwest Regional wins over Cincinnati (66-51), Kansas State (67-66) and Wake Forest (82-68), the Warriors still had the worst record of any in the Final Four.

Joined there by upstarts North Carolina-Charlotte, Nevada-Las Vegas (UNLV) and perennial contender North Carolina, it made for one of the more memorable NCAA windups.

If possible, the semifinals were more intensely fought than the final. Only three points separated the two victors, the closest NCAA semifinals on record. Marquette tipped UNC-Charlotte, 51-49, on Jerome Whitehead's last-second basket after taking a court-length pass off Cornbread Maxwell's fingertips and dropping in an almost-aborted dunk. Run-and-gun UNLV fell before Carolina in a barn-burner, 84-83, to set up the dramatic finale.

The Tar Heels, with Mike O'Koren pouring in 31 points,

overcame a 10-point second-half deficit with 14 unanswered tallies, then hung on the final 14 minutes with their four-corners offense. They shot 70 percent the second half in a preview of the finals—in reverse.

Whitehead's winning shot was decided only after coaches, officials and players surrounded timekeeper Larry Carpenter, clamoring to clarify the call. Television replays of the final seconds, with a clock superimposed on the screen, showed the basket

Marquette's colorful coach, Al McGuire, had taken his team to the NCAA final three years before and had been involved in several important regional games. But 1977 was the year he ascended to earn a long-awaited championship.

in time, inflicting a heart-breaking loss on UNC-Charlotte.

Prior to Atlanta, upsets took their toll during the '77 tournament series. Michigan, No.1 in both final wire-service polls, went down before inspired UNC-Charlotte in the Mideast Regional at Lexington, 75-68. San Francisco, No. 1 most of the season and undefeated until toppled by Notre Dame in the regular season finale, was rudely upended by UNLV, 121-95. Potent but unknown Idaho State stunned mighty UCLA, 76-75.

It was that kind of tournament. And Al McGuire's scratchers and clawers gave it the storybook finish.

Edgar Allen, longtime sports editor of the Nashville Banner and past president of the U.S. Basketball Writers Association, became director of media relations for Churchill Downs in 1979.

1978
THE SEASON WITHOUT A CELEBRATION

By John McGill

At halftime of the 1978 NCAA championship game, Kentucky led Duke by seven points. To commemorate this comfortable turn of events, Kentucky's players lost their temper. In the locker room, emotions sizzled and accusations flew: not enough teamwork, not enough effort, they yelled. Joe Hall, the coach, thought he'd detected a smile on the face of center Mike Phillips and admonished him. "Dammit," Phillips snapped. "Do you think I'm happy?"

At Kentucky, happy was the ultimate sin. Happy meant com-

placent. Happy meant content. Until a title was secured—until its fans were sated and its coach could lift an aging albatross from his neck—Kentucky had no room for contentment.

This was a team of grim purpose, born of the Kentucky tradition which begot four national titles under Adolph Rupp but had come up empty for 20 years.

Nobody felt this pressure to produce more than Hall. This was his sixth season as successor to Rupp, who had died in December but whose presence as the standard for Wildcat basketball excellence was very much alive.

As a kid in Cynthiana, Ky., Hall had grown up listening to Wildcat games on the radio. But his relationship with Rupp—his idol—was to prove uneasy. A reserve on Kentucky's 1951 title team, Hall transferred to Sewanee. And after he returned to Kentucky as an assistant, Hall succeeded Rupp only after the legendary coach had lost a bitter fight against mandatory retirement.

Hall knew that Kentucky's fanatical following would gauge this team as the true test of whether he deserved to follow in Rupp's footsteps. Mix that with a coach whose personality was inherently intense ("Perfection is an attainable goal," Hall once said) and the tone for a season was set.

From the outset, Kentucky was awesome. With King (6-10 Rick Robey) and Kong (6-10 Phillips) joining silky-smooth Jack Givens on the front line and muscular junkmaster James Lee developing into the nation's best sixth man, the Wildcats were a fright inside.

To that, Kentucky added the cerebral control and seamless shot of guard Kyle Macy, a trans-

fer from Purdue, and the quickness of guard Truman Claytor.

Through all of December and most of January, things ran smoothly as Kentucky won its first 14 games. But the Wildcats then lost two of the next five. And with the second loss, "The Season Without Celebration"—as Hall would later term it during a Final Four press conference—began. Kentucky, which had beaten Louisiana State by 20 points at home, lost the road game rematch, 95-94, in overtime despite all five LSU starters having fouled out in regulation.

In its NCAA tournament opening game against Florida State, Hall took the biggest and boldest risk of his career. Trailing 37-27 with 3:30 left in the first half, he benched Givens, Robey and Claytor and replaced them not with top reserves like Lee but with the seldom-used Dwane Casey, LaVon Williams and Fred Cowan. The banished starters didn't return until 10 minutes remained in the game. When they did, Kentucky scored 14 straight points to turn a 53-48 deficit into a 62-53 lead. The Wildcats won, 85-76. Had they lost, Hall said he expected to be fired. The team was 26-2 at the time.

Trailing Michigan State and a freshman named Magic Johnson, 31-22, in the Mideast Regional final, Kentucky survived another serious threat with an improvised offense. Michigan State had stymied the Wildcats with a 2-3 zone. As they walked onto the floor for the second half, assistant coach Leonard Hamilton suggested to Hall that Robey and Phillips break the zone by picking for Macy at the top of the key. Macy wound up with a game-high 18 points and hit seven straight free throws in the final 2 1/2 minutes. Kentucky won, 52-49.

The celebratory net was worn by Marquette forward Bernard Toone (above) as the team received its trophy at mid-court. The emotionally drained coach, Al McGuire, retired to the locker room to compose himself and wipe away the tears.

Maurice "Bo" Ellis fired a jumper over North Carolina's Mike O'Koren (left) as Marquette fought off a second-half surge by the Tar Heels. Ellis and Butch Lee led Marquette to the 1977 title in coach Al McGuire's final game.

Following the legendary Adolph Rupp had been difficult for Kentucky coach Joe B. Hall. As he talked to the team in the locker room before the 1978 championship game, Hall knew he was expected to win. With the pressure gone, the net-cutting was especially joyful.

When the Final Four opened in St. Louis, Kentucky faced a semifinal Arkansas team that boasted a three-guard offense headed by Sidney Moncrief and coached by Eddie Sutton, who in 1985 would become Hall's successor at Kentucky.

Those sensing an Arkansas upset envisioned Razorback quickness overcoming Wildcat size. But to its physical play, Kentucky added Givens, the 6-4 forward whose soft, left-handed jumper was an added dimension to the Wildcats' attack. Givens hit 10 of 16 floor shots and scored 23 points. Kentucky won, 64-59.

In the final Kentucky faced Duke, a 90-86 winner over Notre Dame in a game that saw center Mike Gminski score 29 points, freshman Gene Banks 22 and guard Jim Spanarkel 20. The contrast between the two teams fairly screamed. Expected to win,

Kentucky shouldered that responsibility soberly. Duke, on the other hand, had every reason to regard its entire tournament experience as a trip to Disneyland. The Blue Devils—who started two freshmen, two sophomores and a junior—were on a joyride of unexpected success.

Their glee, of course, made all the more glaring Kentucky's solemn mission. For the media, the scenario was easy to set: The Glad versus The Mad.

Of all the players who were subjected to Hall's tongue-lashings, Givens was the most frequent target. Givens would wind up the No. 2 scorer in Kentucky history with 2,038 points. But Givens had a tendency to disappear in crucial moments, often reluctant to shoot, and Hall reacted with rage—calculated rage, perhaps, but brutal nonetheless.

On one such occasion in the previous season, Hall had called Givens "gutless" at halftime of a game against Alabama and Givens had responded with 18 points in the second half. He was the brunt of similar verbal attacks throughout his senior year. Givens, a bright and soft-spoken man, was perceptive enough not to take it personally, but moved enough to respond where Hall wanted him to—on the court.

In the title game, no such prompting was necessary. Givens was already primed. Because the back line of Duke's 2-3 zone tended to stretch from corner to corner, Hall suspected that Givens would be free in the key for good shots.

As Duke's weakness became evident in the first half, Givens began to flash toward the free throw line more and more. He hit nine of 12 shots in the half and had 23 points by intermission, including Kentucky's last 16

points of the half. The Wildcats led, 45-38.

Duke—which again got balanced scoring from Banks (22), Spanarkel (21) and Gminski (20)—drew within three points on two occasions early in the second half but Claytor drilled a long shot and Macy hit two free throws and then set up Robey for a dunk. The Wildcats led by nine and never wavered.

Givens, meanwhile, never let up. Duke adjusted its defense to cut off much of the lane, but now Givens was hitting from everywhere. He scored 18 in the final 20 minutes and finished with 41 points—the third highest total ever in a championship game. Kentucky, leading 91-80, went to reserves in the final minute and saw the lead whittled down—making the final margin, 94-88, deceptive.

Givens wound up with 64 points and 17 rebounds in his two Final Four games. He was the runaway choice as the tournament's Most Outstanding Player. And Kentucky—grim Kentucky—had won 30 of 32 games and given the school its fifth national title. "Your names have been immortalized," Hall said as the team gathered in the locker room.

He wasn't finished. Maintaining a straight face, Hall looked at

Kentucky's Jack Givens more than rose to the occasion in the championship game, launching a jumper over Duke's Kenny Dennard (33) and Mike Gminski (43). When the game was over, Givens had scored 41 points and was named MOP.

his championship team. "Fellas," he said, "curfew will be at 10 o'clock tonight."

At that, Kentucky's players did something strange. They laughed.

John McGill covered many Final Fours while writing for the Lexington (Ky.) Herald-Leader. Now retired, he still writes an occasional column for the Herald-Leader.

1979

MAGIC'S MOMENT

By Lee Benson

It's hard to imagine now—after all their Biggest Game Ever showdowns; after more sequels than "Rocky"; after never playing together to a single empty seat—that there ever was a time when Magic Johnson and Larry Bird weren't co-authoring the history of basketball.

But it wasn't until the 1979 Final Four that they met.

It was in Salt Lake City. Bird was a 6-9 senior forward for the Indiana State Sycamores; Magic was a 6-8 sophomore guard for the Michigan State Spartans. Their schools, along with DePaul and Pennsylvania, made up the Final Four teams.

As surely as the fates conspired to get James Naismith to hang his peach basket, so did they conspire to get Bird's Sycamores past DePaul (and Mark Aguirre) and Magic's Spartans past Pennsylvania in the semifinal games at the University of Utah's Special Events Center.

That naturally set up the Big Two for the Big One—and set up America in its TV rooms.

If anyone ever needed a reason to justify the invention of television, this was it. Only 15,220 people could attend the confrontation live, leaving millions of Americans on the outside looking in. Literally.

At no time in the history of basketball or television had so many watched a single game, a record still unbroken today. Even as Bird and Magic went on to meet in the NBA Finals on almost annual occasions in the '80s, even as the NCAA game became a Monday night television ritual, even after Villanova upset Georgetown in the NCAA title game in 1985 and sets from coast to coast were clicking on in waves in the second half (the game finished with a 23.1 rating for No. 2 on the all-time list)—no single game in history attracted as much attention as Magic-Bird I.

They were captivating.

They were as different as they were alike. They were both from middle America and had elected to attend colleges near their hometowns. They had each elevated an almost forgotten art—passing the basketball—into the favorite part of their respective games. They were both consummate team players and, as time would tell, they were not only the straw that stirred the drink, but the whole drink. (The following season, after Bird and Johnson had gone on to the NBA, neither Michigan State nor Indiana State made the NCAA tournament field.)

In other ways, they were as different as their skin color. Earvin Johnson, a.k.a. Magic, was the extrovert, a point guard by way of a disc jockey—he was called "EJ the DJ" because of his hobby of announcing records at discos in East Lansing—and the quintessential finesse player who looked like he never even broke a

sweat except on those occasions when he would flash the widest smile in Michigan, which was often.

On a basketball court, Bird looked like a plodder in the Kentucky Derby. He was slow-footed and had no discernible jumping ability. His deft passing and Houdini-like abilities to get open were never appreciated until they were over—like a subtle plot in a mystery novel. Off the court he was an introvert. He had left Indiana University in Bloomington as a freshman recruit because the size of the school didn't suit him as well as the small town atmosphere at Indiana State in Terre Haute, a town closer in both proximity and lifestyle to his native French Lick.

Bird's Sycamores were 32-0 coming into the Final Four. This was significant not only because the record was perfect but because: a) Indiana State had a first-year coach in Bill Hodges and b) the Sycamores had no history of grandeur. They had never before been to an NCAA tournament, period, and now they were the No. 1-ranked team in the country and had made it to the Final Four.

Bird was the heart and soul of everything, averaging 29 points, 14.8 rebounds, six assists and 2.4 steals a game. Where he went, others followed. Guard Carl Nicks—who would go on to a brief NBA career—was the hustle leader, forward-center Alex Gilbert was the leaper, forward Brad Miley was the defensive specialist, point guard Steve Reed was the floor director and the sixth-man Bob Heaton was the designated keeper-of-the-streak. It was Heaton who hit a 50-foot shot at the regulation buzzer in the 19th game of the season to tie New Mexico State and send the game into overtime,

It was the matchup of the year—Larry Bird against Magic Johnson. Despite Bird's best efforts (guarded here by Michigan State's Greg Kelser), the Spartans rolled to a 75-64 victory before the largest television audience to watch a Final Four game.

which Indiana State won. And against Arkansas, he hit the shot that won the game, 71-69, and kept the Sycamores on course for their date with Magic Johnson.

Michigan State's record was less lofty than Indiana State's. The Spartans came into the Final Four at 24-6. More impressive was their 13-1 mark since a mid-season loss to Northwestern, 83-65. It was after that loss that

coach Jud Heathcote and his players had a meeting. "It's not how good you are; it's how good you play," Heathcote told his players after which they developed a locker room ritual. They would spell out the word p-o-t-e-n-t-i-a-l after every game.

Despite being a mere 19-year-old sophomore, Magic had developed into the world's biggest and best point guard. He

averaged 8.8 assists, 16.9 points and 7.3 rebounds a game, and made everyone else look better, particularly forward Greg Kelser—also a future NBA player—who was Magic's favorite target.

By the time the Spartans got to the NCAA tournament, they had come close enough to their p-o-t-e-n-t-i-a-l that Dale Carnegie wanted to adopt them.

A second-half slam dunk by Earvin "Magic" Johnson (right) was the exclamation point in the Michigan State victory. With a decisive lead, Magic cheered the substitutes from his seat on the bench.

They beat Lamar in their Mideast Regional opener, 95-64. They beat Louisiana State, 87-61, and Notre Dame, 80-68, for the right to advance to Salt Lake City and see what the deal was with this Larry Bird.

Meanwhile, out of the East and West Regionals, Pennsylvania and DePaul had arrived at the Final Four in rather miraculous fashion.

Without the shadows of Bird and Magic to contend with, they'd have been the talk to Salt Lake. Here was Penn, an Ivy League team with a GPA almost higher than its scoring average and no athletic scholarships, playing like a Cinderella possessed.

And here was DePaul, an independent school from Chicago that had lost the heart of its team the year before (starters Dave Corzine and Joe Ponsetto both were drafted by the NBA) and was supposed to be rebuilding. Coach Ray Meyer hadn't been to a Final Four since 1943, and his main offensive weapon was a 6-7 freshman from Chicago named Mark Aguirre who hadn't yet shed his baby fat.

But at the Final Four, DePaul had to face Larry Bird, and Penn had to face Magic Johnson, and neither team had enough momentum to contend with all of that.

Michigan State beat Penn, 101-67, and Indiana State beat DePaul, 76-74—and America started popping popcorn.

This was like being tipped off in advance about the landing at Normandy, or that something was going to happen at noon at the OK Corral.

As is often the case with epic showdowns that are advanced as such, the actual confrontation took a dive.

There was little suspense in Michigan State's wire-to-wire

75-64 win over Indiana State. Magic had a marvelous game. EJ the DJ played all requests. He led all scorers with 24 points. Kelser had 19 points and guard Terry Donnelly 15 on a perfect five-of-five from the field. In the meantime, a modified Spartan zone defense that kept 1 1/2 men on Bird the entire game throttled Indiana State. Bird scored just 19 points on 7 of 21 shooting from

the field.

And that was that. Magic and Bird had met for the first time. But it certainly wasn't for the last time; not with those kind of TV ratings. They had brought new meaning to the phrase "prime time," both as it applied to television sports and to the game of basketball.

1980-1989
THE DECADE OF THE COACH

A dominant coach and player took Georgetown to three championship games in the '80s, winning it all in 1984. Coach John Thompson and center Patrick Ewing consulted during a timeout in 1984.

When a former Hollywood movie actor was elected U.S. president in 1980, cynics sneered. Yet in the next eight years, Ronald Reagan at least managed to restore some of the country's sense of pride, confidence and well-being, while generally managing to avoid the traumatic, divisive conflicts of the previous two decades.

The '80s were a sentimental, nostalgic decade in which some rather amazing things made comebacks, including crewcuts, 1950s music (in commercials, mostly), Tina Turner, mini-skirts, the stock market, the institution of marriage, Bill Cosby, patriotism and Life magazine. After decades of confusion, many young people became upwardly mobile again, earning them the tag of Yuppies.

The computer age, born in the 1970s, became a way of life. Many Americans did their writing and kept their books on home computers, and the proliferation of VCRs opened a mushrooming new industry for videotapes. The top rock stars of the decade were Bruce Springsteen, a throwback to the nitty-gritty days of the 1950s, and Michael Jackson, a vision of the future whose frenetic dancing and androgynous sex appeal made him perfect for the new art form of music videos.

In a decade where style was more important than substance, the stars of the college game were the gifted athletes who could glide, soar and stuff. Some of the prime examples were Darrell Griffith of Louisville, James Worthy and Michael Jordan of North Carolina, and Isiah Thomas of Indiana. Even the decade's best big man, Patrick Ewing of Georgetown, was an agile giant whose timing and shotblocking brought visions of Bill Russell to mind.

The game came to be dominated more by coaches than by the players, sometimes much to the chagrin of the paying customers. Eventually, to eliminate such ploys as the stall offense and the pack-in zone, the rules committee attempted to speed up the game to its tempo of the late 1950s and the '60s by installing first a shot clock, then a three-point field goal from 19'9". Still, it will be remembered as a coach's decade, and there were four who appeared on almost everybody's top five list—Bob Knight of Indiana, Denny Crum of Louisville, John Thompson of Georgetown and Dean Smith of North Carolina.

Each won at least one NCAA title in the '80s, and each made at least two trips to the Final Four. But as much as their results were alike, their styles and personalities differed.

Crum was laid-back and cool, much like Wooden, his mentor at UCLA. Smith was the innovator whose ideas were copied by almost every coach in the nation. Knight was the moody genius whose brilliant teaching tended to be overshadowed by his tantrums and altercations. And Thompson was the stern authoritarian who trusted almost nobody outside his family of players and staff.

Not since Iba, Rupp, Allen and McCracken had four coaches had so much impact on the game. And by defining it and refining it with such distinction, they created a legacy of excellence that will be part of the game for at least the next 50 years.

In a decade where style was more important than substance, the stars of the college game were the gifted athletes who could glide, soar and stuff.

The longest pauses are in a quiet locker room, each person with his own thoughts, awaiting the start of a championship game. Indiana waited at Philadelphia's Spectrum, soon to face North Carolina for the 1981 crown.

1980

DARRELL GRIFFITH AND THE DOCTORS OF DUNK

By Mike Sullivan

Reserve Poncho Wright provided a colorful slogan for Louisville's championship run after a preseason scrimmage in November of 1979.

"The Ville," Wright declared, "is going to the Nap."

His reference was to Indianapolis and Market Square Arena, where the Cardinals captured their first NCAA championship in their third Final Four appearance by outnerving UCLA, 59-54, on March 24, 1980.

By the time Darrell Griffith had wrapped up player-of-the-year honors, scoring 23 points against UCLA to go with his 34 in an 80-72 semifinal win over Iowa, Louisville's achievement had acquired a false aura of inevitability.

There was that final 33-3 record, after all. There was Griffith, labeled "Dr. Dunkenstein" and "Louisville's Living Legend," the crowd favorite with the 48-inch vertical leap. And there was never a shortage of folklore. Remember Wiley Brown, the forward who left his artificial thumb on the table at the pregame meal? It was retrieved from a dumpster in time for the title game.

What may be harder to retrieve as the years go by is a firm grasp on the underdog status that coach Denny Crum's Cardinals actually carried into that season and, to an extent, into the tournament itself.

After failing to make the

NCAA field in 1976, Louisville bombed out in three straight appearances. In Griffith's junior season, he had appeared lost in a nationally televised shellacking at Duke, then was badly outshone by Sidney Moncrief in a Midwest Regional semifinal defeat against Arkansas.

Still trying to master the transition from forward to guard, Griffith entered the 1979-80 campaign with much to prove in the eyes of the national media. The 6-3 senior's supporting cast had all but vanished. Forward Bobby Turner, his teammate from

Louisville's Male High School, had career-ending academic problems. Sophomore Scooter McCray, the returning starter at center, was lost to a knee injury in the first week of the season. Senior Tony Branch, the previous year's floor leader, lost his job to sophomore Jerry Eaves and became a seldom-used reserve.

Louisville added a lack of height to its lack of experience, with Brown the tallest player at 6-8. Into the pivot went Rodney McCray, Scooter's younger brother, a 6-7 freshman who had been Crum's only recruiting

Denny Crum, once an assistant to John Wooden, guided his Louisville team to the championship for the first time in 1980. The Cardinals were led by player of the year Darrell Griffith, who was carried from the floor of Indianapolis' Market Square Arena.

signee. The forward opposite Brown, 6-6 Derek Smith, had been tried at guard late in the previous season. Griffith, Branch and reserve guard Roger Burkman, a junior, were the only upperclassmen in the bunch.

"I don't think there's any question that team surprised a lot of people, including myself," Crum said. "I don't think anybody expected us to be very good. Even when we kept winning, I didn't think about the post-season much. There were so many teams with more experience than us that it wasn't realistic."

It also wasn't considered realistic, 16 years after UCLA's pressing dervishes of 1964, to employ a full-court press for every minute of every game. But Crum, in what may have been the most radical coaching decision of his tenure at Louisville, did just that, reasoning that his club could avoid having its size and youth exploited in half-court defense.

"The benefits we derived from the press didn't always surface until late in a game, when the general pace and our conditioning suddenly took a toll," he recalled.

There was more than a touch of irony in the fact that UCLA provided the opposition in the title game. Crum, after all, had played and coached at UCLA under John Wooden and had lost to his alma mater in three previous NCAA trips as Louisville coach—in the national semifinals in 1972 and 1975 and in the first round in 1977.

The matchup itself was something else again. UCLA, like Louisville, made up in quickness for what it lacked in size and had upset its way through the tournament under coach Larry Brown after a fourth-place finish in the Pac-10. Senior forward Kiki Van-

deweghe was the star, abetted by frisky freshmen guards Rod Foster and Michael Holton.

Using the same ferocious defense that had carried them past Purdue and 7-1 Joe Barry Carroll, 67-62, in the semifinal, the Bruins put Louisville in a 50-45 hole on Mike Sanders' layup with 6:28 left in the game.

Vandeweghe made a running interception and steamed toward the basket with a chance to all but finish the Cardinals. Eaves, in a hustling recovery, crossed in front of him at the last second and his altered shot was rebounded by Brown.

The rest of the game was a 14-4 parade to the championship by Louisville, which scored the last nine points. Griffith's soaring three-point play on a pass from Brown made it 50-48, and Griffith trimmed a 52-48 deficit to 52-50 with an 18-foot baseline jumper. Two clutch baskets by Eaves—a 17-footer and a driving layup in traffic—cut a 54-50 deficit in half and finally tied the score, 54-54, with 2:54 remaining.

McCray, the seasoned freshman, collared his game-high 11th rebound when a corner jumper by Holton rattled in and out of the basket, and Griffith struck from the top of the key to break the tie with 2:21 to go. Smith's two bonus free throws made it 58-54 with only 52 ticks left.

Afterward, Crum revealed that he had accused his players of choking at halftime when they trailed, 28-26. "Then I apologized and told them I loved them," Crum said. "I realized they had been trying as hard as they could. I told them to loosen up and give it their best shot."

It was just a hint at how much emotion and dramatics had gone into that glossy 33-3 record. The NCAA opener had been an over-

time test against Kansas State, decided when Branch replaced Griffith, who had fouled out, and banged in a 16-footer at the buzzer. Texas A&M also had fallen in overtime in the Midwest Regional semifinal.

"We had a rare chemistry," Crum said. "Darrell seemed to come through with a basket, a rebound or a pass whenever we needed it most, and all of our younger players seemed to draw strength from Griff and also from Tony Branch, who never gave up his leadership role."

"It wasn't the Darrell Griffith Show, it was the University of Louisville Show," said Griffith, who had appeared on a televised insert before the tipoff to dedicate the final game to his lifelong friend, Jerry Stringer.

The day after the game, Stringer, who was dying of cancer, had strands of the net draped around his head as he lay in bed in his home, surrounded by Louisville players.

Maybe it was inevitable, after all.

1981
KNIGHT GETS HIS WAY AND HOOSIERS WIN

By Bill Millsaps

Variations of primal scream therapy developed by the renowned Indiana University psychologist, professor Robert Knight, quite likely played a major role in the Hoosiers' capture of their fourth national basketball championship in 1981.

In an effort to firmly establish early control of his young team, Knight twice took unusual

The Tar Heels' Sam Perkins (above) dove for a loose ball in what was a very physical game.

rienced as it was talented, could pick up the subtleties of his system. Knight, with only one senior in his starting lineup, wondered out loud if his Hoosiers could pick up the simplicities of his system.

Almost four months later, their wonderings were at an end. The Hoosiers and Tar Heels had made it to the Final Four along with two teams that had few down moments in their run to Philadelphia.

In the first semifinal at The Spectrum, Indiana played Louisiana State, which had won 26 straight games during the season and boasted a 31-3 record.

In the second semifinal, North Carolina played Virginia, which had won its first 23 games en route to a 28-3 record and had beaten the Tar Heels twice during the regular season.

Ralph Sampson, a 7-4 sophomore center bound for a college basketball career that received a grade of "incomplete," had scored 46 points and collected 24 rebounds in the two Virginia victories over Carolina. Each was a bitter pill for the Tar Heels to swallow, for on the first occasion the Cavaliers came from 13 points behind in the second half, and on the second, they came from 16 back in the last 20 minutes in Chapel Hill.

In those first two meetings, almost nobody had noticed that UNC's Al Wood had scored 51 points. Few failed to notice Wood when the Tar Heels and Cavaliers played for the third time.

Wood scored 39 points, 25 in a brilliant second half in which he missed only one of 10 shots from the floor. "Every time Al shot," said Tar Heel forward Matt Doherty, "I got in position for rebounds that never came off. After a while, I knew he was never going to miss."

actions with his best player in December of 1980. These actions were calculated to get the undivided attention of that player and his teammates.

There was the day that Knight, bereft of patience, tossed Isiah Thomas, his precocious point guard, right out of practice in Bloomington.

Then there was the day, later in the same month, that Knight became angry with Thomas for throwing a couple of careless passes in a game with North Carolina in Chapel Hill.

Knight summarily removed Thomas from the game and kept him on the bench long enough in the second half so that it was almost inevitable North Carolina would win by nine points. Some who watched that game still won-

der if Knight didn't lose it on purpose in order to teach Thomas a lesson.

On the last day of 1980, Knight and North Carolina coach Dean Smith met again. This time, the setting was the airport in Kansas City.

North Carolina, having just lost by 16 points to Minnesota in a holiday tournament in Los Angeles, was on its way back to a game at Kansas. Indiana, having lost two straight to Clemson and Pan American at a tournament in Hawaii, was changing planes on its way home to Bloomington with a so-what 7-5 record.

The two famed coaches exchanged lists of woes. North Carolina had lost four starters from the previous year, and Smith wondered if his team, as inexpe-

Returning to Philadelphia's Spectrum, site of an earlier championship, Indiana scrambled against North Carolina. However, it was Isiah Thomas in the second half who dominated, scoring 19 of his 23 points and earning MOP honors. Indiana won, 63-50.

The Hoosiers were joyous in Philadelphia, but things changed before Indiana had a chance to defend its title the next year. Isiah Thomas, who cut the nets, would leave school to begin his NBA career. And Landon Turner, (above right foreground,) would be seriously injured in a car accident, ending his career.

"I wanted to break his arm," said Virginia forward Terry Gates.

Virginia coach Terry Holland tried five different defenders on Wood, and he charbroiled them all. "You almost had to stand up and cheer," said Holland, "even if you're on the opposite bench."

North Carolina won, 78-65, and, considering the setting and the stakes, took the season series with Virginia, 1-2.

The Indiana team that took on LSU had lost nine times, but the lineup Knight started against the Tigers had a perfect record. From Feb. 21, 1981, when Knight put 6-10 sophomore Landon Turner into his starting five, the Hoosiers were unbeaten.

Against LSU, Turner scored 20 points and held Durand Macklin, the Tigers' leading scorer, to a career-low four points. LSU had a three-point halftime lead but Indiana scored the first 11 points of the second half and cruised to a 67-49 victory.

That evening, Knight made some more headlines by getting into a physical confrontation with an LSU fan who, Knight said, had become verbally abusive.

Trying to explain himself the next day, Knight said, at first, that "If it happens tomorrow, I'd do exactly the same thing."

Later that day, Knight defined discipline as "doing what has to be done, doing it when it has to

be done and doing it as well as it can be done and doing it that way all the time." Asked how he squared those words with his actions of the night before, Knight said, "I'm human, and I failed in this situation in reaching the ultimate discipline."

Some six hours before the 1981 championship game, President Ronald Reagan was shot and wounded by a would-be assassin in Washington. The NCAA went ahead with the consolation game, but did not make a decision to play the title match until about 30 minutes before the scheduled tipoff.

This time, Knight didn't have Thomas on the bench in the second half. In the last 20 minutes, Thomas was merely wondrous at both ends of the floor, scoring 19 of his 23 points and earning Most Outstanding Player honors.

North Carolina got no closer than seven points down the stretch and wound up falling, 63-50. The Tar Heels' only consolation is that it was Indiana's closest game en route to the championship. The Hoosiers had won four previous tournament battles by 35, 15, 32 and 18 points.

"Ours is a game," said Knight, "of doing what we want to do the whole game. If we can do that, our ultimate objective is to break down a team over the whole 40 minutes. If we can stay with our defense and pressure the ball and stay with our offense and be patient, we're going into the last part of the game and we've gotten control."

Knight thought that the best days were still ahead for his team. He was wrong. Thomas left school for the NBA after the '81 season, and Turner was terribly injured in an auto accident.

Knight did not get back to the Final Four for six years but his 1987 Hoosiers gave him his third NCAA title in New Orleans.

There was also a certain symmetry to the stories of the other coaches in that '81 Final Four.

Holland never returned to another Final Four with Sampson, but he reached the national semifinals the year after his three-time national player of the year graduated.

Dale Brown also returned in 1986, taking an LSU team that was dead in the water in mid-season and somehow contriving a way to get it to Dallas.

In his seventh Final Four, Smith won his first NCAA title in 1982 in New Orleans.

The '81 Final Four also reflected the tone of the

decade—as coaches took center stage.

Bill Millsaps joined the sports staff of the Richmond Times-Dispatch in 1966, became sports editor in 1973, managing editor in 1992 and executive editor in 1994. A longtime fixture at Final Fours, he now watches the games on television.

1982

THE CITY CARE FORGOT REMEMBERS DEAN SMITH

By Curry Kirkpatrick

Shortly after North Carolina finally won its elusive national championship in New Orleans, a photograph made the rounds in Chapel Hill that defined the emotions swirling around Dean Smith's one and only NCAA title better than words or numbers possibly could.

The classic, raw-thrills 63-62 victory over Georgetown was over; the momentary ecstasy was past. As James Worthy, the shreds of net still clinging around his neck, and Jimmy Black sat vacantly, their bodies exhausted, their senses virtually paralyzed, Smith grimly stared at the floor while Tar Heel publicist Rick Brewer, cognizant there might still be life left on the planet, checked his watch. What time was it? It was about time; 25 years since the last time Carolina had won the NCAA. It was relief time.

"The feeling was whew! What did we just go through?" Matt Doherty would say. "And thank God it was—finally—over." It was a very special time.

The wonder was that such a compelling year as 1981-82 could be outdazzled by its own watershed Final Four. But the nouveau celebrity schools that showed up in the cavernous Louisiana Superdome to challenge old-money Carolina made sure that the colossal record crowds of over 122,000 (61,000 and change both Saturday and Monday) got their strained eyesight's worth. This was the first year college basketball went one-on-one against itself (NBC and CBS having hooked up with competitive weekend games during the regular season) and the last year it went backdoor on the shot clock.

North Carolina came to New Orleans with an amazing lineup of raw talent, not the least of which was freshman Michael Jordan, shooting here against Houston in the semifinals. Two nights later, he shot with 16 seconds left and lifted the Tar Heels to the championship over Georgetown and Patrick Ewing.

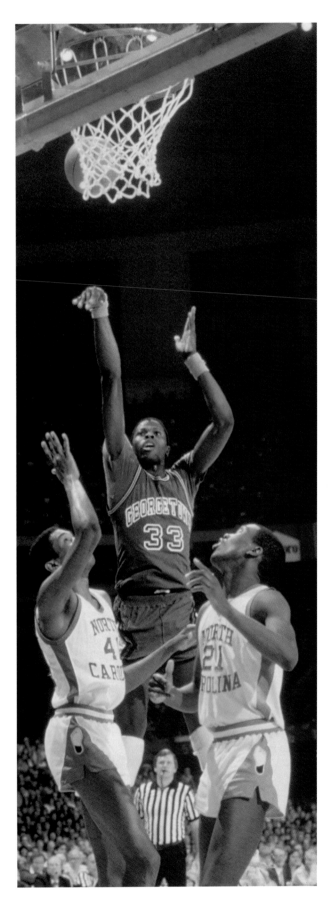

The early rounds of the tournament featured: 1) a famous game that never happened—Louisville vs. Kentucky (Middle Tennessee State upset the Wildcats); 2) a famous team that never advanced—for the third year in a row DePaul, ranked first in somebody's poll, lost in the first round to a nobody; and 3) a famous player who just, well, never—Virginia's Ralph Sampson who was denied again, this time by Alabama-Birmingham.

As a result, the dregs New Orleans wound up with included: Louisville, with four starters off its 1980 championship team and making its second appearance in a three Final Fours in four years run; Houston, starting the first of a three straight Final Fours streak; Georgetown, debuting in its own three-in-four-years roll, which would include the 1984 title over Houston; and Carolina, whose victory would culminate in three championship games in a six-year stretch.

In other words, the dynasties of the decade—that's all. In the '80s, these teams combined for 11 Final Four appearances and four titles. Such a legacy left in '82! Louisville's Derek Smith and the McCray brothers, Houston's Akeem Olajuwon and Clyde Drexler, Georgetown's Patrick Ewing, Carolina's Worthy, Sam Perkins and Michael Jordan.

The star-touched Tar Heels traversed that bewitching season, emboldened from their final loss to Indiana the previous March. They were reinvigorated as No. 1 for most of the winter, rampagers of the Atlantic Coast Conference, slayers of pretender-dragons, Kentucky and Sampson. They were a nifty, resourceful, multi-dimensional and sometimes spectacular crew whose ability to play both fast and slow not only won games

(32 of 34) but was to actually change the rules of the game.

After their stallball defeat of Virginia in the ACC Tournament forced the final blueprint for a shot clock, who could deny they were something extraordinary? Who could stop them from fulfilling Dean—"I've handled it well, I don't feel the emptiness," he said of his zero-for-six trips to the finals—and his dream?

Well, Georgetown seemed a prime candidate. The lean, mean Hoyas, with Ewing premiering his old gray mare of a T-shirt, had absolutely devastated the West Regional, limiting the States, Fresno and Oregon, to 41 and 39 percent shooting while they themselves hit a tournament-record 74.4 percent against the Beavers. No less did Georgetown coach John Thompson have his nasties on, housing his troops far from the playing sites, cutting off the outside world and intimidating referees and the media in kind.

For the Final Four, the Hoyas stayed in that charming French Quarter suburb of Biloxi, Miss. After Georgetown eliminated Louisville in a brutal defensive semifinal, 50-46—Ewing had only eight points and one block but several terrifies—to make Thompson the first black coach to reach the championship game, he bristled: "I don't want to be the first black nothing."

And the Hoyas' Eric Smith, asked if he missed staying in New Orleans, said: "I don't know what I missed. Can't you see? I ain't here."

Carolina's Worthy, meanwhile, was here, there and everywhere when the Tar Heels took a two-touchdown lead, 14-0, over Houston in the other semifinal. Black was to shut out Cougar leading scorer Rob Williams and by the time the infant Olajuwon

THE FINAL FOUR

came on—he scratched for one basket and six boards in as inauspicious Final Four debut as any future legend ever suffered—it was all over, 68-63, to Carolina.

"Choke, Dean, Choke," the kindly Georgetown section roared at Smith on Monday night prior to the championship game. But Deano was loose, even bantering with writers about his depleted cigarette pack. "Fewer (smokes) than for Duke at Duke," he laughed.

It was a full eight minutes after tipoff before Ewing ceased smoking and the Tar Heels finally saw one of their shots actually go down. The Hoyas' monster-child had been that dominating and swatting everything back to Bourbon Street and significantly altering Carolina strategy. To cut the court and challenge the freshman giant would be folly. Eventually, Smith had to take the cuffs off his 6-9 junior, Worthy (who would shoot 13 of 17 and explode for 28 points) and simply let him rush down the floor and tomahawk the ball before Ewing, a human Pac-Man, swallowed all the Tar Heels alive.

Worthy's rebound slam (which turned out to be Sports Illustrated's cover shot) got Carolina a tie at 20-20. But Georgetown maintained an edge midway through the second half until Sleepy Floyd got too cute on a breakaway that would have given the Hoyas a six-point lead at 49-43. As it was, Worthy started swoop-jamming again, the Heels stiffened on defense—"I always felt like the hunted and Georgetown was the hunter," Smith said—and Ewing picked up his third and fourth fouls.

Momentum swayed. Intensity increased. From the spread delay, Jordan made a preposterous switch-hands, rainbow

scoop drive over Ewing and Carolina led, 61-58. But Ewing (23 points, 11 rebounds) scored a turn-around and Floyd coaxed in a jumper from the lane. The Tar Heels were behind for the 12th time in the game when Smith called timeout with 32 seconds left.

Most everybody assumed the ball would go to either Worthy or Perkins in the seams of the Georgetown zone. But Smith, knowing the Hoyas would deny his big men, instructed the Heels to take the first good shot. He also

guessed that shot would be given to Jordan—the freshman, the rookie, the kid who had fantasized about this moment on the bus ride to the Superdome. As his team broke from the huddle, Smith took one step toward Jordan, patted him on the rump and said, "Knock it in, Michael."

Of such are geniuses made, monkeys shot off backs and titles won. At 0:16 Jordan's shot from the left side, smack on a line between his coach and his coach's holy grail, kissed only twine—63-62, Carolina.

Patrick Ewing (left) fired away successfully over a collapsing North Carolina defense. James Worthy (above) claimed the baseline to move for a layup, as both Georgetown and Carolina traded baskets and the lead. As the game ended, most assumed Worthy or Sam Perkins would take the last shot. Instead, freshman Michael Jordan shot the winning goal.

After Georgetown raced downcourt without calling time-out; after Fred Brown froze and threw the ball directly into the hands of Worthy; after Worthy stole away like a phantom from Mardi Gras; even after Thompson embraced the crestfallen Brown on the sideline afterward, the image that lingers clearest from that hazy Louisiana evening is Dean Smith watching Jordan's shot: still seated, hands clasped, jaw set, totally in control.

Just Easin' Off here in the Big Easy. Would it were so. But on the same night Henry Fonda finally won his Oscar, Smith finally won his NCAA. The City Care Forgot ultimately took care of a coach the college game will always remember.

Curry Kirkpatrick was a staff writer at Sports Illustrated covering the Final Fours during the UCLA years of the '70s. He has since worked as a special writer for USA Today and done commentaries for CBS Sports. Today he is a senior writer for ESPN, The Magazine.

North Carolina State's Jim Valvano (above) brought a most unlikely group to the championship in Albuquerque. The Wolfpack took care of Georgia in the semifinals, but then came a seemingly overwhelming obstacle: the physical Houston team, led by Akeem Olajuwon. Olajuwon grabbed the ball from the hands of Thurl Bailey (right) early in the game, but State hung around and won at the buzzer.

1983
THE NINE LIVES OF N.C. STATE

By Bill Millsaps

Nobody's that lucky. Nobody's suddenly that good. Eighteen years later, you still wonder how the entire college basketball melodrama—"The Nine Lives of N.C. State"—could've taken place. It was a blessed, heroic stretch that was roughly the antithesis of Murphy's Law: Everything that needed to happen for the Wolfpack did.

North Carolina State winning the 1983 NCAA championship does not rank in the global/political/patriotic league with the United States' hockey upset of the Soviet Union at the 1980 Olympics. It is not as memorialized in sports history as New York's dual, wholly unanticipated 1969 triumphs of the baseball Mets and football Jets.

But for pure, athletic, never-say-die, long-running achievement by an underdog, North Carolina State might've outdone them all. It was far more than the national final, where N.C. State used one last stroke of fortune/skill to overturn Houston, 54-52. It was the entire, unbelievable, nine-game Wolfpack package that led to the championship moment in Albuquerque.

Consider the elements:

•N.C. State's record at the end of the regular season was 17-10, leaving the Wolfpack unranked, unrespected; a team bettered in its own Atlantic Coast Conference neighborhood by North Carolina, Virginia and Maryland. To even have a chance at an NCAA tournament bid, State had to find a way to make the ACC Tournament final in Atlanta.

•One miracle makes few impressions, but the Wolfpack did come from behind in the second half to survive its ACC playoff opener against Wake Forest, 71-70.

•Against favored North Carolina in the league's semifinal game, N.C. State trailed, 80-74, with 2:13 left in overtime. Wolfpack coach Jim Valvano ordered his players to intentionally foul. The Tar Heels flunked at the free throw line and the Wolfpack never missed a critical shot. North Carolina was outgunned 17-4 down the stretch and became little more than a blue puddle left on The Omni court.

N.C. State won, 91-84.

•Virginia had beaten N.C. State twice during the regular season but in the ACC Tournament final, Ralph Sampson and several shorter fellows wilted and N.C. State rallied in the second half to succeed, 81-78.

•By now, Valvano and his sleight-of-hand artists were getting national attention. The New York coach with the Prince Valiant hair was an All-American quote machine. But, in the first round of the NCAA tournament, the party seemed about over. Pepperdine took the Wolfpack into overtime and led by six points with 0:59 on the clock. Valvano went into his fouling, daredevil scheme and, in the end, State won, 69-67, in two overtimes.

•State had no geographical edge being assigned to the West Regional. It would play no NCAA tournament game east of The Pit, on the University of New Mexico's campus in Albuquerque. On the night of its regional semifinal in Ogden, Utah, the little team in red seemed, one more time, to be on the verge of a crash. Nevada-Las Vegas led the Wolfpack by 12 points with 11 minutes to go. But lightning kept striking the same place, and State hit a shot at 0:04 to win 71-70.

•That gets us to the seventh of N.C. State's "Nine Lives"—the West Regional final against a most familiar opponent, the Virginia Cavaliers. "I think we owe them one," said Virginia coach Terry Holland, referring to the ACC final his Cavs blew back in Atlanta. N.C. State again trailed in the second half, but, in the end, the Pack did it again. Sampson's last chance for an NCAA championship perished in a 63-62 game.

•Luck, no matter how good,

usually runs out. Even with a
stacked deck, nobody deals himself eight or nine straight aces.
Nobody but the 1983 North Carolina State basketball team. But,
in the national semifinal at Albuquerque, the Wolfpack had to use
little of its magic. In comparison,
things went rather methodically
in a 67-60 conquest of Georgia.

OK, it's now Monday night.
The NCAA final. Even with all
that had gone before, N.C. State
remained a lopsided underdog
against a No. 1-ranked Houston
team that was 31-2 with 26
straight victories. In their semifinal, the Cougars took basketball
into the 21st century with their
so-called Phi Slamma Jamma
offense, strangling a talented
Louisville team, 94-81.

Houston had howitzers to fire

against the blessed popguns of
N.C. State. "We'll try to stay
alive," Valvano said, "to keep it
close and see if there's another
stroke of magic in a very over-
used wand." But Houston had so
much size, so much athletic ability and so many killer nicknames
in Akeem "The Dream" Olajuwon, Clyde "The Glide" Drexler,
Michael "Mr. Clutch" Young and
Larry "Mr. Clean" Micheaux.

During pregame warmups,
Houston dunked itself into a
frenzy. It was like basketball bat-
ting practice where every hitter
puts every pitch over the wall.
Nevertheless, N.C. State did
decide to show up.

N.C. State's cast of characters
included husky, 6-7 Lorenzo
Charles and skinny, 6-11 Cozell
McQueen. The best NBA

prospect on the Wolfpack end
was 6-11 Thurl Bailey, who
looked slack-jawed at Houston's
high-flying warmup acrobatics.
One of the great strengths of the
Wolfpack was its guards, a rotation that included Sidney Lowe,
Dereck Whittenburg, Ernie
Myers and Terry Gannon.

Once the game began, Val-
vano had some effective defensive ideas that worked against the
ungodly giants from Houston.
The Cougars weren't gliding and
dunking like they did in the
semifinal against Louisville. N.C.
State stayed close, just as Valvano had hoped. Still, you kept
thinking Houston would over-
power the kids from Raleigh.
Could there really be "Nine
Lives?" The game reached the
final minute. Remarkably, it was

As the clock ticked off the last five seconds with the score tied, Dereck Whittenburg (25) took a 30-foot jumper, which fell short. In one stunning second, Lorenzo Charles (43) grabbed the ball in mid-air for the stuff and the title. Afterward Wolfpack players fashioned a victory celebration from up high (facing page). The late Jim Valvano danced around the floor, looking for anyone to hug.

went off.

State had won, 54-52.

In the 49 NCAA tournaments, there have been extraordinary upsets. Remember 1963, when Loyola of Chicago upset 1961-62 champion Cincinnati, 60-58, in overtime? Or 1966, when Texas Western flailed a giant, beating Kentucky, 72-65?

But when you count them all from top to bottom, nothing compares with the "Nine Lives of N.C. State."

1984
DOMINATION AND INTIMIDATION

By Michael Wilbon

Just a few minutes after his proud Kentucky Wildcats had been obliterated, whipped and humiliated like nobody's business, coach Joe B. Hall was still a might befuddled when he tried to describe the phenomena of his team's defeat and soon-to-be-crowned NCAA champion Georgetown.

Hall stammered and paused and finally said: "It was some kind of extraterrestrial." Georgetown's 53-40 victory over Kentucky that Saturday afternoon in Seattle's Kingdome and the Hoyas' run to the 1984 national championship certainly were not normal earthly stuff.

Two nights later, in an 84-75 victory over Houston, Georgetown and coach John Thompson finished a most impressive season. Houston's Akeem Olajuwon, who had played in the Final Four three times without going home happy, put his finger on just what it was that separated Georgetown

52-52. N.C. State had the basketball. "One shot!" Valvano yelled. The Pit vibrated with excitement. Guy Lewis, Houston's 61-year-old coach, chewed on his famous red-and-white checked towel. He had won 530 games in 27 seasons, but never an NCAA championship. His best of chances was now in unexpected jeopardy.

Lowe whipped the ball to Whittenburg. Time ticked below 15 seconds. The grand try was in motion. But at 0:05, the basketball was too far outside, leaving little chance to work for a high percentage shot, or to get the ball inside and perhaps draw a foul.

Overtime seemed all but assured when Whittenburg heaved a prayer from beyond 30 feet. It was well short, a pitiful game-winning attempt. But, no—the muscular hands of Lorenzo Charles reached above the seemingly stunned Cougars, taking the "air ball" two feet from the hoop and then dunking it as the buzzer

year, it conjured up all the wrong images, many of them racial. But Georgetown did intimidate its opponents, through talent, smarts, unselfishness, relentlessness and toughness. And, yes, Georgetown intimidated physically. From the time the Big East season started, right through the Final Four, teams grew more frightened of the Georgetown Hoyas because there didn't seem to be any way to beat them. In an early round NCAA tournament game against Nevada-Las Vegas, Georgetown couldn't score for 10 minutes and 35 seconds and still beat the Runnin' Rebels by 14 points.

Kentucky and Houston—which was lucky to beat scrappy Virginia in overtime of the first semifinal—would find that out soon enough. Kentucky, after taking a seven-point lead at half-time, made only 3 of 33 shots the second half. The starters, including Sam Bowie and Melvin Turpin, went 0-for-21 in that second half. Georgetown's Gene Smith, one of the best defensive guards who ever lived, chased Kentucky's Dickey Beal and Jim Master like the Chicago Bears' Richard Dent chased quarterbacks.

That is the memory of the '84 Final Four, even though Georgetown wasn't officially crowned until Monday night following the 84-75 victory over Houston. And Thompson, an all-world worrier, could finally enjoy it.

"The only time a team is special is at the end of the season," he said in reflection. "I'm so conservative with my opinions about the team during the season that it's difficult to assess until afterward. But it's not what they gave up that made it a special team."

David Wingate and Reggie Williams, the versatile youngsters who played two and three positions every night, had to sacrifice

One of the great meetings of big men matched Houston's Akeem Olajuwon against Georgetown's Patrick Ewing in the 1984 Final Four in Seattle's Kingdome. The Hoyas destroyed Kentucky and Houston to win the championship.

from the other final three teams, besides Patrick Ewing and one of the best teams ever assembled:

"Georgetown, they don't care who scores, who takes the shots. That's the difference. They aren't a selfish team. The unselfish team won."

The previous two Final Fours had been characterized by the bizarre, the surreal: Georgetown's loss to North Carolina in 1982; Houston getting

Phi Slamma Jamma'd by North Carolina State in 1983.

The 1984 Final Four wasn't one of a moment, or even a game. But the Seattle tournament involving Georgetown, Houston, Kentucky and Virginia, will be remembered for Georgetown's everlasting dominance, and yes, intimidation.

Thompson hated, in fact still hates, the word "intimidate." Used as many people did that

some of their offensive skills, as did point guard Michael Jackson, who was probably the most underrated player on the team. Bill Martin, the elegant power forward, knew his job could change from day to day, depending on the opponent.

Fred Brown and Gene Smith were the quarterbacks, the players who knew Thompson so well they could relay his messages to the team before Thompson opened his mouth. And the centerpiece, of course, was Patrick Ewing, simply the most dependable player in the college game since Bill Walton.

And there were substitutes, including guard Horace Broadnax and center-forward Ralph Dalton, who could have started for other Top 20 teams but did what Thompson asked. It was a team that even an adversary such as Olajuwon could admire.

Also, unforgettably, there was Michael Graham, a 6-9 power forward and the source of much of the criticism aimed at Georgetown. During the regular season, Graham averaged three points and three rebounds per game and was largely an afterthought. In the Final Four, he sparkled: seven field goals in nine attempts, with five rebounds against Houston; four field goals in six attempts, six rebounds and a team-high 33 minutes against Kentucky. Number of bodies slammed: impossible to calculate.

"It shows you the enormous exposure the Final Four gets," Thompson said. "You'd have thought he was a superstar from the attention he got as a result of the NCAA tournament, and specifically the Final Four. He contributed enormously at the right time."

In their own way, the Hoyas were a glamorous team: fast, smart, powerful—and kept away from the television lights just enough to add a dash of mystery. We could never get enough of the Hoyas. It never got boring because we never knew too much about them. And there was so much outsiders didn't know.

"One of the great things about the team was that the kids were so secure in their abilities," Thompson said. "To play that way when the pressure was there and do what is expected of you is one of the toughest things in any sport. Of course, Patrick was special. His attitude was as important as his ability, which of course was enormous.

"They were tough damn kids, competitive athletes. Michael Graham was the only one not mature enough to realize the total responsibility. Those kids fulfilled the whole responsibility."

Ewing, Martin, Wingate, Williams and Jackson—all five starters—have played in the NBA. Everyone from that team except Graham graduated and at least four have done postgraduate work.

Thompson is often asked if he carries a special game or a special moment from that championship season. Those who know Thompson well can anticipate the answer and the moment has no rival.

Georgetown, flat and struggling—"I still can't, to this day, figure out why," Thompson says—was tied at 34-34 with Southern Methodist in a second-round tournament game at Pullman, Wash. Gene Smith was at the foul line in the waning seconds when Ewing ran over to Thompson on the bench.

"Patrick was supposed to go back on defense (and stand under the basket)," Thompson said. "But he asked me if he could stay up on the foul line in case Gene missed the free throw. I just looked at him, then told him 'OK.' "

Smith did miss the foul shot; Ewing put it in. The Hoyas got another free throw and won, 37-36. Thompson says that in every season, even championship seasons, there is a game like that, a play like that. Only this time, it was a special player helping his team complete a special season.

Michael Wilbon joined the staff of The Washington Post in 1980 and has covered 17 Final Fours during that time. Today, he is a writer and a columnist for the Post.

1985
THE PERFECT GAME

"There are only two great plays," an uncomplicated old coach used to say. "Put the ball in the basket and 'South Pacific.' "

By Tom Callahan

How well a team rebounds loses some significance when there are no rebounds. This was the simplest moral of 1985, when the only team with 10 losses met the team with only two, and for the first time in a long time, the early edition newspaper columnists felt they could safely write about dynasties again, being at least as certain of Patrick Ewing as the Chicago Tribune was of Thomas Dewey.

Georgetown University was going to be just the sixth college to repeat a national championship and Ewing's Hoyas were already being measured beside the splendid San Francisco and UCLA teams of Bill Russell and Lew Alcindor. After losing one

One of basketball's greats from the 1955 and '56 tournaments, Bill Russell celebrated with John Thompson, whose Hoyas had just won the 1984 title. Thompson celebrated not with champagne but with swigs of milk.

final to North Carolina, and winning another from Houston, the seven-foot Ewing, and his mountainous coach John Thompson, brought a mood of graduation, if not coronation, to Lexington's Final Four.

Since two of the supporting actors, St. John's and Villanova, were Big East associates twice beaten by Georgetown, the Hoyas' preeminence was a matter of record as well as opinion. Surrounded by all these city Catholics, country coach Dana Kirk cheerfully declared Memphis State the secular national champion, then genuflected to Villanova, 52-45. (The untidiness of the game obscured his parting prophesy: "If they're a Cinderella team, Cinderella wears boots.")

Meanwhile, Georgetown terrorized St. John's a third time, 77-59, terribly disabusing the city of New York. This was a nostalgic season for college basketball in Manhattan. The local papers clutched elfin coach Lou Carnesecca adoringly to their collective breast, and by a clever course of reasoning concluded that freckle-faced guard Chris Mullin was the finest player in the country. Mullin won the John Wooden Player of the Year award emphatically over Ewing, though it would probably be best if nobody asks the old coach's opinion.

Quietly, almost invisibly, another New Yorker remained— an agile, angular fellow named Ed Pinckney. A child of the Bronx, Villanova's 6-9 1/2 center grew up, and up, in the natural way of the neighborhood, dribbling from borough to borough, studying various playground styles like a linguist sampling accents. Uptown, he learned power. In Queens, finesse. Brooklyn showed him flair but it was unlike him to display any.

Driving the baseline between defenders, Villanova's Harold Pressley scored against Memphis State during a 1985 semifinal game.

In the hours before the Monday night final, coach Rollie Massimino—coach Mass—urged the Wildcat players to think in terms of "the perfect game." Pinckney, in particular, was fascinated. "On a one-shot deal," the coach said, "we can beat anyone in the United States."

The scale of their task was evident from the tipoff: Villanova made seven of its first eight shots and still was behind, 20-14. Shot clocks were on order in college basketball, so this was something of a closing night for slow danc-

ing. The custodian of the ball was a sharp little gizmo named Gary McLain, whose patience was equal to his caution. Without yet signaling much of an alarm, he steered Pinckney, Dwayne McClain, Harold Pressley and Harold Jensen (this team was more Harolded than we thought) back to all-even at 20. On a follow-up shot by Pressley at the close of the first half, Villanova actually took a quaint 29-28 lead.

Nothing seemed particularly wrong with the Hoyas, though

his fifth shot of the game and made his fifth field goal. Villanova did the rest of its uncanny shooting from the foul line. As soon as Pinckney and Jensen each made a pair, the score was 59-54. The 24-10 Wildcats, fourth-best in their conference, eighth-seeded in their region, 23-point losers to Pittsburgh on the last day of the regular season, became the champions of the world, 66-64.

Missing just one of 10 attempts in the second half, they shot 78.6 percent for the game. With 16 points, six rebounds and five assists (to Ewing's 14, five and two), Pinckney was named the tournament's Most Outstanding Player. "Really and truly, I don't know if we thought this would ever come true," Pinckney said, "but we did dream it." In 40 minutes Gary McLain turned the ball over only twice. On the eve of the final, the expressive eyes of coach Mass had filled with water as he heard McLain describe him as "a brother, a friend, a father, your boss, your coach." Massimino murmured, "I've screamed at this group more than any other, not because they are such good players, but because they are such good kids. They could take it."

So could Georgetown. Through all their many glories, the Hoyas never looked as becoming as they did that night in Lexington standing at their bench applauding Villanova.

Tom Callahan covered Final Fours in the '80s for Time magazine. Today, he lives in Charlottesville, Va., writes for the New York Times, and authors books.

Ed Pinckney became the Final Four Most Outstanding Player as he scored 16 points. Dwayne McClain scored 17 for the Wildcats. And Villanova, which took fourth place in the Big East Conference, finished the game with an unlikely 66-64 win over Georgetown.

their spindly young forward, Reggie Williams, was slightly hobbled by a tender ankle. Beyond that, he looked spent from the 35-2 season and a 17-game winning streak. Used to dominating whole teams, Ewing was so utterly occupied by Pinckney, that at no time in the first half did he get to the free throw line. (Ewing didn't know it yet, but he would never go there again as a collegian.)

Come the second half, it was Villanova that spurted ahead a couple of times, and the full extent of Georgetown's emergency was perfectly plain by the time David Wingate's banked basket reclaimed a scarce 54-53 lead. After Villanova fumbled the ball out of bounds, coach Thompson ordered the Hoyas to delay. About three and one-half minutes remained.

It is probably too easy, then, to say that the championship bounced off somebody's foot and into the arms of Harold Jensen, but in a manner of speaking, it did. Jensen tried

Reunion Arena in Dallas hosted the 1986 Final Four, where Duke and Louisville eliminated Louisiana State and Kansas to play for the championship. Duke's David Henderson drove toward the basket (above) in front of the bench and the watchful eye of Duke coach Mike Krzyzewski.

1986

BIG D STANDS FOR DENNY

By Billy Reed

As the tournament unfolded, it had so many plots and subplots that at times it seemed a prime-time soap opera, which was rather fitting considering the Final Four was to be held in Dallas, known to millions of television viewers as the home of J.R.

Ewing and his fellow wheeler-dealers in the oil business.

Was the Big East really dead or was it just a dream? Was Michigan only tired or too big-headed for even a 10-gallon hat? And while North Carolina was the answer to one question— Who got J.R. (Reid, the nation's best high school prospect?)—it also had everyone wondering how a team that was No. 1 so much of the season could be so flat at tournament time.

While the experts pondered these and other mysteries, they

also agreed that the city known as "Big D" would be where classy Duke and its rowdy fans finally would claim the title. But they forgot that in the 1980s, the "Big D" of college basketball was Denny, as in Crum, the laid-back coach at Louisville. When the Cardinals arrived in Dallas, it marked their third trip to the Final Four in five years, their fourth in the seven years of the decade, and their sixth in Crum's 15 seasons since leaving John Wooden's side at UCLA. In the age of parity, this was about as close to a, uh, Dynasty as anybody could get without hiring Joan Collins as pom-pon coach.

Before the season, Crum's team looked to be just another big player. The previous season's 18-17 record had been: (a) the worst of Crum's career, (b) the first time he failed to win 20 games, and (c) unworthy of even an NCAA bid. But Cardinal fans had some reasons to expect improvement. The guard corps would be helped by the return of 6-5 Milt "Ice" Wagner, a cool veteran of two Final Fours who had been redshirted as a senior because of a foot injury. In Pervis Ellison, a 6-9 freshman from Savannah, Ga., Crum had found a center precocious enough to invite comparisons with North Carolina's Sam Perkins because of his physique (all legs and arms) and ability to clean the boards ("Windex," he was promptly dubbed by Wagner).

Invited to play in the inaugural preseason NIT, Crum's team played well enough to join Kansas, Duke and St. John's for the final rounds in New York's Madison Square Garden. Although the Cards dropped tough losses to Kansas and local favorite St. John's, Crum was typically undismayed. "Those teams are as good as any in the country," he said. "This would have been a good Final Four."

That proved to be prophetic. The survivors who arrived in Dallas did, indeed, include Louisville, Duke and Kansas. The fourth member was surprisingly Louisiana State, which lost to Kentucky three times during the season but beat the Wildcats when it mattered the most, in the final of the Southeast Regional.

While the season proved that Wagner's foot (and his shooting touch) were as good as ever and that Ellison was the best freshman center in the nation, the Cards didn't really begin to look like a champion until 6-7 senior forward Billy Thompson finally began showing the consistency and leadership that Crum had been patiently awaiting for three and one-half years, or since he came to Louisville from Camden (N.J.) High School ballyhooed as the best prospect in the nation. Booed at home after key mistakes in tough losses at Kansas and Memphis State, Thompson got his multi-dimensional act together just in time to help the Cards to a 26-7 season that included an 11-game winning streak heading into the NCAAs.

Named the No. 1 seed in the West, Crum's team rolled to easy wins over Drexel and Bradley to advance to Houston. Omen-watchers noted what this team and U of L's 1980 champions had in common were freshman centers (Rodney McCray in '80), their final loss to teams coached by Jim Valvano (Iona in '80, N.C. State in '86) and a regional played in Houston. Finding the Summit as much to his liking in '86 as he had in '80, Crum watched his team finally put North Carolina out of its misery, 94-79, before withstanding a fine individual effort by Auburn's Chuck Person to beat the Tigers,

84-76, and earn (ho-hum) another trip to the Final Four.

And ending LSU's fairy tale run to glory with an 88-77 victory, the Cardinals watched top-ranked Duke get a last-second basket by freshman forward Danny Ferry to pull out a 71-67 win for coach Mike Krzyzewski, who had played and coached for Bobby Knight at Army.

More than one writer saw the final game as a matter of students

(Duke) vs. jocks (Louisville), an unfortunate and unfair stereotype. If Crum's program deserved more credit for its academic successes, then it also was true that Duke's players were hardly just a bunch of eggheads.

Preppy though he looked, forward Mark Alarie would trade elbows with anybody. In Johnny Dawkins, the Blue Devils had a flame so quick and deadly that Wagner, befuddled, was forced to

In the second half of the 1986 championship at Reunion Arena in Dallas, Louisville's Herbert Crook (41), Mark McSwain (10) and Pervis Ellison (43) had position for the rebound and shot. Ellison became the first freshman since 1944 to win the Most Outstanding Player award.

the bench in the first half of the title game.

In retrospect, it's difficult to figure out how Louisville won. Twice, once in each half, Dawkins took the game into his own hands and burned the Cards so severely that the game teetered on the brink of dissolving into a Duke rout. But like the Louisville native Muhammad Ali taking punches from Joe Frazier, the Cards managed to stay on their feet, hang tough and remain within striking distance.

With only 48 seconds left in the game and 11 on the shot clock in Reunion Arena, Louisville was clinging to a 66-65 lead when Crum called a timeout to set up a play. The idea was to get the ball to either Wagner or the other senior shooter, Jeff Hall, and let them go one-on-one in the hope of either a basket or a foul. Under heavy pressure, Hall threw up an off-balanced air ball. But suddenly, Ellison arose from the pack under the basket to wrap his hands around the ball and drop it in.

Cards 68, Devils 65.

Then, after rebounding a wild miss by Duke's David Henderson, Pervis showed why he was known as "Never Nervous," dropping in a couple of free throws for a 70-65 lead with 0:27 remaining. The Blue Devils quickly got four straight points, but finally were buried when "Ice" Wagner coolly swished two free throws with only two seconds to go to clinch the 72-69 win.

While Ellison became the first freshman since Arnie Ferrin of Utah in 1944 to be named the tournament Most Outstanding Player, Thompson was the catalyst. In six tournament games, he averaged 18.3 points and 7.8 rebounds while hitting 69 percent from the floor.

But it was the coach who drew

Bob Knight (above), "The General," contemplated many strategies and game plans. His rolled-up red sweater became a trademark as the Hoosiers moved into New Orleans' Superdome for another title attempt. Indiana's Keith Smart (right), who grew up in nearby Baton Rouge, scored 21 points, including the game-winning jumper. He was named the Most Outstanding Player.

the biggest hand from the jubilant Cardinal fans. On a night that "Big D" stood not for Dallas or Duke, but for Denny (and Dynasty), Crum smiled and said, "I'm really going to enjoy this one … it kinds of puts you in select company."

1987
HOLLYWOOD SCRIPT COMES TO LIFE

By Bob Hammel

In Hollywood, NCAA tournament championship night was also Oscar Night. Writer Angelo Pizzo's first movie, "Hoosiers," was nominated in two categories. It was the story of an Indiana high school team's improbable championship, won on a last-second basket. Pizzo, who grew up in Bloomington, Ind., had his Oscar tickets, his tuxedo, his limousine ... "but it just killed me that I wasn't in New Orleans," he said. He stayed home and watched the NCAA final on television. "You go back to your roots in times of stress," he said.

In New Orleans, Keith Smart was back to his roots. Ten years earlier, as a Boy Scout from nearby Baton Rouge, Smart had worked Sunday afternoons as a volunteer usher at New Orleans Saints football games in the Superdome—"so far up you needed television just to watch the game."

When Smart returned, television watched him. With five seconds to go in the championship game, Smart's 16-foot jump shot from the side swished through and made Indiana a 74-73 winner over Syracuse.

It was Indiana's fifth NCAA basketball championship in a glorious tradition that stretches to Everett Dean and Branch McCracken, decades and generations ago. In all that Hoosier history, there never was a single shot to rival Smart's.

And, of course, it worked the other way as well. Syracuse, which had felled a giant, North Carolina, to get to New Orleans, had its first championship in its grip, until:

● After hitting a free throw to put his team up 73-70, Howard Triche missed a free throw (0:38);

● Smart, lined up third on the right side of the lane, picked off the rebound and drove to a basket that cut the lead to 73-72 (0:30);

● After a timeout and an inbounds pass, Smart fouled freshman Derrick Coleman (0:28);

● Coleman missed a one-and-one free throw; Daryl Thomas rebounded for Indiana (0:27);

● Smart got the ball in the post to Thomas, who was covered by Coleman (0:08);

● So the ball went back to Smart … and into history.

"What do I remember most?" Smart said months later. "How quiet the arena got when the ball left my hand.

"And all of a sudden it went in."

It was an improbable finish, if only because Indiana's vast preference would have been to get the ball in the hands of its other guard for such a vital shot. Steve Alford had been taking those for Indiana for four years, and hitting most of them.

Four weeks earlier, in a game crucial to Indiana's Big Ten championship hopes, Alford felt the burden of last-second leadership and tried to create a shot with his team two points down at

Syracuse coach Jim Boeheim (above) had brought his team to the tournament nine consecutive years. His 1987 team was best positioned for a championship, but it was Indiana that celebrated that night in the Superdome. Steve Alford, Dean Garrett, Tony Freeman and Daryl Thomas (right) rejoice in the moment.

less game. In the final minutes of the biggest game of the year, the fifth-leading scorer on Indiana's team put together his own highlights film. "It was just all Keith down the stretch," said Dean Garrett, who will have everlasting trivia fame standing alongside Smart as answers to the questions:

Who were the two junior college players who Knight, of all people, recruited and made starters on a national championship team?

Why "Knight, of all people..."?

That's a question Knight himself asks, though he knows the answer involves a collision of images more universal than absolutely accurate—his own, for a rigidity in all things, including recruiting; that of the "jucos," for turning out borderline students.

His change from a previous disinclination to recruit in the junior colleges came simply because the regional high school talent pool that fueled his program for its first 14 years went unexpectedly dry. "We have been able to get the exact kind of kid we need coming out of high school, work with him a year or two and then he's ready to play," Knight said at a press conference in Cincinnati prior to the Midwest Regional final. "That pool kind of dwindled numerically, and that will happen."

At the time he spoke, Indiana was halfway down its tournament road—Fairfield, Auburn and Duke hurdled, Louisiana State up next.

The first two games had come in friendly environs for the Hoosiers: at the Hoosier Dome in Indianapolis, where tournament-record crowds watched home-state hero Alford lead the way over Fairfield and then score 31 points to rally the Hoosiers from a

Illinois. He tried to get free for a three-point try but couldn't; he worked his way into the deep corner, then out just far enough to force up a two-point try that missed, and Illinois won.

Back home, it didn't take exacting film study to show that Alford's best play would have been to give the ball up because defensive concentration understandably had swarmed around

him. The Illinois game was the 118th of Alford's Indiana career, but not too late for him to learn. With the national championship game on the line, Alford moved to the far side of the court —available if the defense ignored him; maneuvering room opened for the others if it didn't.

Smart had been using any room left open to him for the entire last 12 minutes of a breath-

24-10 deficit to a 107-90 win over Auburn.

The Duke game was the first to match Knight against a team coached by one of his former players. Mike Krzyzewski, who took Duke to the 1986 final game, was captain of a Knight team at Army. This game was a rousing matchup of friendly philosophies and Indiana survived it, 88-82.

It all seemed over for the Hoosiers, however, when LSU opened a 12-point second-half lead and was up 75-66 with four and one-half minutes to go when Indiana's Rick Calloway drove to dunk and missed—spectacularly. The ball ricocheted off the rim and out of bounds. Indiana took a timeout, and somehow the Hoosiers found the answers for a 77-76 win.

Calloway, playing in his hometown, pulled teammate Daryl Thomas' missed shot out of the air and banked it in for the game-winner at 0:06.

From early February on, the nation's No. 1-ranked team was Nevada-Las Vegas. Jerry Tarkanian's Runnin' Rebels entered the tournament 33-1, the loss by a point at Oklahoma. Indiana went into the tourney 24-4, No. 2-ranked in one poll (UPI — coaches) and No. 3 (behind North Carolina) in the other (AP — media). If there was a surprise in the semifinal matchup at the Superdome, it was that Indiana chose to run with the Rebs. Despite 38 points by UNLV guard Freddie Bands and 32 points by center Armon Gilliam, Indiana sped to a 97-93 victory.

Syracuse had its own three-point concerns in the semifinal round. Its Big East partner, Providence, had used the shot freely and well in leaving a shocking trail of higher-ranked victims, most notably No. 9 Alabama

(103-82) and No. 4 Georgetown (88-73). The Friars, with Billy Donovan leading the way, took 78 three-point shots and hit 40 in the four victories that sent them to New Orleans. Unimpressed, Syracuse used guard Sherman Douglas to cool Donovan, and the Orangemen maintained their dominance (15 straight victories) over Providence, 77-63.

Syracuse went after Indiana with a variety of defenses but basically two: man-to-man, with Greg Monroe on Alford most of the time, or a box-and-one—a four-man zone defense with Douglas assigned to Alford. Alford got his points (23, including 7-for-10 from the three-point range), but Syracuse—never a finalist before and a Final Four team only once in its 14 previous NCAA tournament trips—got 20 of them back from Douglas himself, 19 from center Rony Seikaly, and backboard domination from the game's only freshman starter, Derrick Coleman. The 6-9 forward from Big Ten country (Detroit) had 19 rebounds, nine more than anyone else in the game.

Syracuse was in the box-and-one, and Douglas was dogging Alford, when Smart—who had 21 points (15 in the last 12 minutes) to win the Most Outstanding Player award—found the opening that won for Indiana.

When it was over, the Hoosier story seemed almost scripted. Alford had led the way through Indianapolis; the game-winning basket at Cincinnati was by Cincinnatian Calloway; the game-winning basket at New Orleans was by Louisianian Smart.

And in Hollywood, Hoosiers scriptwriter Angelo Pizzo smiled.

1988
KANSAS CAPS STORYBOOK FINISH

By Bob Hentzen

University of Kansas fans had the script for April of 1988 in their minds months, even years, in advance. There were two givens: (1) the 1988 Final Four would be in Kansas City's Kemper Arena, 40 miles down I-70 from Lawrence and (2) 1988 would be Danny Manning's senior season as a Jayhawk. What better place for Manning to end his brilliant college career than a Final Four "at home?"

But it did not happen the way that Kansas fans had first envisioned. Heck, even the most ardent supporter had given up on the script midway through the 1987-88 campaign.

Kansas was leading the nation only in adversity—with injuries, ineligibilities and suspensions decimating Manning's supporting cast. At one point the troubled Jayhawks were a so-so 12-8 and there was genuine doubt that they would even finish good enough to

As players and coach Bob Knight waited for the 1987 trophy celebration at game's end, Knight and senior point guard Steve Alford shared the moment. Alford, son of a coach and a student of the game for his four Knight years, has since put those lessons into practice as an accomplished head coach.

qualify for the NCAA's 64-team starting field.

They made it safely, finishing the regular season 21-11. But they hardly came into the tourney with momentum, having been drilled by Kansas State 69-54 in the Big Eight Tourney semifinals in Kemper Arena.

History, along with common sense, said they would not be celebrating a national championship there 23 days later; no team with that many losses had ever won it all.

First stop on the tourney trail was Lincoln, Neb.,—not a particularly good omen because Kansas had blown a 16-point lead and lost to Nebraska there during the regular season. But in somewhat of an upset—Xavier was ranked No. 17—the Jayhawks won decisively, 85-72. They were fortunate to escape Lincoln alive, though. Murray State missed a potential go-ahead bucket at the end and Manning hit two free throws with one second left for a 61-58 victory.

Then is was on to the Silverdome in Pontiac, Mich., and Kansans were busy resurrecting the Jayhawks' script and also writing one for another state Cinderella, Kansas State.

Doggone, it worked out that Kansans could not lose in the regional finals—they were going to have a team in Kansas City after KU rode Manning's 38 points to a 77-64 win over Vanderbilt and K-State stunned third-ranked Purdue 73-70.

Kansas had lost two of three previous confrontations with the Wildcats, but at the end the KU pep band was playing "Goin' to Kansas City"… and coach Larry Brown was high-fiving Manning and congratulating other seniors Chris Piper and (the injured, but inspirational leader) Archie Mar-

shall … and Athletics Director Bob Frederick was picking up the black bag with 1,625 Final Four tickets. The Jayhawks had prevailed, 71-58.

The field for the 50th anniversary NCAA championship could not have turned out to be more attractive for folks in the host city. There was fifth-ranked Duke (24-6), which had knocked off No. 1 Temple in the regional final. There was second-ranked Arizona (31-2). And there was fourth-ranked Oklahoma (30-3).

Kansas City had been preparing for this Final Four for three years. It was the 10th time the city had hosted the championship, but the first time since 1964 and the first time in Kemper Arena.

The first semifinal matched Kansas against Duke, a nemesis to the Jayhawks and an albatross that Manning had carried for two years. In the Final Four at Dallas, remember, Mike Krzyzewski's Blue Devils knocked off Kansas, 71-67, when Manning experienced a nightmarish four-point game.

Larry Brown was not thinking so much about that before the tipoff, but of the season he had spent yelling and criticizing his troops. He decided in his pregame pep talk that it was time for him to tell them they were doggone good.

"I thought our kids thought they could win, but I thought they needed to hear it from me," Brown said.

Kansas bolted in front 9-0, then 14-0, and, unbelievably, 18-2. It held on for a 66-59 victory to even the score with the Blue Devils. "This is like a dream season," said Manning after a dream game—25 points, 10 rebounds, six blocked shots and four steals.

Then Oklahoma made another dream, an all-Big Eight final, a reality by dispatching Arizona with surprising ease, 86-78. Lute Olson's Wildcats got 31 points from Sean Elliott, but were done in by the Sooners' inside combination of Harvey Grant and Stacey King, who both scored 21.

Oklahoma had beaten Kansas twice during the season, 73-65 and 97-85, but the Sooners—like the rest of the basketball world—were realizing that the Jayhawks were on an amazing roll. "They're on a high right now; they know they can beat anyone," said Sooner guard Ricky Grace.

On Easter Sunday, the off day, Billy Tubbs' runnin', pressin' Sooners were being tabbed by coaches and media to win the championship. Kansas' only chance, most agreed, hinged on being able to slow the tempo as North Carolina State and Villanova had done (in pre-shot clock days) in scoring memorable upsets in the finals.

The first half ended 50-50—perhaps the most furious, exciting 20 minutes in college basketball history.

"I remember looking at the referees and seeing them shaking their heads and grinning," said Brown afterward. "I think they thought it was an excellent game, too."

No way could the two teams keep up that pace in the second half, and they did not—especially since Kansas did not want to. But the excitement, the drama, the electricity, lingered until the end.

Manning, appropriately, salted away the 83-79 victory with two free throws with five seconds left. He finished with 31 points and 18 rebounds, numbers that probably were in the original script when he first put on a Jayhawk uniform.

In 1988, the NCAA saluted the 50th anniversary of the Final Four. Kansas City's Kemper Arena became the unlikely celebration spot for the Kansas Jayhawks, whose campus is only 40 miles down the Kansas Turnpike. Coming off an inauspicious season that included 11 losses, even reaching the Final Four seemed unlikely for Kansas.

This NCAA championship was the Danny Manning Show, but as Brown said to the media later, "We wouldn't be sitting here talking to you right now if it wasn't for the rest of the kids. We got an unbelievable performance from a lot of kids."

In the title game, undersized 6-4 forward Milt Newton hit all six shots from the field, scoring 15 points. Guard Kevin Prichard hit six of seven shots from the floor and turned in a great floor game down the stretch. Piper, a rock throughout the season, capped his basketball career with eight points and seven boards.

The celebration, of course, started in Kemper Arena. It soon extended to the streets outside and then to the suburbs, lasting until the wee hours. The Jayhawks were back atop the basketball world.

1989

FISHER AND COMPANY GRAB NCAA GOLD

By Bill Halls

The news hit the Michigan campus like a bombshell. On

"Danny Manning and the Miracles" was how Kansas was known when it played Oklahoma in the 1988 championship game. Manning scored 31 points, including two clutch free throws, and grabbed 18 rebounds to be selected as the Most Outstanding Player.

For Kansas coach Larry Brown, high-five time arrived with seconds remaining as Danny Manning came from the game. As streets of Kansas City erupted into parties, the sometimes introspective and unpredictable Brown celebrated quietly in his hotel suite.

March 15, four days after the regular season had ended and two days before the Wolverine basketball team was to play its first NCAA tournament game, coach Bill Frieder resigned.

"We were shocked," said center Loy Vaught. "He never let on he was leaving."

Frieder made the announcement at a hastily arranged press conference in Tempe, Ariz. He was leaving Michigan following nine seasons and 191 victories to become head coach at Arizona State. Frieder said he planned to coach Michigan in the tournament.

Back in Ann Arbor, Bo Schembechler, the football coach and recently appointed athletics director, made a decision of his own. "A Michigan man will coach Michigan," he announced and immediately named Steve Fisher, Frieder's top assistant, interim head coach.

There had been high expectations among Michigan's basketball followers all summer. Michigan was coming off a 26-8 season and had a lineup overflowing with talented players, led by Glen Rice, a 6-7 senior with exceptional shoot-

ing range. Rice and Mark Hughes, a senior backup center, were named cocaptains. The 6-10 Terry Mills, who had never lived up to his high school rave notices, started at the other forward with Vaught in the pivot. The guards were Rumeal Robinson, a physically powerful and aggressive playmaker, and 6-6 Mike Griffin, a solid all-around player who specialized in defense.

Hughes and Sean Higgins, a 6-9 sophomore who was a taller version of Rice, were the primary reserves. Backing up Robinson at the point were juniors Demetrius Calip and Kirk Taylor.

The Wolverines roared out of the blocks by winning the Maui Classic in Hawaii, including an impressive 91-80 victory over highly regarded Oklahoma in the final. Michigan was 11-0 and ranked No. 2 nationally when it was stunned by Alaska-Anchorage, 70-66, in the first round of the Utah Classic in Salt Lake City on December 28.

When Indiana nipped Michigan, 71-70, in Ann Arbor, it was the third loss in four games for the Wolverines. Feeling the heat, Frieder gave his team a lecture, saying it lacked leadership, mental toughness and concentration. Michigan won its next three games, but Indiana pulled out another one-pointer, 76-75, on Jay Edwards' buzzer beater in Bloomington. That virtually eliminated Michigan from the Big Ten championship race. That is when the normally taciturn Rice made a brief speech.

"From that point on we were on a mission," said Vaught. "Glen started it and he usually doesn't say much. So when he talked about being on a mission to shock the world, we listened."

Michigan won its next five games before Illinois pounded out a resounding 89-73 triumph

in Ann Arbor on the final day of the Big Ten season. Michigan finished third in the conference, but its 24-7 record earned the team an NCAA tournament bid.

Fisher hardly had time to gather his thoughts. Michigan was scheduled to play Xavier (Ohio) in the first round of the Southeast regional in Atlanta. Fisher, a low key, soft-spoken man, had never been a head coach at the collegiate level. Schembechler hastily made arrangements to attend the game. He gave the players a rousing pep talk.

The Wolverines struggled through most of the game, but took an 84-82 lead on a three-point field goal by Rice with 3:32 remaining and held on down the stretch for a 92-87 victory. Rice and guard Rumeal Robinson each scored 23 points. Forward Terry Mills added 18.

"I'm probably no different than anyone else cast in this situation," Fisher said. "I was scared to death prior to walking from the locker room onto the floor, but after the ball was thrown up I think I settled into a routine that was business as usual."

After the Xavier game, Michigan seemed to settle down. Rice scored 36 points and Mills added 24 as Michigan eliminated South Alabama, 91-82. The Wolverines headed for Lexington, Ky., for a regional semifinal date with powerful North Carolina.

Dean Smith's Tar Heels had eliminated Michigan from the NCAA championship two years running. But Rice would not let it happen again. The talented senior scored 34 points, making 13 of 19 floor shots, including eight three-point field goals as Michigan prevailed, 92-87.

"I'm just going to hang on for the ride as long as I can," said a smiling Fisher.

In the Southeast regional final, Michigan crushed a solid Virginia team, 102-65, as Rice scored 32 points and Higgins added 31. Michigan was on its way to the Final Four in Seattle.

"We're playing with a lot more confidence," said Mills, who raised his game to a new level during the championship. "Coach Fisher found the right chemistry and the right combinations. It doesn't matter to us anymore who scores. We just want to win."

Lou Henson's Illinois team was awaiting the Wolverines in the Emerald City. But Fisher was becoming a Wizard of Oz for his Tin Man (Vaught), Cowardly Lion (Mills) and Scarecrow (Robinson). Vaught had been mired in a tourney-long slump but his coach stood by him. Fisher quietly told

Mills that he had not come close to scratching the surface of his talent. And Robinson needed to play under a bit more control and, for crying out loud, watch the silly fouls.

Each of the three players rose up to play their best basketball against Illinois. The smaller, quicker Illini raced in front, 16-8, in the early going. But Michigan closed behind the heart of Vaught (16 rebounds, 10 points), the courage of Mills (nine rebounds, eight points) and the heady play of Robinson (14 points, 12 assists) to take a one-point halftime lead.

Rice continued to pop rainbow jumpers through the nets with amazing regularity (28 points on 12-for-24 shooting). But it was left to Higgins to wear the hero's halo.

Michigan had taken an 81-79 lead on a three-point play by Hughes with 1:09 remaining. Ken Battle, who led the Illini with 29 points, tied the score with a 12-foot jumper with 50 seconds left on the clock.

Fisher set up a final play, but the Illini defense thwarted the Wolverines and Mills was forced to fire up a wild 18-footer with the 45-second clock running out. The ball caromed off the rim and landed in Higgins' hands. He tossed in a soft six-footer to give Michigan the victory with two seconds left on the clock.

"If this is a dream," Fisher said, "don't wake me up until Tuesday morning."

Now the stage was set for the championship game. Seton Hall, completing a Cinderella story of its own under P.J. Carlesimo, was

Physical Michigan arrived in Seattle for the Final Four facing a team it knew well— Illinois. Michigan forward Mike Griffin dove for a loose ball (above) and, with the score tied, the game came down to a last-second shot by Sean Higgins. The shot went in and the Wolverines were ready to face Seton Hall for the championship Monday night.

Seton Hall, putting together a Cinderella story with coach P.J. Carlesimo writing the script, faced Duke in the semis, where forward John Smith (above) leaped high attempting to block a shot from Anthony Avent (32). But the glass slipper broke two days later as Michigan made two free throws with three seconds remaining to claim the crown, 80-79. The Wolverine bench cleared as the celebration began (far right).

making its first appearance in the final. And what a final it was.

Michigan led 37-32 at halftime and built a 12-point bulge early in the second half. Seton Hall, behind some miraculous shooting by John Morton, battled back and sent the game into overtime on Morton's three-pointer.

Morton nailed another three-pointer to give Seton Hall a 79-76 lead with 2:50 remaining in overtime. He finished the game with 35 points, but it was his last gasp in the championship.

Michigan trailed by a point when Rice's defense forced Morton to toss up an airball. Rice grabbed the rebound and fed a pass to Robinson, who was fouled with three seconds to play. Robinson calmly sank both free throws to give Michigan an 80-79 victory and the school's first NCAA basketball championship.

"You have to believe you're going to make them," said Robinson. "Because if you don't, you won't."

Rice finished the game with 31 points and 11 rebounds and was named the championship's most outstanding player. Fisher had coached his team to six-straight victories under incredible pressure. "Don't pinch me," he said. Days later, Fisher was hired by Schembechler as Michigan's coach.

"It seems like a story," said Mills. "It seems like something someone would make up. But it came true for Michigan. You couldn't tell this story to anyone else. They wouldn't believe it."

Bill Halls covered eight Final Fours throughout his 30-year career at the Detroit News. After his last Final Four in 1981, he covered professional basketball. He has won numerous awards from the U.S. Basketball Writers association and the Professional Basketball Association. He is currently retired and living in Michigan.

1990-2000
THE EMPIRE STRIKES BACK

In 1994, the Razorbacks' Corey Beck reveled in the moment as he cut the game nets. Arkansas was victorious over Duke in a close final game attended by Arkansas' No. 1 fan— President Bill Clinton.

In the final decade of the 20th century, America fought a high-tech war in the Persian Gulf, witnessed the crumbling of the Soviet Union, and rode the soaring stock market to a new level of prosperity. Actor Tom Hanks emerged as the Jimmy Stewart of his generation, starring in such movies as "Forrest Gump," "Philadelphia," "Sleepless in Seattle," and "Saving Private Ryan." In the record industry, compact discs rendered 33 rpm albums obsolete, and youngsters embraced a new kind of music known as "rap" that many of their elders insisted wasn't music at all.

In the burgeoning computer world, along came the Internet, which provided unprecedented access to an incredible amount of information, in addition to electronic mail (e-mail). Cable TV grew and proliferated to the point that around-the-clock coverage was available for major news events such as the deaths of Princess Di and John F. Kennedy Jr.

Among the more stunning developments in the sports world were: the inclusion of NBA players on the U.S. Olympic basketball team; the cancellation of the 1994 World Series because of a dispute between players and owners; and boxer Mike Tyson twice biting Evander Holyfield's ears during a heavyweight championship fight in Las Vegas. A couple of erstwhile bush-league sports—stock-car racing and professional wrestling—experienced surges in popularity that challenged the traditional "ball" sports for TV time and the entertainment dollar. Early in the decade, Michigan's "Fab Five" adopted long, baggy shorts, and it began a trend that swept throughout the basketball world and the nation's playgrounds.

From 1992 through the end of the decade, the White House was occupied by Bill Clinton, a native of Arkansas who presided over a tumultuous and controversial presidency. For college basketball fans, the most important thing about Clinton was that he was an avid and knowledgeable fan. He frequently watched games and he annually invited the men's and women's champions to the White House to be honored. When his favorite team, the Arkansas Razorbacks, won the 1994 NCAA title, Clinton attended the championship game in Charlotte, N.C.

Yet with all due respect to Arkansas and three other first-time champions—UNLV (1990), Arizona (1997) and Connecticut (1999)—the decade will be remembered as one dominated by the traditional powers. In 1991 and '92, Duke became the first back-to-back champ since UCLA won its seventh consecutive title in 1973. In 1993, the Blue Devils' arch-enemy, North Carolina, won its third title and in 1995, UCLA won its first title since the John Wooden era.

But the team of the decade may well have been Kentucky, the college game's all-time winningest program. When Rick Pitino became the Wildcats' coach in 1989, the program was at its lowest ebb due to NCAA sanctions stemming from rules violations. In only four years Pitino had the Wildcats back into the Final Four. Then from 1996-98, Kentucky went to three consecutive championship games. The Cats beat Syracuse for the title in '96, lost to Arizona in '97, and then won again in '98, their first season under Tubby Smith, who became the third African-American coach to win a national title. (Others were John Thompson of Georgetown and Nolan Richardson of Arkansas.)

Entering the new millennium, no sport was more popular or healthy than college basketball.

Early in the decade, when Michigan's "Fab Five" adopted long, baggy shorts, it began a fashion trend that swept throughout the basketball world and on to the nation's playgrounds.

Duke came to the finals five times in the '90s, winning twice and always contending. In 1999, Connecticut reached high to achieve its championship goal. Jake Voskuhl (above, right) soared for this rebound as UConn took the 59th title, 77-74.

As the nation's basketball attention turned to Denver in 1990, UNLV's Larry Johnson went to the basket in the semifinal game against Georgia Tech. The Runnin' Rebels raced to a 90-81 victory to advance to the final.

1990

RUN, RUN, RUN, RUN AWAY

By Bob Sands

It was 1:30 in the morning and two ol' guys short of hair but long of basketball savvy were walking down the corridor of the Denver Sheraton Tech Center.

Smoke from an El Ropo victory cigar billowed toward the ceiling. Blush wine lapped at the glass with each step of Nevada-Las Vegas coach Jerry Tarkanian. James Madison coach Lefty Driesell, Tark's long-time buddy, was waving his arms like a band conductor gone mad. The two

coaches stopped, Driesell offered more congratulations and they parted.

Tarkanian took a drag on the cigar and let out a puff of smoke. He liked that. So he did it again. Then a Cheshire Cat grin and another drag.

This was a happy man.

The coach of the 1990 NCAA championship team certainly had reason to be. The Rebels had buried the Duke Blue Devils, 103-73, in the title game four hours earlier at McNichols Arena.

A 30-point victory—the widest margin in a championship game. The Rebels registered three 30-point victories during the NCAA championship, but this one … oh so superb. And Driesell, a Duke graduate, had stopped by to offer his congratulations.

Tark, indeed, was in a euphoric, reflective mood in these wee early hours. National champions, what an awesome statement. Only 28 other universities had won the title since the NCAA championship started in 1939. At the beginning of the 1989-90 season, 293 schools had an opportunity to win the trophy. Nevada-Las Vegas became the one, the only.

But a 30-point margin … what in the world? Tark explained the Rebels were able to get a good start on the Blue Devils.

Tarkanian was surprised that slight-of-build Duke point guard Bobby Hurley started defensively on bigger, stronger Greg Anthony. With the physical advantage, Anthony could penetrate and either dish it off or shoot the jumper.

The anatomy of an impending blowout. Oh, it didn't take long for Duke coach Mike Krzyzewski to change his scheme. But it was too late. The foundation was in

place. The Rebels were off and running—for 103 points.

But in analyzing the Rebels, you must first address the defense. The Rebels could play a hangman's-noose-choking-pressure defense. They also could play a quick-hands-and-feet-in-the-passing-lanes zone defense, which Tarkanian called the Amoeba. The Amoeba globbed on the Blue Devils in the first five minutes of the second half as the Rebels went on an 18-0 tear in three minutes to forge a 75-47 lead at 13:38.

Anderson Hunt, the championship's Most Outstanding Player, scored 12 of those 18 points on the way to a 29-point game.

Still, it was that early situation between Hurley and Anthony that launched the Rebels.

And, please, do not forget the defense. The Blue Devils had 14 of their 23 turnovers in the first half and they averaged 17 for the entire game during the season.

Anthony scored 10 of his 13 points in the first half and for the game, had five steals.

Hurley, who logged only two free throws and three assists, was not the only Devil in the doldrums. His guard running mate, Phil Henderson, made just one of eight three-point attempts, committed six turnovers and had no assists.

The Rebels had been through a lot to get to the championship—all sorts of off-court battles. But this victory cushioned the blows.

But on the court, they ruled—supremely, majestically. Larry Johnson and Stacey Augmon became all-Americas. Anthony and Hunt became highly complementary guards.

Tark did not have a set lineup in the regular season because of

Anderson Hunt rose above the Duke defenders in 1990. Hunt led UNLV with 29 points, was named MOP and, in the epic blowout of all the tournament years, helped defeat Duke, 103-73. For Duke, the stunning defeat may have provided special resolve. For the next two years, the Blue Devils won back-to-back championships.

As the game wound down, the UNLV bench began its celebration with Jerry Tarkanian still coaching his players.

win, 69-67. The Cardinals had a chance to win it, but Rebel center David Butler intercepted a weak pass inside just before the buzzer sounded.

Then came the awaited classic: two teams not afraid to run and gun, Nevada-Las Vegas and Loyola Marymount. But wouldn't Nevada-Las Vegas' defense be the difference here? Yes, it would. The Rebels won, 131-101—the second of their 30-point victories.

After Loyola Marymount, it was on to the Final Four to face Georgia Tech in the national semifinals. The Rebels overcame a 53-46 halftime deficit to win, 90-81.

It was another shootout. But the Rebels overcame everything thrown at them. Georgia Tech's Dennis Scott was launching bombs, scoring 20 of his 29 points in the first half. But at the half, the Rebels regrouped and came out with defense on their minds.

Georgia Tech did not score the first six minutes of the second half as Tarkanian reverted to his hangman's-noose-man-to-man defense.

Yellow Jacket coach Bobby Cremins said: "The turning point came in the first five minutes (of the second half), when we seemed to lose our composure. They really played defense on us. They got into our jocks and really got after us."

The pressure defense triggered the explosive offense. The Rebels put five players in double figures and they were in the finals.

Duke beat Arkansas, 97-83, to gain the other championship berth. Arkansas had made it to the Final Four with a defense the Razorbacks called "40 Minutes of Hell." Heck, that was just fine for the Devils. They shredded the

Razorbacks with 54 percent shooting as Henderson scored a heavenly 28 points.

So it was Duke and Nevada-Las Vegas. And, once again, Duke was the runnerup. Four times the runnerup. And the first NCAA championship title for the 30-5 Rebels.

It was Johnson who said: "You can call us bad. You can call us thugs. You can call us hoodlums. But at the end of that, please, call us national champions, too."

Bob Sands covered seven Final Fours while writing for the Kansas City Star, the Las Vegas Review-Journal, the Manhattan (Kan.) Mercury and the Evansville (Ind.) Courier and Press. Sands is now retired from newspapers and is living in Las Vegas.

1991
DUKE IS KING

By Caulton Tudor

It was on the night of April 1, 1991, that Duke, having overthrown Nevada-Las Vegas two days earlier, finally was able to declare itself the king of collegiate basketball.

But was the NCAA championship clinched on that cool, windy night in Indianapolis, or did it actually occur way back on a humid afternoon in June of 1990?

Many Blue Devils, and virtually all of their fans, say the answer to that question is "both."

Certainly, the tangible evidence did not surface until the 72-65 win against Kansas in the Hoosier Dome was complete. That is what the official record will show—the win, and Grant Hill's antenna jam off a Bobby

eligibility and sickness problems. The Rebels lost five regular-season games, but down the stretch, they meshed, winning the Big West Conference regular-season and tournament titles.

Their "NCAA Championship Trail" began with a 102-72 romp over Arkansas-Little Rock in Salt Lake City. Yes, the first of the three 30-point blowouts. The Rebels then beat Ohio State, 76-65.

On to Oakland, Calif. And wouldn't you know it, the Rebels found trouble where they least expected. Ball State of Muncie, Ind.

The Rebels missed the front end of three one-and-one free throws, the back end of a one-and-one and the second of a two-shot intentional foul in the last two minutes, but still managed to

Hurley feed, and leg-dead Christian Laettner's 12 straight free throws, and Bill McCaffrey's 16 points off the bench, and Brian Davis' defense and a dozen other things.

What the official Final Four record book will not show is that perhaps none of it would have happened if Mike Krzyzewski had not withdrawn his name from consideration for the Boston Celtics' coach search almost a year earlier.

"We wouldn't have been here without him," Laettner, the Final Four's Most Outstanding Player, said of Krzyzewski that night in Indianapolis. "What kind of team we would have been, I don't know. But we wouldn't have been anything like this, I know that."

In truth, the Blue Devils were not entirely anything like that as late as a week before the NCAA run began against Northeast Louisiana, Iowa, Connecticut, St. John's and Nevada-Las Vegas and culminated with Kansas.

Duke won those six games by an average margin of 14 points. But in its last game prior to the NCAA Championship, the Blue Devils were reduced to shambles by archrival North Carolina, 96-74, in the championship game of the Atlantic Coast Conference tournament in Charlotte, N.C.

"The low point of the season," Hurley recalled, a piece of the Hoosier Dome nets in one hand. "That was the lowest. You can't get lower than that."

On January 5, Duke began its Atlantic Coast Conference season with an 81-64 loss at Virginia. Eventually, the loss at Virginia and the ACC championship defeat to North Carolina brewed powerful incentive within the Blue Devils.

Following Virginia, Krzyzewski convened a practice

session that ended with star freshman Grant Hill nursing a broken jaw and the remainder of the players united in a new mission.

"One of the things we learned that day was it's not good enough just to have some talent," Hurley said. "Talent's no good without the right kind of incentive."

Duke then won 12 of its next 13 games by an average margin of 20 points.

"During that stretch we saw our potential," Krzyzewski said. "The way the guys responded to that loss at Virginia made me feel very positive about what they could accomplish."

The storm ended with narrow

Christian Laettner drove through UNLV traffic for a layup in 1990. There were too few moments like this for the Blue Devils, and UNLV took control of the game. A year later Duke avenged the championship loss.

losses at Wake Forest and Arizona. After three more wins, the
complete collapse against North
Carolina hit. Historically, the losing team in the ACC title game
does not fare well in the NCAA
championship, particularly teams
that lose by an unsettling margin
of 22 points.

But Duke was different.

"Losing that game like that
didn't depress us," Hurley said.
"It made us mad at ourselves.
But it didn't depress us because
we knew we'd been just that low
before and had bounced back.
We thought back to Virginia."

For the second time in one
season, Duke recovered from a
one-sided loss to play a brilliant
stretch of basketball—one that
would end three decades of Final
Four frustrations.

"The ninth time's the charm,"
Laettner said, jokingly referring
to eight previous Duke trips to
the Final Four.

It was obvious from the opening tip in Saturday's semifinal
against the Rebels that the Devils
had no trouble forgetting the
103-73 humiliation they suffered
a year earlier in Denver against
Nevada-Las Vegas in the championship game.

Hurley was the most glaring
difference. Older, tougher and
stronger, he did not wilt under
the defensive heat that came from
Nevada-Las Vegas' Anderson
Hunt and Greg Anthony. Just the
opposite, in fact. He flourished—
12 points, nine assists and only
two turnovers.

And poetically, it was also
Hurley who hit the biggest shot of
the game, perhaps the biggest
single shot in Duke history to that
point. Duke was behind 76-71
with less than three minutes to
play when Hurley found himself
with the ball and shooting room.
His three-pointer put the outcome back in doubt, and maybe

created some in the Rebels.

Whatever, Duke forced a turnover. Davis then drove the lane, hit a shot, was fouled and converted the free throw. A free throw by Larry Johnson tied it at 77. Duke, on its last possession, went to Laettner. He was fouled with 12.7 seconds left, converted both chances and after a long miss by Hunt, Nevada-Las Vegas' undefeated season ended one game short of its target.

Duke celebrated in the most serious sort of way. But above the cheers and hugs, Krzyzewski could be heard screaming, "Our work's not finished! It's not finished!"

For artistic purposes, the Monday victory against Kansas paled. "I think players on both sides played a lot on guts," Krzyzewski said.

The Jayhawks, long-shots to go so far, were coming off an equally emotional semifinal win against North Carolina. "They had a little more left than we did," said Kansas star Mark Randall. "Not much, but a little."

Caulton Tudor has covered 22 Final Fours for the Raleigh News & Observer, both as a basketball writer and a columnist. Selected to the National Basketball Writers Association Hall of Fame, he wrote a book about North Carolina State's 1983 championship team.

1992
TWICE IS NICE

By Eddy Landreth

One year later, many of the same Duke players who had won the 1991 title sat in the locker room at the Minneapolis Metrodome, visibly exhausted,

worn from a pressure-packed season of being No. 1, relieved their quest for a second title had come to an end.

"It took me a week to get over it," guard Thomas Hill said several months later.

No team since John Wooden's UCLA clubs (1967-73) had won back-to-back titles. And when Duke completed its run, the Blue Devils understood why.

"I know how hard it is to win even one national championship," Hill said after Duke beat Michigan (71-51) for the title. "Then to win it back-to-back, that is incredible. I'm just sitting here in awe of our team and what we've gone through."

When the season began, the Blue Devils made it look easy. They rolled over most of their opponents in December and January by 20 or more points.

Their fastbreak resembled a high-wire act, with point guard Bobby Hurley tossing long, high lobs to Grant Hill. Except for reserve Greg Koubek and transfer Billy McCaffrey, Duke had returned all the key actors from the previous year. The experience showed. So did the confidence. The Blue Devils expected to win. They knew they would win.

Losing never entered their minds.

Then Hurley suffered a stress fracture in his foot during the Blue Devils' first game against North Carolina. Duke not only lost its first game of the season, but one of the two most important parts to its machine.

Then bad luck struck again. On the night Hurley returned to the lineup, Grant Hill missed the first of several games with a sprained ankle.

Somehow the Blue Devils persevered. They finished the regular season atop the Atlantic Coast

Conference standings and headed to Charlotte for the Atlantic Coast Conference tournament to make their latest title official.

The ACC's recognized champion is the tournament winner. And for all seniors Christian Laettner and Brian Davis had accomplished, this one achievement had eluded them.

In addition, they had been embarrassed by archrival North Carolina the year before (96-74).

This time Duke breezed through with little resistance, resembling the team that had rolled across everyone at the beginning of the season as it beat North Carolina 94-74 to win the ACC championship.

"We played intelligently, aggressively," coach Mike Krzyzewski said.

With the preliminaries aside, Duke could now move on to the business of winning another national title.

"We're excited about the opportunity of doing something that's special, that's unique," said Krzyzewski. "I don't see where that should ever be perceived as pressure. What a fantastic opportunity for us. If we get beat, I hope somebody plays a great, great basketball game against us and we haven't defeated ourselves."

Kentucky almost made a prophet of Krzyzewski in the East regional final in Philadelphia. Just when it appeared Duke would run away with the game, the Wildcats found the resolve to come back.

They erased a 12-point Duke lead with a swarming full-court press, the kind of press that had been ineffective against the Blue Devils before.

With 2.2 seconds left in overtime, Kentucky's Sean Woods drove into the lane and flipped

Duke coach Mike Krzyzewski (top) and Kansas' Roy Williams directed their teams in the 1991 final. Williams, who had been an assistant to Dean Smith at North Carolina, crafted his Kansas program similar to his mentor's.

In Minneapolis' Hubert H. Humphrey Metrodome in 1992, Duke dominated Michigan for its second-straight title. Bobby Hurley (11) fired from three-point territory (above), but Christian Laettner, Grant Hill and Thomas Hill shared the scoring load.

the ball over Laettner, off the glass and into the basket.

Timeout Duke.

With 2.1 seconds left, Kentucky led 103-102.

History, it seemed, would have to wait for a repeat champion.

As his team gathered around, Krzyzewski assured his players they were going to win. Although the Blue Devils had great faith in

their coach, Krzyzewski pushed the limits a bit on this occasion.

"Coach told us we were going to win," Hurley said. "I doubted him a little."

Grant Hill inbounded the ball. He threw a perfect, three-quarter court pass to Laettner. Kentucky coach Rick Pitino had stationed Deron Feldhaus behind Laettner and John Pelphrey as a rover at the free-throw line. Pelphrey was

supposed to break for the ball like a defensive back. Instead he allowed Laettner to catch it.

With his back to the basket, Laettner faked to his right, dribbled once, spun left and released the ball with four-tenths of a second left in the game.

Woods lay face-down on the court, stunned as the scoreboard told the improbable story—Duke 104, Kentucky 103.

"All I could say for 10 minutes after the game was: 'This is unbelievable. This is unbelievable,' " Hurley said. "I asked (Duke associate coach) Pete Gaudet if I was alive or in a dream. He smacked me upside my head and said: 'You're alive.' "

So were the Blue Devils, thanks to Laettner.

Laettner finished 10-of-10 from the field, with one three-pointer, and 10-of-10 from the free-throw line for 31 points.

"It was totally incredible," Laettner said. "I just thank God for giving me the opportunity to take the shot and win the game."

With just two games left, Krzyzewski decided his team needed a refresher course on defense. Unlike the previous season, when the Blue Devils played defense with a passion, the 1992 team had been offensive minded. So with Indiana waiting ahead, Krzyzewski declared war in practice. The Blue Devils must play defense again.

"They were really rugged," Grant Hill said of the workouts. "Coach had to stop practice early because they were becoming too physical. People got bruised. Tony (Lang) got stitches (in his head). Christian elbowed me in the mouth. I went up in the air for a dunk over Cherokee (Parks), and he undercut me and I landed on my butt.

"The Kentucky game showed us if we don't play defense, if we don't play tough, we can lose. So we just went out there and played hard."

Yet for all their desire and effort, the Blue Devils could not get going in the first half against Indiana. Indiana hit 12 of its first 16 field goals and led 29-21 at the outset. By the half, the margin stood at 42-37.

Perhaps Kentucky had beaten Duke after all.

Laettner, the savior against the Wildcats, went 1-of-6 from the field in the first half. He finished with just eight points.

Hurley, however, looked more like himself than he had since returning from his broken foot. He scored 26 points on 7-of-12 shooting.

As he had the year before, when he played all 80 minutes in the Final Four, Hurley made the difference.

The Hoosiers pulled to within 78-75 with 24.6 seconds left, but the Blue Devils hung on to advance to their third-straight championship game.

Michigan and its "Fab Five" freshmen had almost beaten Duke in a December game. The Blue Devils escaped with an 88-85 win. The memory of that game remained fresh in the minds of both teams.

"I think that served as a bit of a wake-up call," Hurley said. "We had some easy games and all of the sudden we were in a sit-

uation where we could have lost."

The two teams played the first half of the title game the way they had the waning moments of their December encounter. They were rarely separated by more than a point. But Laettner's poor play carried over from the Indiana game. He committed a career-high seven turnovers, went 2-of-8 from the field and scored five points—in the first half.

Hurley exploded with a rare emotional outburst at halftime, ripping Laettner for his uninspired performance.

"Bobby doesn't speak out all that often," Lang said. "It sent chills down my spine to see Bobby do something like that. He said: 'I'm out there giving 110 percent. Why can't you give 110 percent?' "

Laettner responded as soon as the second half began. He scored on a driving layup—on an assist from Hurley—and sank a three-pointer on Duke's next possession.

Hoisting the championship trophy, Duke and its coach Mike Krzyzewski celebrated its 71-51 victory over Michigan.

A seemingly stoic Christian Laettner held aloft the victory net matter-of-factly. The senior had two championship rings, a place in the Blue Devils record book and a video clip from a regional victory over Kentucky. That clip will be replayed at Final Fours for many years to come.

The Blue Devils gradually pulled away, turning a close game into a rout. Their final game reflected their season, a hard-fought, but successful, struggle.

"This is the greatest year I've ever had as a coach," Krzyzewski said. "To beat such an outstanding team for the national championship, and Indiana, Seton Hall and Kentucky in these last four games, makes it feel even better—like we deserve it."

Eddy Landreth is the sports editor of the Chapel Hill News and a columnist for ACC Today. Covering ACC sports since 1987, he has covered Duke for the Durham Herald-Sun and college basketball for the Charlotte Observer and the Winston-Salem Journal. He also has written for The Sporting News, Basketball Digest and Basketball Weekly.

1993
A PICTURE OF PERFECTION

By Gary McCann

Before the season began, North Carolina coach Dean Smith gave each player a photo of the Superdome. It said, "North Carolina, 1993 NCAA Champions." It was taped in lockers and other places, never very far from sight and never out of mind.

"It's on the wall over my bed," said 7-0 center Eric Montross. "I was always looking at it, because throughout the season (getting to New Orleans) was our goal."

It was such a thrill that Montross, when the Tar Heels played a regular-season game in January against Louisiana State in the Superdome, got chills when the

bus rolled past the mound of metal on Poydras Street.

"I'm going to carry that memory with me for a long time," Montross said.

Smith's photo was, if you will, a kind of paint-by-numbers blueprint for the Tar Heel season. Smith's goal each season was to have his team be a national contender.

But with archrival Duke winning back-to-back titles in 1991 and 1992, there was added incentive.

"By Duke being able to accomplish that," senior George Lynch said, "it has driven us. There is a lot of pride. If you are a player at Carolina, people expect you to win a national title."

From Montross in the middle, Donald Williams on the wing, Derrick Phelps on the point and Henrik Rödl on the bench, there was only one goal.

"It would have been a disappointment not to get there," Lynch said. "We only had one dream. Get to New Orleans."

The trip wasn't without its bumps, bruises and disappointments. Or its amazing performances. Down 21 to Florida State with 11:48 to play at home and behind 19 with 9:01 to play, North Carolina rallied for an 82-77 win.

The next time out, the Tar Heels went to Wake Forest and reached a turning point on their road to New Orleans. The Deacons ended an 11-game losing streak to the Tar Heels with an 88-62 blowout.

"That," Dean Smith said, "was our wake-up call."

Duke beat the Tar Heels three days later, giving them their longest losing streak of the season.

But Smith was pleased with the effort at Duke. His team was

coming on. The offense began to click in February. And as was his custom, Smith met with each player at mid-season and talked about their play.

One key conversation was between Smith and Rödl, the senior guard. The talk was about giving up the starting slot to Williams.

"It hurt not to start," Rödl said, "but Donald was coming on and the chemistry was working."

Phelps was a walking injury most of the season. Along the way he injured an ankle, elbow, foot and back. He bruised his tailbone on a hard fall in the ACC Tournament semifinals, didn't play in the title game and North Carolina lost to Georgia Tech. It was the only goal the Tar Heels didn't reach.

Phelps played with pain throughout the NCAA championship, but when it came time to play hard, he somehow found the strength.

Williams' shooting ran hot and cold, until he got his act together in March and April when it mattered. Montross started slowly and peaked at the end. Forward Brian Reese limped around through half of the season, too, then played the best basketball of his career in the last 15 games.

Still, the Tar Heels were almost an afterthought when they joined blazing Kentucky, steady Kansas and high-flying Michigan for the Final Four.

Kentucky ran through the regionals without a real test. Kansas, playing spectacular defense and getting excellent guard play from Adonis Jordan and Rex Walters, reached the Final Four for the second time in three seasons. And Michigan, riding those fabulous sophomores, moved to the Final Four for the second-straight season

The national semifinal matchup against Kansas sent Smith against his former assistant coach, Roy Williams. Both quickly defused thoughts that the game was Dean versus Roy or that the teams were mirror images of each other.

While the two were almost evenly matched in New Orleans, North Carolina won, 78-68, thanks to superior size in the middle.

And Donald Williams.

For the third-straight game, the 6-3 sophomore knocked down a crucial three-point shot. With 2:48 left, the Jayhawks were still hanging around despite 40 percent shooting. North Carolina led, 68-65.

At a time when it appeared the Tar Heels might be content to run some clock, Phelps lofted a looping pass to Williams running down the right wing.

He pulled up and swished a three-pointer from the right of the key.

"Every player has to know his role," Williams said. "Coach has told me that's the best time to take a three. The other team is trapping and we can usually get good rebounding position. I wanted to take it."

Williams finished with 25 points, making seven-of-11 shots, including five-of-seven threes.

While the Tar Heels were getting past Kansas, Michigan was beating Kentucky, 81-78, in overtime. Like the Tar Heels, the Wolverines, who had lost to Duke in 1992 finals, had pointed toward the Superdome all season. Anything less than a title, they said, would not be worth the trip.

The Wolverines had won the Rainbow Classic in December, beating North Carolina in the second round, 79-78, on a follow shot by Jalen Rose at the buzzer.

North Carolina's George Lynch slam-dunked (left) in the first half of the championship game against Michigan. The game see-sawed with bench strategies providing intrigue to go with spectacular plays. But the game became notable when, with 11 seconds left, the Wolverines' Chris Webber called a timeout when Michigan had none left. Coach Steve Fisher asked him why, but it was too late—two technical shots by Donald Williams wrapped up the North Carolina victory.

determined to complete the job it had failed to do against Duke in 1992.

North Carolina reached the regional semifinals after routs of East Carolina and Rhode Island. While the routs gave Phelps time to get healthier, they did not give the Tar Heels a test.

North Carolina erased an 11-point deficit in the first half of the East regional semifinal to beat Arkansas, 80-74. Williams scored North Carolina's final nine points to set the tone for what was to come in the next three games.

Cincinnati led by 15 in the first half of the regional final, with Nick Van Exel scoring 21 first-

half points on six-of-10 three-pointers.

But at halftime the Tar Heels made a switch. Phelps took Van Exel head to head without help.

He told his teammates: "he's mine."

Phelps, despite a sore tailbone and blisters, dogged Van Exel. Van Exel hit one-of-11 shots in the second half, and North Carolina survived, 75-68, in overtime. Williams, finishing with 20 points, had two crucial three-pointers in the extra period.

"We're where we want to be," Montross said, "but we're not finished yet."

The Wolverines played that game without Ray Jackson, who injured a shoulder.

"I just hope it's a close game like it was in Hawaii," Smith said.

It was close and more. It was a game of runs early. It was physical inside with Montross, Lynch and Reese battling Chris Webber, Juwan Howard and Jackson.

North Carolina led early, but the Wolverines put together a spurt to take a 23-13 lead. North Carolina fought back to tie it at 25 and took a 42-36 halftime lead.

With 4:12 to play, Jimmy King hit a perimeter jumper to put Michigan ahead, 67-63. But the Tar Heels had gone to an effective zone defense, and Smith liberally went to his deep bench, using 37 subs in the final 20 minutes.

And Donald Williams continued his remarkable string of bailing out the Tar Heels, hitting his fifth three-pointer of the night with 3:50 left to cut the lead to one.

On his way to another 25-point night and the Final Four Most Outstanding Player award, Williams had 12 points in the last seven minutes.

Two quick missed three-point shots by Michigan opened the door and North Carolina barged in. Phelps scored on a drive, Lynch hit a difficult shot over Howard and the Tar Heels led 70-67. When Rose tried to drive into the teeth of North Carolina's defense, Montross knocked the ball away to Williams.

After a timeout and two Michigan fouls to get North Carolina into the one-and-one, Montross slipped behind the Michigan defense, took a pass from Lynch and slammed home a five-point lead.

Facing each other in the semis (above), Kansas' Roy Williams met his mentor, Dean Smith, in a fateful meeting. A shot at the national championship was on the line, and Carolina won, 78-68, to advance to the final. A memorable moment came when Smith's players insisted he cut the last strand of the net (right) after the Tar Heels' championship win over Michigan.

The Tar Heels had run off nine unanswered points.

"Basketball is a game of runs," Williams said. "We were playing good on offense and told each other to concentrate on stopping them on defense."

It almost backfired.

A basket by Jackson, a North Carolina turnover and a follow shot by Webber cut the lead to 72-71 with 30 seconds left.

But the game's turning point came with 46 seconds left, although Michigan didn't know it at the time. Coach Steve Fisher

had used his last timeout.

With 20 seconds left, North Carolina's Pat Sullivan made the front end of a one-and-one. Webber rebounded the second shot and headed up court. He dribbled hard to the corner where Lynch and Phelps turned him into a defensive sandwich right in front of the Michigan bench.

With nowhere to go, no shot to take and no passing angle, Webber called time.

"I just called timeout," Webber said. "It was one we didn't have. It probably cost our team the game."

Perhaps.

But the Tar Heels, aware of the situation, had two fouls to give.

"We were going to keep fouling," Smith said. "It would have been hard for them (to score). We had Webber covered pretty well."

It was a bizarre ending to a superb game.

"Chris said he heard someone holler to call timeout," Fisher said. "We talked about not having any timeouts (during the timeout with 46 seconds left), but apparently we didn't make it clear."

With 11 seconds left, it was up to Williams to finish off the title. Standing there with no other players around him in the cavernous Superdome, he hit both shots of the technical.

Fouled with eight seconds to go, Williams made two more free throws.

"I never could have imagined this," Williams said. "Every kid dreams about making the game-winning shot, but last year (during an up and down freshman year) this didn't seem possible."

North Carolina won its second NCAA title in the Superdome, the other coming in 1982. And like that 1982 game, when Georgetown's Fred Brown threw a pass to James Worthy in the final six seconds, the ending left some people wondering about what might have happened if Webber hadn't called time.

"Say we're lucky, yes," Smith said. "I've always said you have to be lucky to win the NCAA championship. Say we're fortunate. But it still says we're national champions."

Smith had endured criticism about winning only one NCAA title in his 32 years at North Carolina, despite countless all-America players and repeated Sweet 16 appearances.

"This talk about coach Smith not winning enough championships," Montross said, "had better stop. He's caught too much flak. It's not fair. We told him as soon as the game was over that this one was for him and the seniors."

In 1982, Smith's players wanted him to climb the ladder and snip the last thread of net. Instead, he stepped aside to allow senior guard Jimmy Black to cut the cords.

But in New Orleans, at his players' insistence, Smith cut the last threads.

Sullivan recalled the photo that began the season.

"I looked at it every day," Sullivan said. "I didn't really allow myself to think about winning the national championship until we won the East Regional. No one on this team thought it would be easy. But I looked at that picture a lot. *A lot.*"

Gary McCann was a writer at the Greensboro News & Record when he covered the 1993 tournament.

1994
DUKE PROVES NO HAZARD TO HOGS' TITLE RUN

By Bob Holt

After the Arkansas Razorbacks beat Michigan, 76-68, in Dallas to win the 1994 NCAA Midwest Regional, exchanged high-fives with President Clinton and cut down the nets, their Reunion Arena locker room seemed strangely subdued.

No one threw a bucket of ice water on coach Nolan Richard-

son. There were smiles, but no whooping or hollering. If you had walked in and didn't know better, you might have thought the Hogs had just beaten Alabama or LSU or another one of their Southeastern Conference foes.

"We've still got something to prove," sophomore forward Scotty Thurman said. "We want to play the last game of the season—and win it."

The Razorbacks did, thanks to Thurman's last-second heroics. His three-point basket with 50 seconds remaining in the game broke a 70-70 tie and propelled Arkansas to a 76-72 victory over Duke for the Hogs' first NCAA basketball championship.

Thurman now has a place in Final Four history, along with players such as Michael Jordan and Keith Smart, whose last-second shots lifted North Carolina (1982) and Indiana (1987) to national titles.

The Hogs followed presidential orders in putting the ball in Thurman's hands.

"I kept screaming to get the ball to Thurman," said Clinton, the former Arkansas governor and unabashed Razorback fan, who watched the game from a Charlotte Coliseum skybox. "He's a tremendous clutch player."

Thurman, who during the season hit game-winning three-pointers at Tennessee and LSU, saw the 35-second shot clock tick down to three seconds as junior point guard Corey Beck passed the ball to junior center Dwight Stewart.

Stewart, who hit 11 of 20 three-pointers in the NCAA tournament but was 0 of 5 against Duke, was looking for a game-winning three of his own when he caught Beck's pass at the top of the key. But Stewart fumbled the ball, so he passed it to Thurman on the wing.

Arkansas' Corliss Williamson went up for a close-up jumper as Duke's Cherokee Parks fell backward to the floor in a key second-half run by the Razorbacks. Williamson's 23 points and commanding play earned him the Most Outstanding Player award as Arkansas claimed the national championship.

"When the ball came to me," Thurman said, "I felt like the shot clock was going to run out. I had no choice but to put up the shot."

And Thurman figured he was due, considering he had missed his previous two attempts from the field.

"In practice, I hate it when I miss three in a row," he said. "I knew in the game I had missed my last two, so it was time to hit one."

Thurman's shot barely got over Duke forward Antonio Lang.

"His whole body was in my face," Thurman said.

Replays showed Lang's outstretched arm missed the ball by an inch or two.

"I still don't know how it went in," Lang said. "I was right there and I thought I could tip it. Obviously, I didn't get a hand on it.

We've made big shots to win games. I guess it was just Arkansas' turn to make a big shot."

The Blue Devils still had a chance to win their third NCAA championship in four years, but sophomore guard Chris Collins missed a three-pointer with 37 seconds left. The Razorbacks then clinched the victory with free throws by junior guards Clint McDaniel and Alex Dillard.

Arkansas overcame a 13-0 Duke run that put the Blue Devils ahead, 48-38, with 17 minutes to play. Richardson called timeout to rally the Razorbacks.

"Our guys know the fat lady hasn't sung with 17 minutes to play," Richardson said. "It's all about being on a mission."

Richardson told his players three things: "One, we were taking too many early shots; two, I wanted Big Nasty (all-American sophomore forward Corliss Williamson) to touch the ball before we took a shot; and three—most important—I told them they'd better get their butts after it on defense. We did all three."

The Razorbacks, who were led by Williamson's 23 points, tied the game at 52 and moved ahead, 62-57, but Duke came back to tie the game, 70-70, on all-American senior forward Grant Hill's three-point basket with 1:29 to play.

"That was a heavyweight championship bout," Richardson said. "My turn, your turn. My turn, your turn. My turn."

Duke coach Mike Krzyzewski said it was hard to be disappointed.

"It was a great game," he said. "Everybody won and nobody lost."

The Hogs held Hill to 12 points on 4-of-11 shooting from the field.

"Hill is their workhorse, and we tried to keep pestering him," Richardson said. "I think fatigue set in."

Several Razorbacks alternated guarding Hill.

"Every time I looked up," he said, "they had a different guy on me."

One player Hill probably didn't expect to see guarding him was Ken Biley, a senior forward who averaged 5.2 minutes during the season, but started against Duke as a reward for four years of service.

"I want to thank coach Richardson for allowing me the opportunity to go out there and see what it feels like to be on the court during the national championship game," said Biley, who played the first three minutes, in which Hill didn't score. "I wouldn't necessarily say I stopped (Hill), but I did have a good time out there. I played as hard as I possibly could, because deep down I knew this was my last opportunity.

"Once I settle down and get married and have a family, I can tell my kids, 'Hey, I guarded Grant Hill!' "

Arkansas was ranked No. 1 for nine weeks during the regular season, twice as long as any other team, and finished 31-3, including 14-2 in the Southeastern Conference to win its second regular-season conference title in three years.

Williamson was voted the Final Four's Most Outstanding Player by the media and was joined on the all-Final Four team by teammates Beck and Thurman, and the Blue Devils' Lang and Hill.

Richardson compared beating Duke in North Carolina to his first Tulsa team beating Syracuse in New York's Madison Square Garden to win the 1981 National

Invitation Tournament championship.

"When you beat a team in its own backyard, that's sweeter than any juice you'll ever drink," he said. "I thought it was a game between two of the smartest coaches in the country—I was one of them—and two talented basketball teams. They had three players with gold rings (for NCAA titles in 1991 and '92) and we had a bunch of young guys trying to keep them from getting another one and trying to get one for themselves."

Arkansas advanced to the championship game for the first time in five Final Four appearances with a 91-82 victory over Arizona in the semifinals.

The Wildcats led 67-62 with 8:02 to play, but the Razorbacks then applied their full-court pressure defense and went on a 12-0 run in a 2:04 span to move ahead 74-67 to take control of the game.

"That wasn't 40 minutes of

Duke senior Grant Hill kept his team alive, tying the game with less than two minutes to go on a three-point play. Hill ended his Duke career an all-time great in college basketball.

Arkansas coach Nolan Richardson yelled instructions from the bench (above), and Corey Beck (right) took a rebound, leaped high and passed back outside to restart the offense. Arkansas had been rated No. 1 in the nation for nine weeks during the regular season, but proof came in Charlotte, N.C., with the Razorbacks' No. 1 fan in attendance— President Bill Clinton.

hell," said Richardson, referring to his catch phrase to describe Arkansas' intense style. "That was eight minutes of torture. We had to go for the jugular at that point. We had no choice."

Williamson finished with 29 points, 13 rebounds and five assists.

"My teammates challenged me to take over," Williamson said, "and I love it when somebody makes a challenge to me."

When Williamson was double-teamed, he was able to find his teammates for baskets.

"He did a good job of finding the open people," Arizona coach Lute Olson said. "Most players lose their poise when they're doubled, but he didn't."

The Razorbacks had been focusing on going to the Final Four since ending the 1992-93 season with an 80-74 loss to North Carolina, the eventual NCAA champion, in the East regional semifinals at East Rutherford, New Jersey.

Two days after the loss to the Tar Heels, the Hogs were back on campus in Fayetteville playing pickup games in Barnhill Arena.

"We felt like we were cheated out of the rest of the season when we lost to North Carolina," Williamson said. "We felt like we should have kept playing. So, we went out and played in Barnhill the first chance we got."

The Razorbacks returned the nucleus of their Sweet 16 team, and added the missing pieces to the national championship puzzle with freshmen centers Darnell Robinson, Lee Wilson and Dillard, a three-point shooting specialist who hit an SEC-record 12 treys against Delaware State.

The 6-7 Williamson had been forced to play center as a freshman, but was able to work at power forward with the arrival of Robinson and Wilson,

both 6-11.

"We all felt if we had a big man, we could have won that game against North Carolina last year and gone to the Final Four," Williamson said before the Razorbacks played Arizona. "That's not a problem now."

Arkansas moved into Walton Arena in 1992 and went 16-0 at home, including a 120-68 pounding of Missouri, which then went 14-0 in the Big Eight Conference and advanced to the West regional final, where it lost to Arizona.

North Carolina A&T made things interesting in the Hogs' first-round game at Oklahoma City, but the Razorbacks used a late 18-2 run to pull away for a 94-79 victory.

Arkansas then literally fought off Georgetown—Thurman was ejected in the first half when he went on the court to try and break up a scuffle that broke out— 85-73 by hitting 61.4 percent from the field, a season-high by a Hoyas' opponent.

The Razorbacks advanced to familiar territory in Dallas, where they used to dominate the Southwest Conference tournament and also where they had won the 1990 Midwest regional to advance to the Final Four in Denver.

Tulsa took Arkansas to overtime in a regular-season matchup before the Hogs won, 93-91, on Williamson's short jumper. At Reunion Arena, however, the Golden Hurricane was no match for the Razorbacks, who won, 103-84, with Thurman and Williamson scoring 21 points each.

Arkansas then denied Michigan a third consecutive Final Four trip by making all the key plays in the last five minutes to win, 76-68. Williamson was held to 12 points but served as a

decoy much of the game, allowing Thurman and McDaniel to combine to hit seven-of-14 three-point attempts and Robinson to score on the inside. The 6-11 freshman center tallied 14 points and was named to the Midwest regional all-championship team.

"If we believed all the stats about Michigan, they'd be on their way to the Final Four," Richardson said. "But our guys believe in themselves. When Michigan came back, as we knew they would, we kept our composure and kept playing."

It was a big day for Richardson, who before the game was named the Naismith National Coach of the Year and after the victory gave Clinton a high-five and then hugged the president.

Bob Holt covers Arkansas from Fayetteville for the Arkansas Democrat-Gazette and has written of the Razorbacks' trips to Final Fours in 1990, 1994 and 1995.

1995

BRUINS ADD AN 11TH TITLE TO LEGACY

By Bud Withers

It has happened before, and it happened to UCLA and its coach, Jim Harrick. The winning of an NCAA basketball championship confers a glory onto its perpetrators far beyond the simple acts that may decide it—a missed shot, a fluky rebound, a hairline call on a foul.

So, too, with UCLA in 1995. This had been a team and a coach that couldn't seem to fulfill reasonable expectations, let alone

Fans who can't get tickets monitor the Final Four through CBS Television with play-by-play by Jim Nantz and analysis from Billy Packer (once a Final Four player at Wake Forest). CBS was awarded the Final Four rights in 1988. A contract signed in 1999 will take that network through the 2013 tournament.

UCLA's Charles O'Bannon leaped high to block a Razorback shot in 1995 as the Bruins made their first appearance in the Final Four in 15 years. It was a hard-fought game with one special spectator watching from the stands—John Wooden.

the ones attached to the Bruins' outlandish 10 national championships in the '60s and '70s under John Wooden.

UCLA had bottomed out of the tournament just a year before, giving up 112 points to Tulsa to lose in the first round. In 1991, again in the first, a 13th-seeded Penn State team dropped the Bruins.

Meanwhile, Harrick had made an intemperate remark in 1992, to the effect that if people wanted big-time results, he needed to be paid like Lute

Olson or Denny Crum.

But all that seemed to wash away with UCLA's ascent to the championship. In coaching his first Final Four team, Harrick handled gracefully the press inquiries about being a successor to Wooden. And his team got not only extraordinary play, but leadership from three seniors—Ed O'Bannon, Tyus Edney and George Zidek—plus contributions from some freshmen like J.R. Henderson and Toby Bailey who were just happy to be a part of things.

And so it was that on the night of April 3, the Bruins rented a limo in Seattle and got crazy, their race won. In the spotlight of college basketball, Harrick suddenly seemed very capable, and the Bruins were everything a champion should be: Resilient, captivating, classy.

The Bruin run through the tournament featured the near-miss and the full-bore blowout. It began innocently, in Boise, Idaho, against a backdrop that stole any attention from UCLA.

For one, the Bruins played in the last game of the day, in the Pacific time zone. They also were following the Indiana-Missouri game, when Hoosier coach Bob Knight made headlines during a postgame interview.

UCLA's opponent, Florida International, had made the tournament, despite an 11-18 record, by winning the Trans America Athletic Conference tournament. Its coach, former Mississippi and Texas coach Bob Weltlich, had already announced his resignation.

UCLA put to rest any notions of a Cinderella run by the Golden Panthers, breaking to a 20-point halftime lead and coasting to a 92-56 victory. Henderson had 16 points and Charles O'Bannon 14, but the game was more notable for every Bruin playing at least six minutes and the postgame jocularity of Weltlich, who said, "If anybody knows of any jobs out there, my number is …"

There was little to suggest UCLA would have any serious difficulty negotiating Missouri and thereby move on to Oakland, where it would have a big following in the regional.

What evolved was a game for the ages. Missouri took the fight straight to the Bruins, leading 42-34 at halftime, UCLA's largest deficit at the break all season. A familiar Bruin run in the second half seemed to make them comfortable, up six, but with Tiger guard Paul O'Liney having an unconscious shooting afternoon (nine of 13, five of six treys for 23 points), Missouri scratched ahead, 74-73, with 4.8 seconds left. The go-ahead basket came on guard Kendrick Moore's dish to Julian Winfield under the hoop.

All that remained was some of the most riveting 4.8 seconds in NCAA history. Cameron Dollar, the UCLA guard, inbounded to Tyus Edney and could only watch and implore silently: "Go, Tyus, go."

Edney wound a behind-the-back dribble that redirected him to the right. Ed O'Bannon, the all-American forward, shoved Winfield to clear space for himself. Still, Edney kept motoring.

"When I got around the free-throw line, I saw an opening," he said. "No guys were coming to take me."

Finally, Edney encountered Missouri forward Derek Grimm as he hurtled toward the goal from the right. Grimm raised his arms dead vertical, intent on not fouling. Edney cast up sort of a half-hook, half-layup, half-prayer from five feet away. It kissed the backboard and hit net just about the time the horn sounded.

After UCLA mobbed Edney and fell into delirium, the little guard remembered having seen Danny Ainge's five-second court-length drive to beat Notre Dame by one in a regional semifinal game in 1981.

"I've seen clips of that," said Edney. "I knew it could be done."

In Oakland, they simply dismantled a good Mississippi State

team that had won both at Arkansas and Kentucky. The Bulldogs couldn't match the Bruins' athleticism and facility for the running game and UCLA won, 86-67, after having a 65-29 lead midway through the second half.

That gave the Bruins a berth in the regional final against Connecticut, a team that earlier had been No. 1-ranked, and one seen as being as good—perhaps even better—at the running game.

But UCLA thought it detected a flaw in the Huskies' defense against the break and the Bruins continually took advantage with edges in numbers.

UCLA started quickly and led through most of the first half. Then Edney, having a monster tournament, struck again. Taking the ball in backcourt, a la Missouri, with 3.6 seconds left in the half, he blew downcourt, stopped at 25 feet and whistled in a trey at the buzzer to give the Bruins a 48-41 halftime lead.

In the second half, Connecticut stayed close, within four, six, eight, but it seemed like the most mountainous four, six, eight. The Huskies got 36 points from Ray Allen in a marvelous performance, but they simply couldn't stop UCLA's offense, which shot 62.5 percent.

At the finish, it was 102-96, UCLA, and the Bruins had made their deepest push into the tournament since their runnerup finish to Louisville in 1980.

The Bruins basked. They had won a trip to Seattle, where, on their February trip to play Washington, Harrick had asked the bus driver returning them to the hotel from a practice to detour to the Kingdome, just to send a little message.

The national semifinal game featured two programs of extreme contrast. It was the Bruins, most

of them from frenetic Los Angeles or nearby, against Oklahoma State's seven-foot Bryant "Big Country" Reeves, pride of Gans, Okla. It was UCLA's preference for the fast pace against the Cowboys' grinding, half-court approach.

"We've played that tempo before," insisted Dollar, the UCLA back-up point guard. "We know how."

It was 37-37 at halftime, and the Cowboys were playing at their speed. UCLA edged out by eight in the second half, but midway

Ed O'Bannon took control of the game in the second half, driving past Arkansas' Corliss Williamson on the way to the basket and to the Most Outstanding Player award.

The Bruins' victory was a sweet one for many, including MOP Ed O'Bannon, who climbed the traditional ladder to clip the nets and record the view from the top. For coach Jim Harrick, the hugs on the bench at game's conclusion were special.

through it, Reeves led Oklahoma State back to within 50-49.

Soon, it became Edney's game again. He drove for a layup around Reeves for a 64-61 UCLA lead with a little more than two minutes left, and the Bruins sealed an uneasy 74-61 victory with 10 free throws down the stretch.

Edney finished with 21 points and five assists. Little did the Bruins—and those anticipating a drag-race Arkansas-UCLA final game—know that his work in the tournament was done.

On a hell-bent drive to the basket against the Cowboys, Edney had fallen hard after an Oklahoma State foul. He played affectively the rest of the day, but that night, his right wrist swelled up, and while his Bruin teammates attended press conferences on Sunday, he was at the University of Washington, getting treatment for a sprain.

Belatedly, Edney was on the floor Monday night for warmups, but it was obvious he could not use the wrist. As if Arkansas, the defending national champion with the breakneck speed and the wilting pressure, needed any favors.

Edney started the game, but it was a courtesy. He played three minutes, and it was apparent he could not go. Dollar replaced him and was immediately stripped of the ball for a layup by the Hogs' Clint McDaniel.

"When I first came out there," admitted Dollar, "I was a little tense."

After an early 10-0 Arkansas blitz led to a 12-5 lead, Dollar and the Bruins—now only six deep in proven players—began warming to the game. UCLA beat the Razorbacks downcourt for points and Dollar was increasingly pressure-proof.

UCLA led 40-39 at halftime,

and quickly assumed control after the break. Ed O'Bannon, who had a dynamite game, powered in a rebound basket and with 16 minutes left, the Bruins led by eight.

But the question was, when would UCLA cave? Arkansas sent players out in waves. A year earlier, the Razorbacks had chased down Duke in the title game, and surely, UCLA's thinned—if immensely talented—numbers would be vulnerable as well.

There was one frail moment, when UCLA led only 67-63 with eight minutes left and Scotty Thurman, hero of the 1994 championship, cast up a long trey attempt for Arkansas. It bounded in and out, and UCLA nursed the lead back to eight with 4:06 left.

Whereas Bailey, the UCLA freshman guard, had been frustrated by the methodic Oklahoma State game, he was unshackled against Arkansas, scoring 26 points, including one emphatic, stratospheric slam that found its way to sports pages across the nation.

Ed O'Bannon was magnificent, with 30 points and 17 rebounds. The other component was UCLA's defense—center Zidek and no small amount of help—on Arkansas' 6-7, 250-pound all-American Corliss Williamson, held to a three-of-16 shooting night.

The Bruins thus completed circles. Edney had done so much to get them here, and now they finished his labor. Ed O'Bannon, the Final Four Most Outstanding Player, had begun his college career with a significant knee injury, and he ended it by kneeling to kiss the Kingdome court.

And there was Harrick, once considered too small a coach for this job. He now seemed much larger, his place in history, and

his team's, cemented.

Bud Withers has covered Northwest college sports for many years, first on the staff of the Eugene (Ore.) Register-Guard and most recently at the Seattle Times.

1996

KENTUCKY REACHES PINNACLE WITH SIXTH TITLE

By Rick Bozich

This is what they were saying about the University of Kentucky basketball team before the Wildcats touched down in the 1996 NCAA Final Four at Continental Airlines Arena: Can't win the big one. Haven't done anything remarkable in the Final Four since Jack "Goose" Givens was golden and Kyle Macy was wiping his socks at the free-throw line in 1978. You can depend upon the Wildcats to turn in one performance that gets them beat.

This is what they were saying about Kentucky coach Rick Pitino before he took a team into the Final Four for the third time since 1987: Can't win the big one. Didn't do anything remarkable in the Final Four with Providence in 1987 or with the Wildcats in 1993. Makes you wonder if you can win a championship playing his trademark shoot-the-three, press, press, press style.

This is what they were saying about a Kentucky team that started the season ranked first in the nation and carried that No. 1 ranking for part of the season: The preseason favorite rarely wins the title anymore. Too much pressure. Too many worry lines caused by all the expectations. Better to slip through a side door and get the job done when nobody is expecting perfection. Anything but that preseason kiss-of-death No. 1 ranking, please.

Then the Kentucky basketball team, the seventh team Pitino put together in Lexington, went to East Rutherford, N.J. They dispatched Massachusetts, one of two teams to defeat them during the regular season, 81-74, in the national semifinals. Then they outlasted, outplayed and outfought Syracuse, 76-67, in the championship game.

They won Kentucky's sixth national title and Pitino's first. They answered all the questions, all the skeptics and all troubles.

They did it with pressing and three-point shooting and inside play and poise and balance and unselfishness like we hadn't seen in the college game in many years. They did it in a season when they were supposed to do it, never entering any arena, including the one in East Rutherford, through the side door.

Any questions?

The Wildcats won 34 of 36 games. Nobody beat them during the regular-season portion of Southeastern Conference play. Their average margin of victory in six NCAA tournament games was more than 21 points. They were ranked No. 1 during the preseason and during four other polls during the year. And despite all the expectations, they never stopped smiling.

"We had fun from Day One," Pitino said. "I've been asked a hundred times about the pressure of having to win. I told the players, 'You can't say there is no pressure. You have it. I have it.'

"I told them, 'If you're worried about it, if you have fear of fail-

ure, if it gets you nervous, it's bad pressure and you're not prepared.' "

A great team that had a great time—beginning in August 1995, when this Kentucky team was put together during a preseason trip to Italy. That's where the Wildcats learned that Anthony Epps would emerge as the team's point guard, that senior guard Tony Delk would be unstoppable on the perimeter, that sophomore forward Antoine Walker would emerge as Pitino's go-to guy, that senior Walter McCarty could play forward or center, that center Mark Pope, the team's third sen-

ior, would step forward as a dependable leader and that all the other important pieces would fit together.

It was in Italy, where the Wildcats won four of five games, that Pitino experimented with a variety of lineups. It was also in Italy where Pitino showed the valuable ability to deflect the expectations that had started building upon his team moments after the Wildcats had been upset by North Carolina in the championship game of the 1995 Southeast regional in Birmingham, Ala.

It was in Italy where Pitino and his wife, Joanne, had the

Kentucky guard Tony Delk scored a layup on his way to a 24-point game and the Most Outstanding Player award. Rick Pitino rebuilt the Wildcats into a national champion, winning Kentucky's sixth title, second only to UCLA. Another title would be added before the century ended.

As the Wildcats circled around, Rick Pitino accepted the 1996 trophy with mascots, kids and television cameras all in attendance.

good fortune to meet Pope John Paul II at The Vatican. As Pitino later told the story, and kept telling it during the many speeches he made around the state, he asked if he could kiss the Pope's ring. The Pope complied. Then the Pope asked the Kentucky coach if he could see his ring.

"I'm sorry," Pitino said. "But I don't have a ring."

That tells you the enormity of the expectations the Wildcats lived with during the 1995-96 season. They started the year in mid-November holding the nation's No. 1 ranking and then rallying from an 11-point deficit to defeat Maryland, 96-84, at the Hall of Fame Tip-Off Classic in Springfield, Mass.

So much for perfection. The Wildcats lost the top ranking the next time they played. All-American center Marcus Camby stopped them with a 32-point, nine-rebound performance, leading Massachusetts to a 92-82

upset victory in Auburn Hills, Mich. What was surely a jarring moment for Kentucky fans turned out to be the best thing Pitino could have written into the Wildcats' script. Just ask him if the defeat helped him get the attention of his players.

"If we win that game, we don't win the national championship," Pitino said after the season. "That loss taught us more about our team than any win on our schedule."

They would not be beaten again until they faced Mississippi State in the championship game of the SEC tournament at the Louisiana Superdome. That 84-73 Mississippi State victory reminded the nation of two things—that Mississippi State was supremely talented, which the Bulldogs proved by winning the Southeast regional and making the Final Four; and that Kentucky was guaranteed nothing when the 64-team tournament field was finally announced.

The Wildcats began their tournament run at Reunion Arena in Dallas. Getting 24 points from McCarty, 22 from Delk and non-stop applause from mega-fan actress and Kentucky alum Ashley Judd, the Wildcats inflated a 47-41 halftime lead into a 110-72 victory over San Jose State. It was Walker, with 21 points and 11 rebounds, who carried the Wildcats past Virginia Tech, 84-60, in the second round, providing clues that every night there would be another hero.

In Minneapolis, where the Wildcats met Utah and all-American forward Keith Van Horn in the semifinals of the Midwest regional at the Metrodome, it was time for Epps to prove precisely how underrated he was. Epps drilled three three-point field goals, and Derek Anderson added 18 points as the Wildcats spurted away from the Utes for a 56-34 halftime lead and a 101-70 victory. "If we played them 90 more games, we would probably lose 89 more times," Utah coach Rick Majerus said.

Now the world wondered if Wake Forest, which had edged Louisville in the Midwest semifinals, was the team that could stop Kentucky. The Demon Deacons were led by all-American center Tim Duncan. Camby had destroyed the Wildcats around the basket in November. Maybe Duncan could do the same thing in March.

Wrong. Wrong. Wrong.

Duncan shook loose for only three field-goal attempts in the first half. He made only 2 of 7 shots all afternoon. Kentucky raced to a 38-19 lead and cruised over the ACC tournament champs, 83-63. This time it was Delk's turn to blaze, and he torched the Demon Deacons with 25 points. For that he was named the Most Outstanding Player in the regional.

Finally, the Final Four. As fate scripted it, another crack at Massachusetts, which met Kentucky in the second national semifinal game after Syracuse defeated Mississippi State.

This time Kentucky showed it had learned how to defend Camby. He scored only eight points in the first half, making only 3 of 9 shots. Camby finished with 25, but many of them came after the Wildcats surged to a 15-point lead in the second half.

Massachusetts cut Kentucky's lead to 63-60, but the Wildcats pushed their lead back to 68-60. Minuteman guard Edgar Padilla hit a 22-foot jumper to pull Massachusetts within 73-70 in the final minute-and-a-half. But two free throws by Mark Pope and a slam by Walker gave Kentucky an 81-74 victory—and its date with destiny. Once again it was Delk delivering a team-high 20 points, even though he missed more than two minutes with leg cramps.

"We made a couple of turnovers down the stretch that I wish we wouldn't have made, but we maintained our composure," Epps said. "The key was that we had confidence in each other that we would win the game."

In the championship game, it was something old and something new that carried the Wildcats to their first national title in 18 years. Something old was Delk. The veteran guard from Brownsville, Tenn., delivered six three-point shots in the first half, pushing Kentucky to a 42-33 halftime lead. Something new was Ron Mercer, a freshman forward from Nashville. He came off the bench to score a career-high 20 points and help Kentucky withstand a furious rally by Syracuse, which rode the 29 points and 10

rebounds of rugged senior forward John Wallace.

In fact, the Orangemen cut Kentucky's lead to 64-62 with 4:46 to play. But McCarty came through with a follow-up and Anderson drained a three.

Although the Wildcats shot only 38 percent from the field, they made 12 of 27 three-point shots, getting seven from Delk and three from Mercer.

"Not that many players get that many open looks," said Delk, who was also named the Most Outstanding Player of the Final Four. "If I wasn't penetrating and looking for them, it wouldn't have been possible. But when you shoot so many threes in practice and you're open, you take them. That's the way we play."

"We won our last two games in an untypical Kentucky style," Pitino said. "We just bumped and grinded it out …"

Syracuse coach Jim Boeheim, who once employed Pitino as an assistant coach, was impressed by the new national champions.

"Everybody said we needed to play a perfect game to beat them," he said. "I didn't think that. But we had to play a little better than we did."

You want to talk about a team effort. In six NCAA tournament games, three different Kentucky players led the team in scoring. Four players—Delk, Walker, McCarty and Anderson—averaged double figures. Mercer contributed his breakout game against Syracuse. Pope played the physical defense against Camby and Duncan. Epps played six NCAA games with an astounding 38 assists and only five turnovers. The list goes on and on, making the Wildcats one of the deepest championship teams in NCAA history.

Kentucky's average victory margin in six NCAA games was

21.5 points, fourth-best in NCAA history. Their 89.17 scoring average ranked as the sixth-best in tournament history. And the 34-2 record reigned as the school's best since the 1953-54 squad finished 25-0.

"There was an incredible amount of pressure on us, but that just made it even sweeter to win it all," reserve guard Jeff Sheppard said. "Everyone expected us to win it, and we did."

The victory had to be particularly sweet for Pitino. No longer would he have to tell the joke about the Pope and the ring. No longer would he have to hear the jabs about being a "championship coach" whose only championship was the SEC tournament. And no longer would he have to answer questions about whether his frenetic style of play could hold together for six difficult games in March.

"We're like the Green Bay Packers," Pitino said. "Our basketball team belongs to the whole state of Kentucky."

Rick Bozich has covered Final Fours since his days as a student and writer for the Indiana student newspaper. At The (Louisville) Courier-Journal, he has covered many sports and is now a sports columnist.

1997
ARIZONA CATS CRADLE FIRST NCAA TITLE

By Corky Simpson

Faith slam-dunked the skeptics at the 1997 NCAA Division I Men's Basketball Championship. Not once, mind you, but three times.

Arizona guard Mike Bibby (10) shot a jumper over Kentucky center Nazr Mohammed (13) as two teams of Wildcats clawed for the 1997 championship.

Arizona, perhaps the most unlikely champion ever, became the first team to defeat three No. 1 seeds when it upset tradition-rich Kentucky, 84-79 in overtime at the RCA Dome in Indianapolis.

It gave Arizona a national championship in its third advance to the Final Four under coach Lute Olson. The others were in 1988 and 1994.

Nobody could have predicted it.

Nothing about the Wildcats' trip to the tournament gave the slightest hint they would proceed through the championship. But like a fierce summer wind burning across the Sonoran Desert,

Olson's kids made believers of a nation of basketball fanatics.

Kansas, the No. 1 ranked team in the nation, fell to these Wildcats on March 21 at the Birmingham-Jefferson Civic Center in Alabama. Clawing their way to the Final Four, the Wildcats then toppled North Carolina. And in the title game, they beat their more illustrious Wildcat opponent, Kentucky, in overtime. Just like that! Three top seeds fell to a bunch of sprouts.

Arizona started a freshman point guard (Mike Bibby), a sophomore center (A.J. Bramlett), and three juniors (shooting guard Miles Simon, wingman Michael Dickerson and power forward Bennett Davison).

"This is one tough group of Cats," said Olson, his famous silver thatch of hair hidden by a "National Champions" ball cap slightly askew. "All along, we tried to impress upon them that the strongest will survive, that the toughest group of players out there would get the job done."

The final game was a microcosm of the season.

There was a point when it looked as if the Arizona bubble might burst. Kentucky had forced overtime when Anthony Epps hit a three-pointer with 13 seconds left. Shots by Simon and Bibby had rimmed out.

"When Kentucky tied it up, though, I looked in everybody's eyes and I knew we'd come up with a victory," said Arizona guard Jason Terry, one of the best sixth men in America.

"Coach Olson told us that the strong would survive."

Only three and a half weeks earlier, though, there were those who wondered if Arizona would even be invited to the championship. The Wildcats were 19-9 and had just lost both games on a trip to the San Francisco Bay

Area, 81-80 at Stanford and 79-77 at California. But Olson saw things differently.

"Those are two very tough teams, extremely hard to beat on their home courts," he said. "We had chances to win both games, and I think that's a 'positive' we can take into the postseason."

Just the same, the losses dropped Arizona to fifth place in the Pacific-10 Conference, with an 11-7 record. Ahead of the Wildcats in the final standings were champion UCLA (15-3) and three schools who tied for second place with 12-6 records, Stanford, California and Southern California.

Simon, the soul if not the heart of the team, had sat out the first 11 games, on academic suspension. When the team rolled up an 8-3 record during that time, at least one media critic, wandering down an unpaved side road, speculated that the Wildcats might be better off without Simon. Olson laughed out loud at the suggestion. Simon went on to become the NCAA championship's Most Outstanding Player.

For Arizona in 1997, the way to the NCAA tournament was nowhere near as amazing as the stay there. The "toughness" Olson spoke of was never more evident than in the opening round, against a splendid South Alabama team. With less than four minutes left in that first-round game, Arizona trailed South Alabama by 10 points. Somehow, the Wildcats rallied to win, 65-57.

From that point on, there was no stopping Olson's version of the "Desert Swarm" a nickname given to a particularly rugged Arizona football team earlier in the decade.

College of Charleston, a fearsome bunch of outstanding ath-

The moment of celebration was sweet for junior guard Miles Simon, who left the court with the game ball—not officially awarded—and the Most Outstanding Player award, which was official. Arizona coach Lute Olson and his wife walked off with their own souvenir, another game ball.

letes, followed South Alabama. But Arizona won again at The Pyramid in Memphis, 73-69.

Then came the upset that stunned the nation: Arizona's 85-82 victory over top-ranked Kansas. If it wasn't the biggest win in the history of Arizona basketball, it was the greatest effort.

Kansas trailed by 13 with 3:28 remaining but put on a finishing kick that cut Arizona's lead to a single point, 83-82, with 21 seconds left. But a pair of free throws by Bibby, the coolest and probably best Wildcat freshman since Sean Elliott, clinched the shocking upset.

"This wasn't the biggest win," Olson said, perhaps propheti-

cally. "The biggest win is the one that gets you to the Final Four."

Two nights later, Arizona toppled a rugged, physical Providence team, 96-92, and advanced to the Final Four. North Carolina fell on March 29, 66-58, setting up the national championship game against the Kentucky Wildcats.

Cornell coach Scott Thompson, a long-time assistant to Olson, said he thought Arizona's national championship began one cold, dismal night 14 years earlier, in Kansas City. Olson was coaching Iowa at the time and Thompson was on his staff.

The Hawkeyes had just lost a heartbreaker to Villanova, 55-54,

in the Sweet 16 at Kemper Arena in Kansas City. Into the Iowa locker room came a fellow named Cedric Dempsey. He said he was from Arizona and wanted to talk to Lute Olson.

Dempsey, later the president of the NCAA, was at the time Arizona's athletics director. He was looking for a basketball coach, a man to take over a team that had just gone 4-24 for the season, 1-17 in the tough Pacific-10 Conference.

Thompson said when Olson strolled into the Iowa basketball offices a week or so later and announced he had decided to accept the offer at Arizona, "I thought he had lost his marbles."

Seven Pacific-10 championships and three trips to the Final Four later, Olson was on top of the basketball world with an NCAA championship. His decision was validated.

"It is Lute's vision that has built the program," Thompson said.

"I went with him from Iowa, and when we first got to Tucson, honestly, I could not believe a program could be so terrible. I remember going with Lute to dormitories and fraternities, trying to get support from the students. When we first got there, people looked at us like we were crazy when we told them what our goals were. They told us they took recruits to hockey games rather than basketball games, because there was some excitement at hockey. The Arizona baseball team always drew more fans than basketball. The first season, at our games, there couldn't have been more than 3,000 people in an arena that seats nearly 15,000.

"Lute and I looked at each other like, 'What did we get ourselves into?' Now look at it: National champions!"

Olson's family-approach to his program had a lot to do with winning the NCAA title.

"When we talk with the team on what makes champions, the first thing we discuss is family," Olson said. "Trust is the second, and team-support is right there, too.

"The first thing I do each day is check to see how Kenny Lofton (Cleveland Indians outfielder and former Arizona basketball player) did in baseball ... how Sean and Steve and Jud and Damon and Khalid (Reeves) did in the National Basketball Association. They are still Wildcats. That never ends."

Kentucky coach Rick Pitino

NCAA Senior Vice President Tom Jernstedt has presided over the recent evolution of the Final Four.

said Arizona's victory was no fluke. "This is a great basketball team," he said. "Arizona just got better and better as the season and the tournament wore on."

It was a six-game winning streak in the NCAA, of course, that launched the Wildcats into the winner's circle. But interestingly enough, that was the longest winning streak of the season for Arizona.

Corky Simpson began covering Final Fours in the 1950s as a sportswriter at the Carthage (Mo.) Evening Press. For the past 26 years, he has covered college sports at Arizona and many NCAA events as the sports-columnist for the Tucson Citizen.

1998

KENTUCKY GRABS TITLE NO. 7

By Janet Graham

The first time Scott Padgett heard that his University of Kentucky team wasn't going to win the 1998 national title was in the summer of 1997. Padgett was at the USA Basketball tryout camp when Maryland's Laron Profit strolled by and delivered the challenge to Padgett and Nazr Mohammed.

"What are you going do next year when your two best players are gone, Ron Mercer and coach Pitino?" Profit said, taunting the two Kentucky players.

The usually loquacious Padgett didn't have much of a comeback. He and the Wildcats saved all those for later. But to himself, he thought, "We'll just see about that."

It's hard to think of Kentucky in underdog terms. With six play-

ers on the roster who had not played the previous season, they did not have the embarrassment of future NBA riches they had the previous two seasons, and they had to break in new coach Tubby Smith.

In the most endearing way possible, the "Comeback Cats" made a scintillating run to the national championship, capturing each game in heart-stopping fashion in an NCAA tournament filled with a number of intriguing games.

"I think the way we did it was so special," Smith said. "That's what I always think about when the subject of the championship comes up."

When the season began, there was much consternation in Kentucky. It had taken a while for Rick Pitino and his brash New York style to work their way into the hearts of the fans, but eventually they couldn't get enough of the frenetic, high-powered basketball his teams created. Pitino capped his storybook run by leading the Wildcats to their first national title in 17 years in 1996, then returning the Wildcats to the title game the following season.

Then, the event many fans considered inevitable happened. Pitino departed for a return to the NBA and the East Coast. With Pitino gone to the Boston Celtics and a new coach in Smith, fans figured it might be a few seasons before the Wildcats would be holding a national championship trophy above their heads again.

Although Smith had been a Pitino assistant and liked some of the principles of Pitino's coaching, a transition period was inevitable because Smith definitely had his own style.

On the court, Smith implemented the ball-line defense, a

The 1998 championship game featured surprising Utah and its picturesque coach Rick Majerus (above), against Kentucky, led by coach Tubby Smith. Guard Jeff Sheppard (left) drove for the basket and two of his 16 points against Utah. Kentucky took control in the second half, surprising the nation with a title crafted by Smith.

more conservative style than Pitino's full-court press. Although Pitino's teams were characterized by a deep bench, there was more of a star system bolstered by role players. Smith likes a balanced attack and always tells his players to make the extra pass. At practice and off the court, Smith's personality was less high-octane than that of the excitable Pitino. But Smith was more hands-on when it came to checking up on the players' classwork and whether or not they were making his strict curfew times.

There were adjustments, but the players eventually bought into what Smith was preaching.

Before the season began, the Wildcats would hear nothing of the term "rebuilding year."

This was a group of players unaccustomed to anything but a Final Four appearance. But an early season blowout loss (89-74) to Arizona in the Maui Invitational was a wake-up call for the Wildcats.

The run for the title (and here, a loose ball) sent Kentucky's Scott Padgett (34) and Jeff Sheppard (15) racing to retain possession. But the real possession of the night was the trophy, which belonged to first-year head coach Tubby Smith. Smith watched the clock tick off the final seconds of the game, and players Jamaal Magloire and Heshimu Evans savored the winning moment.

Kentucky followed the Arizona loss with eight straight wins and it appeared Smith and his staff were making headway with installing their own variations on the schemes that had worked so well for Pitino.

But a shocking December loss in Rupp Arena to unranked Louisville proved just how far the Wildcats had to go. That loss shook up the team and its coach. Smith started making some drastic changes. He shuffled the starting lineup by replacing

sophomore center Jamaal Magloire with Mohammed, a 6-10 junior, and the team began to come together.

Mohammed's inside scoring skills were beginning to dominate the Southeastern Conference in a way that would earn him honorable mention all-America honors by season's end.

As the SEC season opened, Kentucky was still a heavy favorite and eventually proved it by going unbeaten on the road in the league. That included some

compelling victories, such as Smith's first trip back to Athens, Ga., since he left the head coaching post and his eldest son, G.G., Georgia's starting point guard, behind for the position at Kentucky.

In an incredibly emotional night for Tubby, his wife Donna, who wore the colors of both schools, G.G. and middle brother Saul, Kentucky's backup point guard, Kentucky won, 90-79.

Kentucky breezed through the SEC tournament, beating Georgia, Arkansas and South Carolina by an average of 18 points per game. It was the Wildcats' sixth SEC tournament title in seven years.

A few hours after the SEC championship game, when the NCAA tournament draw was announced, Kentucky found out it would be coming right back to Atlanta and the Georgia Dome to play its first two rounds of the NCAA tournament. Undefeated in the building with a 7-0 record, including two SEC titles, the Wildcats were ecstatic at their draw, even as a No. 2 seed.

Kentucky continued on its roll, powering past South Carolina State, 82-67, in the first round and Saint Louis, 88-61, in the second round.

Then it was on to St. Petersburg and Tropicana Field, the baseball stadium turned basketball arena. In a matchup of two of college basketball's perennial power programs, Kentucky dominated UCLA, 94-68, in the South regional semifinals. But it was nearly overlooked in the race to hype the final—Kentucky-Duke.

It lived up to every expectation as the Wildcats came back from a 17-point deficit with just over nine minutes left, thanks to three-pointers by Kentucky natives Mills and Padgett. Again the game came down to the final play with Duke having the chance to win it with 4.5 seconds left. Smith elected not to guard the inbounds pass, just as Pitino hadn't in 1992. This time, however, it worked as William Avery's shot bounced harmlessly off the backboard. Kentucky was headed back to the Final Four for the third straight year with an 86-84 win.

In San Antonio, the Comeback Cats lived up to their now widely known reputation for heart-pounding escapes. Against Stanford in the national semifinals, the game was tied at 73 at the end of regulation. Kentucky scored the first five points of the extra period and held off the Cardinal to win, 86-85, in overtime and become the first team since UCLA in 1973 to reach its third straight championship game.

Again in the national final, Kentucky fell behind, 41-31, at halftime against a valiant effort by Utah. But mid-season 6 a.m. conditioning drills paid off in the final five minutes as the Utes failed to make a field goal, missing 11 consecutive attempts. Kentucky held on for the 78-69 victory and the school's seventh national championship.

This ice-water-in-their-veins performance had become almost routine during the second half of the season. In games decided by 10 points or less, Kentucky was 10-3 on the season. In games decided by three points or less, the Wildcats were 7-1.

"All year long, I felt like the team for us to beat was going to be Arizona," Padgett said. "Then they fell. And then I'm thinking, we're going to have to beat North Carolina and then they fell. It was like all these little things kept happening and it made me think we were the team of destiny."

The most memorable sight in

the Alamodome after the game was the impromptu celebration by the Wildcats as they hoisted their first-year coach onto their shoulders and carried him off the court. It was as good a piece of evidence as any of the continuity of the Big Blue dynasty. This wasn't about a coach or a player leading the team where they wanted to go. It was about a program where winning transcends the change of power.

Nearly every major player on the 1997-98 team had been through some sort of crisis in his Kentucky career. Sheppard was forced to redshirt in 1996-97 because of the overload of talent. Mills, a walk-on, endured almost three seasons of sitting on the bench. Turner sat on the bench the entire 1996 national championship game against Syracuse. Mohammed was put through Pitino's version of Weight Watchers, dropping 70 pounds while Pitino forced him to play on the junior varsity team as a freshman. Magloire lost his starting job to Mohammed at the start of the season. Allen Edwards lost his mother to breast cancer right before the SEC tournament. Heshimu Evans, who had been a star at Manhattan before transferring to Kentucky, was relegated to the role of sixth man. Saul Smith had to endure the chants of "Daddy's boy" from opponents' fans and the insults of the talk-show callers around the Commonwealth.

Smith made them believe that the team was the bond that could not be broken. As Turner said, Smith was the "MVP" of the team.

Janet Graham covered four Final Fours and two championship Kentucky teams in 1993, '96, '97 and '98 for the Cincinnati/Kentucky Post. As a sports writer she has covered a variety of

sports, including tennis and the 1990 baseball playoffs. She is also a backup Benglas beat reporter. Today she writes primarily feature stories for the Cincinnati/Kentucky Post.

1999
CONNECTICUT
PERSISTENCE
PAYS OFF

By Ken Davis

"We shocked the world!"

That's what point guard Khalid El-Amin screamed at a national television audience as the buzzer sounded on Connecticut's 77-74 victory over Duke in the national championship game at Tropicana Field in St. Petersburg, Fla. That was the delirious emotion as the Huskies won one of the most intensely fought championship games.

But before the Huskies could reach that plateau they had to wind through a maze of obstacles that began a year earlier. Along the way they encountered disappointment, flirted with perfection, confronted self doubts, lost a special friend, lifted an enormous monkey off their coach's back, and finally held off a rival who was responsible for so much of their heartache.

"To beat someone like Mike Krzyzewski and the Duke basketball team, I couldn't be prouder," Connecticut coach Jim Calhoun said. "Our kids had done so much for us, the only thing we needed to tell them was what they needed to do to beat a great team. They did it to perfection."

It was that type of year for the Huskies, who finished the season 34-2. In this unsettled age of col-

Connecticut guard Ricky Moore (21) scored a second-half layup as the Huskies upset the No. 1 ranked Duke Blue Devils for their first championship. Connecticut beat Ohio State in the semifinals to reach its goal.

lege basketball, Connecticut kept together all the basic ingredients for a winner—and just barely missed perfection. Richard Hamilton, the Big East Player of the Year, was a pure scorer and clutch performer. There was Ricky Moore, a senior playing the defensive specialist role that is so important to Calhoun's system. El-Amin was the ball-han-

dler and the engine that made things run. Jake Voskuhl played center like a goalie protecting the net. Kevin Freeman quietly pounded away at power forward, doing the dirty work that was part of Connecticut's blue-collar work ethic.

Calhoun recruited and planned this team with the Final Four in mind. There was no

doubt when it came time to take aim on the final destination.

The process had started a year earlier, in the losing locker room at the East regional final at the Greensboro (N.C.) Coliseum. It was March 21, 1998, and the Huskies had lost to North Carolina, 75-64, ending a 32-5 season, just shy of the Final Four—again.

This was the third time in the decade the journey for Calhoun and Connecticut ended one step from the Final Four. Calhoun was gaining the reputation as "Greatest Coach Never to Reach the Final Four," but that thought didn't enter his mind in Greensboro. He looked around the locker room and saw a young and talented team that could return all of its starters and would add some needed depth the following year.

"I want you to remember the hurt," Calhoun told his team. "Remember the pain. Keep it. Remember how it feels. You don't want to feel that way again."

The Huskies held on to Calhoun's words throughout the summer and cherished them on an August exhibition tour to England and Israel. Hamilton, who injured his right foot during tryouts for the World Championships in July, didn't make the trip. But there's no doubt the early work gave the Huskies a head start on their chemistry and a chance to develop their depth.

"The week we practiced before going to London, we set goals out," Moore said. "We were more into making it to the Final Four but, most importantly, we wanted to win a national championship. We felt we had the guys to do it."

The Huskies were rewarded with the No. 1 seed in the West region, and what seemed to be a favorable draw.

"From the day Connecticut lost in Greensboro, everybody said, 'Well, they'll be back next year. They're good enough,'" said Big East Commissioner Mike Tranghese. "They probably played with as much pressure as any team that's ever played in this conference. They've handled it very well. They've dealt with all the challenges"

In Denver, the Huskies posted easy victories over Texas-San Antonio, 91-66, and New Mexico, 78-56, and advanced to the Sweet 16 for the seventh time since 1990.

Two games away from the Final Four, Connecticut moved on to Phoenix along with No. 5 seed Iowa, No. 6 Florida and No. 10 Gonzaga. The pressure intensified.

"I'm no better or worse a coach than I was last week," Calhoun said. That became his theme, as he tried to deflect the attention away from his team's quest for the Final Four.

But the motivation was there, and so was the opportunity. Connecticut handled Iowa, 78-68, in Tom Davis' final appearance as coach of the Hawkeyes. That left Gonzaga, Cinderella of the tournament.

Stanford, the No. 2 seed, had fallen to Gonzaga the week before. That prompted a call to Voskuhl from his Stanford buddies Tim Young and Ryan Mendez.

"Look out, they're real good," was the message to Voskuhl.

With El-Amin in early foul trouble, Gonzaga looked even more imposing. But Moore, who wasn't about to let Connecticut fall short of its preseason goals, took charge on both ends of the floor and kept the Huskies in the game. And after Gonzaga took a 41-37 lead in the second half, the Huskies won the game on the backboards.

"It came down to a matter of heart," said Freeman, who had 15 rebounds. "I think we really underestimated their inside play in the first half. Then it was a matter of winning the game or losing."

Hamilton scored 21 points as the Huskies defeated Gonzaga, 67-62. As the buzzer sounded, El-Amin embraced Calhoun and kissed him on the cheek.

Finally Four. There were tears all around as the Huskies cut down the nets in Phoenix. Co-captain Rashamel Jones snuck up on his coach and emptied a cooler of ice water on Calhoun's head and back.

The Connecticut coach, who for years said it didn't matter if he ever reached the Final Four, broke down and cried with his team before the Huskies left Phoenix. A mellow smile broke across his face.

Before the Huskies met Ohio State in their national semifinal game, Calhoun shook hands with Tranghese.

"It's not enough just to get here," Tranghese told Calhoun. "You've got to try and win. That's what this is about. You don't get here that often."

The Huskies, comfortable with their success, turned to the usually reliable components for a 64-58 victory over Ohio State. Hamilton scored a game-high 24 points; El-Amin had 18 points and six assists. Moore, Connecticut's defensive specialist all season, held Ohio State's all-America guard Scoonie Penn to 3-for-13 shooting from the field.

"I think they're the best team, probably, in the country," Penn said.

Even though the Huskies had spent more weeks at No. 1 than Duke during the regular season, there weren't many who shared Penn's feelings. Calhoun didn't mind. This is when he could turn the underdog role to his favor.

Instead of a grueling two-hour workout the day before the game, the Huskies held a walk-through and the coaches handed over a game plan.

The first key was doubling

Connecticut's Ricky Moore left the court after the last minute and coach Jim Calhoun cradled the trophy moments later. The celebration was one of the tournament's most enthusiastic.

down defensively on Blue Devils center Elton Brand. Voskuhl
and Freeman had been playing
this type of defense together for
so long, they knew exactly what
each other was going to do.
Connecticut kept it simple.
Brand, the national Player of
the Year, was held to 15 points
on eight shots.

Throughout the season, opponents and observers alike mar-
veled at Duke's depth. But

Connecticut's bench flexed its
muscles. The Huskies got mis-
take-free contributions from
Souleymane Wane, Albert Mour-
ing, Edmund Saunders and Jones
as Connecticut's bench outscored
Duke's, 17-8.

The Huskies never had an
offensive lull. At the end of the
game, it was Duke that was
panicking, rushing shots, turning the ball over and playing
like the challenger instead of

the champion.

Connecticut's final key was to
keep pressure on guard William
Avery and make Trajan Langdon
handle the ball. Moore did that to
perfection, especially on the final
two possessions of the game—
both of which resulted in Langdon turnovers.

When Moore forced Langdon
to travel with Connecticut leading, 75-74, the Huskies could
taste victory.

"It came down to crunch time, him against me," Moore said. "He tried a spin move and I was right there."

El-Amin was quickly fouled and hit two free throws to make it 77-74. Duke raced up the floor but Langdon fell down and lost his dribble as the buzzer sounded.

"I just picked that ball up and held it," Jones said. "And it was a great, great feeling."

After 14 ties and eight lead changes, Connecticut became the first team since Texas Western in 1966 to win the championship in its first Final Four appearance. And the Huskies did it against a Duke team that had blocked their path three times in the NCAA tournament—including twice in the 1990s.

"You really can't describe the feeling," Hamilton said.

Ken Davis covers Connecticut sports for the Hartford Courant.

2000

IT'S ALL ABOUT PLACEMATS

By Billy Reed

The road to the 2000 national championship began with placemats.

In 1996, when second-year Michigan State Tom Izzo was trying to convince Mateen Cleaves, Morris Peterson and A.J. Granger to cast their lots with the Spartans, he always had special placemats at each recruiting dinner.

Each mat was tailored to a specific player's personality. They included photos, fictitious career stats and predictions of stardom in East Lansing.

For example, Granger's placemat included a headline: "Granger makes buzzer-beater against Kentucky as Michigan State wins NCAA crown."

But as Granger told writer Steve Grinczel of the Saginaw News, he thought the mats were rather cheesy. "Yeah, right," Granger remembers telling himself. "What can this Tom Izzo possibly know?"

Yet Granger, a power forward, signed with the Spartans, as did two products of the bleak industrial city of Flint—Cleaves, a highly recruited point guard, and Peterson, a late-blooming small forward. Their careers didn't exactly get off to the start they envisioned.

As freshmen, they belonged to a Spartan team that was eliminated in the second round. Of the NIT, that is.

Said Cleaves, "That was the lowest point of my career. There's nothing wrong with the tournament (NIT), but it was tough to sit in front of the television and watch the teams in the NCAA tournament. All the media attention they get and how much fun it is and the smiles on the players' faces. And I said to myself, 'I'm going to play in the NCAA tournament. I'm not going to the NIT anymore.'"

And he didn't. Before Cleaves' sophomore year, the Spartans added another product of Flint, shooting guard Charlie Bell.

The media dubbed Cleaves, Peterson and Bell the "Flintstones," but they really were the cornerstones of a team that brought the Spartans their greatest glory since Earvin "Magic" Johnson led Michigan State to the 1979 national title.

In their final three years, Cleaves, Peterson and Granger led the Spartans to victory in more than 80 percent of their

games. They won three Big Ten regular-season titles and two Big Ten tournament championships.

Then, after being eliminated by Duke in the 1999 national semifinals, they all came back as seniors to lead the Spartans to the university's second NCAA title.

"The night we lost to Duke, we were down," Cleaves said, "but we still had some guys who felt that we had accomplished something just by getting to the Final Four. But Antonio stood up and said, 'Hey, learn from this. Don't feel like you've accomplished something until you've won it all.' And I talked to the guys and said we've got to get hungry. We can't just want to get to the Final Four."

The aforementioned Antonio, last name Smith, was the beginning of Izzo's pipeline to Flint. He exhausted his eligibility without fulfilling his dream, but he kept in constant contact with his former teammates during the 1999-2000 season, helping them cope with adversity.

Early in the season, for example, Cleaves, who had turned down an opportunity to be a cinch NBA first-round draft pick, missed 13 games with a stress fracture in his right foot, forcing Bell to move to the point. The Spartans lost some games, including a memorable one to Kentucky on the road in December, but they held themselves together until Cleaves returned.

During the regular season, the Spartans defeated Wisconsin twice. Then they eliminated coach Dick Bennett's ball-control, defensive-minded Badgers again during the Big Ten tournament. So they weren't exactly thrilled when they learned that their Final Four semifinal opponent would be—you guessed it—Wisconsin, which was making its first Final Four appearance since

Magic Johnson, now a fan, watched his Spartans duplicate his team's feat of 21 years earlier.

Michigan State coach Tom Izzo encouraged his team in the 2000 final as he faced off with Florida coach Billy Donovan, both enthusiastic and sometimes volatile bench coaches. The game was controlled by Michigan State even though Mateen Cleaves was out of the lineup briefly with an ankle injury.

winning the third NCAA tournament in 1941.

"You think you're finally finished with a team like that," said Cleaves, "and the next thing you know, you're playing them again. It's like, 'Oh, my God.'"

And that was pretty much the feeling of the RCA Dome crowd of 43,116 and everyone who watched the telecast of the Wisconsin-Michigan State game.

At halftime, the Spartans led, 19-17. At the end, their margin was 53-41. For fans who think the game revolves around the slam dunk and the three-point shot, it wasn't exactly state-of-the-art basketball.

Despite a sub-par performance by Cleaves, who made only one of his seven shots from the floor and committed four turnovers to only one assist, the Spartans won with rebounding (a 42-20 advantage) and superior defense. They also were blessed

with an outstanding second half by the 6-7 Peterson, who scored 11 of his game-high 20 points during a 13-3 MSU run in the second half.

Still, it was such an unsatisfactory game that the Spartans' locker room was subdued. Then again, that might have had more to do with the team slogan that was rooted in Antonio Smith's comments after the loss to Duke the previous year:

"We haven't won anything yet."

As Izzo put it, "They really are excited about what they've accomplished, but they have a dream. Everybody has dreams, but few of us ever get to live them. And it's here. They get to live it."

The Spartans' championship-game opponent was a team about as different from Wisconsin as salsa music from the waltz. Under young coach Billy Donovan, the Florida Gators had mastered the uptempo style that Donovan had learned under Rick Pitino.

In 1987, Donovan had been the point guard for Pitino's Providence team that made it to the Final Four in New Orleans. Later, when Pitino took the job at Kentucky, Donovan was one of his assistants.

Like Pitino, he believed in uptempo basketball—full-court pressure on defense, running and gunning on offense. After clawing their way to a 43-32 halftime lead, the Spartans appeared to suffer a fatal blow when, with 16:18 remaining, Cleaves was shoved out of bounds and came down hard on his right ankle, forcing him to hobble to the locker room.

But Bell, drawing on the experience he gained during his fellow Flintstone's 13-game absence, moved to the point and

held things together until Cleaves returned with 11:51 remaining. Perhaps inspired by their fellow senior, Peterson and Granger combined for MSU's next 16 points to give the Spartans a 71-58 advantage with 7:36 remaining.

At the end of the Spartans' 89-76 victory, Peterson had 21 points, Granger 19, and Cleaves 18. The three seniors also combined for 13 of Michigan State's 32 rebounds and contributed 10 of the Spartans 19 assists.

Peterson said he was playing for his grandmother, Clara Mae Spencer, who had died the previous week in Mississippi, and Cleaves said he realized his dream of winning the NCAA title while CBS played the song, "One Shining Moment," in its postgame montage.

And naturally, both, along with Bell, said they were happy to give the citizens of Flint something to be proud of.

But the enduring lesson of the Spartans will be the value of staying in school.

Many of their rivals were decimated by early defections to the pros. Indeed, State was one of the few senior-dominated teams in the nation.

Yet because Peterson, Granger, and, especially Cleaves, had a unique commitment to education, to a school, and to a coach, the Spartans prevailed. If it was a great triumph for Michigan State, and it surely was, it was just as great a triumph for college basketball.

In only his fifth year since replacing the popular Jud Heathcote, who coached the Magic-led Spartans to their 1979 title, Izzo had Michigan State back atop the college basketball world.

Forward A.J. Granger (43) of the Spartans finished this dunk, two of his 19 points, as Michigan State moved into the lead and won the title. He and Morris Peterson, both seniors, combined to cinch the game away when Cleaves was side-lined momentarily. This was all pro-duced during clutch time, assuring a win.

ACKNOWLEDGEMENTS

Many individuals were responsible for this and previous books highlighting the early years and the uniqueness of the NCAA tournament. Walter Byers, the early executive director, helped gather and edit the first book about the tournament. His successor, Dick Schultz, commissioned the next version in 1988 on the occasion of the 50th anniversary celebration. That project, including the book published by Host Communications, was organized by Bob Sprenger.

This book, covering the first 60 years of the tournament, was instigated by Tom Jernstedt, the NCAA senior vice-president. Others within the NCAA staff who contributed included the project manager, David Pickle, and Dennis Cryder, Danita Edwards, Jim Marchiony and Wally Renfro.

Host Communications, longtime partner with the NCAA, manufactured the book and provided advice and assistance, particularly from W. James Host himself, a true fan of the tournament. Other key individuals in that group included Mark Coyle, David Kaplan and David Cawood, who himself presided over many Final Four press rows for the NCAA.

Other special thanks go to Steve Fine and Karen Carpenter of Sports Illustrated and to Brian Gadbery, Mike Dickson, Will Hart and Stephen Nowland of Rich Clarkson and Associates LLC.

CREDITS

Rich Clarkson made all photographs in the book with the following exceptions: Wide World Photos, 24, 27, 31, 44, 48 (2), 58, 63, 69; Bettman Archives/UPI, 34, 48; University of Oregon, 23; West Virginia University, 77; The (Louisville) Courier-Journal, 43, 66, 67; Seattle Times, 41; Richard Mackson for Sports Illustrated, 142, 143; Jim Gund for Rich Clarkson, 137, 139; Brian Gadbery for NCAA Photos, 1, 181 (rt), 191; David Gilkey for Rich Clarkson, 155; David Gonzales for NCAA Photos, 183 (2, left), 184 (2); 187 (top), 192; Ryan McKee for NCAA Photos, 190.